THE ENGLISH MYSTICS

FEW modern authors have achieved distinction in so wide a field as Gerald Bullett—novelist, poet, critic, biographer, and broadcaster. He was born fifty-six years ago in London, but is a countryman by ancestry and adoption, having for the greater part of his life made his home in Sussex, where he now lives. His first-published book, a novel written in his twenty-first year, appeared early in 1916, while its author was on active service in France. After three years at Cambridge, where he took an Honours degree in 1920, he resumed his interrupted career as a novelist and short story writer and began writing criticism for the literary weeklies. His many novels include *The Jury, The Pandervils, Judgment in Suspense,* and *Men at High Table;* and his anthologies *The Testament of Light* and *The English Galaxy of Shorter Poems,* are widely known. His own contribution to poetry is contained chiefly in two volumes: *The Golden Year of Fan Cheng-ta* (from the Chinese), and the more recently published *Poems.* Readers of the long poem called *Winter Solstice* in the latter volume will find it no matter for surprise that Mr. Bullett should at last have been constrained to write the present critical and biographical study of *The English Mystics.*

GERALD BULLETT

The

ENGLISH MYSTICS

London

MICHAEL JOSEPH

First published by
MICHAEL JOSEPH LTD
26 Bloomsbury Street
London, W.C.1
1950

Set and printed in Great Britain by Unwin Brothers Ltd. at the
Gresham Press, Woking, in Bell type, eleven point, leaded,
on paper made by John Dickinson and bound by James Burn

To
M. & K. M.

PREFACE

I HAVE tried to make this account of the lives and writings of some representative English mystics as objective and impartial as possible, presenting the facts as I find them and leaving it to the reader to pronounce judgment, if he must. The book is offered not as a contribution to the scholarship of the subject, but as a means of first approach to it.

G. B.

CONTENTS

CHAPTER I
THE SUBJECT DEFINED
(*p.* 13)

CHAPTER II
THE MEDIAEVAL BACKGROUND
(*p.* 37)

CHAPTER III
GEORGE FOX
(*p.* 65)

CHAPTER IV
SOME SEVENTEENTH-CENTURY POETS
(*p.* 94)

CHAPTER V
THE CAMBRIDGE PLATONISTS
(*p.* 113)

CHAPTER VI
WILLIAM LAW
(*p.* 129)

CHAPTER VII
BLAKE
(*p.* 161)

CHAPTER VIII
WORDSWORTH
(*p.* 186)

CHAPTER IX
COMMENTS AND CONCLUSIONS
(*p.* 214)

ILLUSTRATIONS

BLAKE'S FRONTISPIECE TO 'SONGS OF EXPERIENCE'
(*Frontispiece*)

RICHARD JEFFERIES BY WILLIAM STRANG R.A.
(*Facing p. 33*)

POEM AND DRAWINGS BY WILLIAM BLAKE
(*Facing p. 49*)

GEORGE FOX BY ALFRED TURNER
(*Facing p. 81*)

DR BENJAMIN WHICHCOTE BY MARY BEALE, 1682
(*Facing p. 119*)

A PAGE FROM 'SONGS OF INNOCENCE,' 1789
(*Facing p. 169*)

WILLIAM WORDSWORTH IN 1798
(*Facing p. 193*)

SAMUEL TAYLOR COLERIDGE IN 1799
(*Facing p. 209*)

[*Permissions in respect of the above illustrations are gratefully acknowledged as follows: to* MR DAVID STRANG *for the portrait of Richard Jefferies; to the Librarian of the* SOCIETY OF FRIENDS, *for George Fox; to the Master and Fellows of* EMMANUEL COLLEGE, CAMBRIDGE, *for Benjamin Whichcote; to the* NATIONAL PORTRAIT GALLERY *for William Wordsworth; to the Master and Fellows of* JESUS COLLEGE, CAMBRIDGE, *for Samuel Taylor Coleridge* (*a modern copy of 'the German Portrait' of* 1799); *and to the Keeper of the Prints*, BRITISH MUSEUM, *for the three Blake items.*]

Chapter One

THE SUBJECT DEFINED

§ 1

IT cannot be strictly defined, for the experience it treats of is beyond statement. Only poetry, or music, can say anything quite to the point, and they not directly but obliquely, in image and cadence, in sound and silence. Poetry is 'true' by virtue not of what it says but of what it is: to translate it into doctrine is to destroy the winged life. And poetry is the ultimate language of mysticism.

We are obliged, nevertheless, to ask what mysticism is, and to attempt an answer. To the Greeks, it seems, a 'mystic' was one to whom secret knowledge of 'divine mysteries' had been or was being imparted. In Victorian verse the word is used adjectivally as a whispering synonym for mysterious. Today, in the mouth of the militant secularist, it commonly means irrational, delusional, or merely silly. Let us begin by ridding ourselves of all these preconceptions; for the mysticism we are to examine here is not secret knowledge, is not supernaturalism, is not simple credulity, is not an enemy to reason. It is not even concerned with mystery, if by mystery is meant darkness or obscurity. If in its verbal deliverances it resorts much to symbolism, paradox, and even some apparent self-contradiction, that is not with intent to mystify but because what it seeks to report is beyond the compass of plain prose statement. But, so far from being enamoured of darkness, it is in its essence, so mystics believe, a mode of illumination. The claim can be neither allowed nor disallowed until we have heard the witnesses and considered their evidence.

The English mystics, then, are those men and women of

our country who give the impression—to put it no higher than that—that they have enjoyed contact and communion with something more real than is given in everyday human experience, an utterly indubitable quickening power, as it were a fountain of light and joy. Here, at once, our troubles begin; for what does 'real' mean, it may be asked, and what is more real than the world of things, the world we see and touch? One answer must be that for all practical purposes that is most real which can least be doubted, and that though it is possible to doubt the existence in themselves of what we see and touch, by supposing (for example) that we are dreaming, we cannot doubt the seeing and the touching, or, to speak more exactly, we cannot doubt our own consciousness, the I behind the eye; for not even an illusion can be experienced without consciousness. The mystic bears testimony to something that seems to him to be both 'within' and 'beyond', something in which he both 'loses' and 'finds' himself, loses his small isolated identity and finds himself 'at one' with the life of the universe. Or so it seems: it will be noticed that all the words I have put in inverted commas are metaphorical and therefore inexact.

Here, as always, one is in danger of confusing the given fact with the interpretation, the experience with the groping afterthought. The mystic's own account of the matter is coloured, is indeed determined, by the notions and preconceptions supplied to him by his environment. If before the event he is attached to the doctrines of Christianity, he will inevitably tend to identify the 'light' that has visited him— probably the most frequently recurring image in mystical literature—with the light that shone in Nazareth two thousand years ago; and if he was already an adherent of some other religious faith it is in terms of that other faith that he will interpret it. Whether mystical experience as here defined can establish any truth at all except for those who have shared it is the first of the questions that will confront us; but we can say at once, for it is obvious, that if it does establish anything it will be something that the great religions have in common, not the dogmas peculiar to any one of them. To this fact is due the evident if unconfessed enmity which the subject is apt to arouse in some sectarian bosoms. Ignoring its etymology, and divesting it so far as we may of the atmosphere of solemn hush in which it is too often clothed, let us accept the word mysticism for what it now is: a more or less arbitrary label for a certain kind of human experience, and the most convenient one because established by long usage.

But, though we must accept the word for lack of a better, it is important that we should avoid defining it in terms that prejudge the question by assuming a readymade system of philosophical or religious belief. To begin, for example, by saying that mysticism is 'the attempt to realize the presence of the living God in the soul and in nature'* would be out of place and unhelpful, because it would deliver a premature verdict and plunge us into confusion by introducing the enormous diversity of notions attaching to the term *God*, from eighteenth-century deism at one extreme to thorough-going pantheism at the other, and from the most ingenuous anthropomorphism to the unimaginable Absolute of Plotinus or the 'superessential Nothingness' of Eckhart's conception. A man may arrive at theism by a process of reasoning from first principles; and he may, if he so chooses, relate the notion so arrived at with what we have agreed to call a mystical experience; but the notion and the experience remain strictly separate. The one, being a product of reasoning, must remain subject to challenge, criticism, and modification by reason. The other, a psychological event, exists in its own right, like any other fact, but has no bearing on the truth or otherwise of particular theological preconceptions.

In reading the life-stories and recorded utterances of

* W. R. Inge, *Christian Mysticism*. Methuen, 1899.

religious mystics, therefore, allowance must constantly be made for the local and personal bias that colours their language and determines their choice of image and metaphor. Concrete imagery is the life of language; that which by its nature eludes exact expression can only be suggested, or hinted at, by resort to symbolism; and between symbolism and mythology there is a strong natural affinity. The function of the mythos, like that of symbolism, is to bring metaphysical ideas within reach of the imagination by presenting them in a dramatic or pictorial form. Something is lost as well as something gained in the process; but it is an inevitable one, and we can no more be surprised that the mystic expresses himself in terms of his own religious tradition than that he uses his own language. What *is* surprising, or at any rate impressive, is that, wherever and whenever he turns up, whether in our Christian era and hemisphere or in the ancient civilizations of the East, and whatever his personal antecedents, he always tells us more or less the same thing—that he has enjoyed a sense of communion or 'at-one-ment' with a reality infinitely transcending himself.

Here is perhaps the chief reason for holding that mysticism is worth serious study: the great diversity of its witnesses and the substantial unanimity of its witness. Men and women widely separated in time and space, of various religious faiths or of none at all, and utterly different from each other in social environment and personal character, have unknowingly collaborated through the ages in testifying to one and the same mystical fact. This phrase 'mystical fact' may seem to beg a large question, the question whether the experience we are considering does, as the mystics believe, involve perception of an object or is a purely subjective affair. But that question, as put, is a drastic oversimplification of the problem and depends for its meaning on several debatable assumptions, the chief of them centring in that tricky word 'subjective'. The 'subject' of the experience is the person or self that enjoys it. But what is the 'self'? The nineteenth-century notion that 'each self is a unique existence which is perfectly impervious to other selves' (Pringle Pattison, quoted by Inge) is one that cannot be seriously entertained today in the light of what modern psychology, belatedly catching up with ancient thought, has to tell us about the 'unconscious' or subliminal self and the well-established phenomena of telepathy, extra-sensory perception, and (possibly) precognition, to say nothing of such familiar pathological conditions as schizophrenia. The mediaeval notions about guardian angels and devil-possession, though untenable literally, are far nearer the truth of human psychology than the cast-iron assumptions of nineteenth-century materialism. And if the everyday conscious self is in fact continuous with a larger or even (as the Vedantists hold) with the Universal Self, how are we to say where subject ends and object begins? Church Christianity, in its dread of pantheism, has always stressed the transcendence and 'otherness' of its God; but Christian mystics, as well as their non-Christian predecessors in ancient India and elsewhere, have not hesitated to declare that by love, by the willing loss of self, we realize our true nature and become partakers in the being of God. The ego may be said to represent a stage in a spiritual process. By breaking out of its shell we can be born again, into a boundless freedom. That is the doctrine implied in all mystical philosophy.

If we could survey the whole vast field we should find among mystics, especially in mediaeval times, a high proportion of psychopaths and neurotics, and it is true that the line between ecstasy and self-deceiving hysteria may be sometimes no broader than a razor's edge. But we cannot build much on these pathological considerations. For few if any of us are entirely free from temperamental oddities, and it is notorious that men of genius in all fields often (though not always) exhibit signs of instability in their personal behaviour, without the high value of their work—their poems, pictures, music, scientific discoveries—being thereby affected. The 'religious genius', or whatever we choose to call him, is no exception to the general rule. His eccentricities prove nothing but that the human organism cannot without danger to mental balance sustain too many moments of 'burning bliss', and that mountaineering in realms of 'the spirit', as he calls it, is a hazardous enterprise. They provide no good reason for refusing to listen to those who, at least in their own belief, have from time to time, or perhaps only once in their lives, attained to a state of being beyond our normal reach.

§ 2

Some further definitions are necessary. Though mysticism has no direct bearing on theology, and so can neither prove nor disprove theological propositions, it does undeniably belong to the realm of religion in the more vital sense of the term. Religion can mean either a specific system of dogmas and observances or something at once more intimate, dynamic, rudimentary, and less easy of definition. Is it possible to put one's finger on that which all particular religions, as we know them, have in common, not only with each other but with the religiousness of people who are attached to no Church or creed? We can dismiss at once any definition that equates religion with mere theism; for we have only to look round us to see (a) that it is possible to be religious without professing a belief in God, and (b) that belief in the existence of a God does not in itself make a man religious. In everyday speech it is legitimate to define a man's religion in terms of the values that command his instinctive loyalty, or, more concretely, the objects to whose service he wholeheartedly devotes himself, whether they be personal aggrandizement, moneymaking, business efficiency, art, literature, science, social reform, political power, sport, travel, erudition, physical health, philanthropy, or what you will; but that sense of the word is too general for our present purpose. Religion in these chapters, then, will mean something rather more definite: not indeed a definitely formulated belief, but a sense or apprehension of an immortal reality in and beyond appearances, and, no less, in and beyond oneself. If this is religion, it is also what we have agreed to call mysticism. The two, so far, are one and the same.

It is clear that mysticism, thus defined, admits of many degrees. At one extreme there are the ecstatics who by personal austerities, by the discipline of singleminded contemplation, or even (as it sometimes seems) by means of events quite beyond their own contriving, have put themselves in the way of what they believe to be a supernatural revelation. At the other there are those who, while claiming to possess no peculiar insight, and having no dramatic experience to report, are nevertheless aware of an inward light, a shining mystery, to which they may or may not be willing to give a name. All these, all types and degrees, are relevant to our inquiry. For many readers today the testimony of the poets will have a more persuasive appeal than that of religious devotees whose ways of thought and expression are sometimes archaic, myth-ridden, and even crude, and always, except to their co-religionists, relatively unfamiliar. It would be unwise, however, to let mere habit or prejudice get in the way of understanding; unwise to reject illumination because we do not care for the design of the lamp-shade. Whether we happen to be believers or unbelievers in any given religious system of thought, our aim must be to cut through the accidental accretion of dogma to the hard core of luminous fact (if such there be) in mystical experience. Mysticism is essentially empirical, not theoretical. Any theories built upon it can be, and should be, judged in the light of pure reason. The miscalled 'supernatural' revelation which it sometimes involves does not imply an interference with the natural order from outside: it is rather the perception, as by a sixth sense, of something beyond nature *as we ordinarily know it*. Extraordinary visions and voices come only to those to whose habit of mind such things are congenial and 'natural', or at any rate expectable. It is not surprising that to a mind that has dwelt long and lovingly upon the Christian story a vision of Jesus should appear. * But to other minds, steeped in other religious traditions or in none at all, the revelation will take other forms. The forms are various and in the strict sense accidental: which should, I suggest, make it all the more impressive that their innermost content is always virtually the same. The root of mysticism is an experience, in greater or less degree an ecstatic one. It is feeling rather than thought (though coloured by thought): not a 'mere' feeling, not a sentimental or fanciful feeling, but a spiritual sensation as real and concrete as hunger and thirst, and one in which a man's whole being is engaged. That it may, after the event, be sentimentalized and distorted by fancy is obvious enough; but in its naked essence it is as actual as eating and drinking. The difficulty for those of us who have not had the experience, is how to get at this naked essence, how to distinguish between the event and its necessarily inadequate verbalization. For the mystics themselves, and for them alone, its validity is absolute.

Let us take our first examples from modern times. They are not the best that could be found, but they are the best

* This point has been succinctly made by Miss Sackville-West in her biographical study of Saint Teresa of Avila. 'Is it or is it not conceivable that in the hypothetical case of a person who had never heard of God, Christ, the Communion of Saints, the Devil, or any of the accepted appurtenances of religion, the phenomenon of divine visions or locutions should occur? Is it possible to imagine a stigmatist to whom the story of the Crucifixion should be totally unknown? Is it possible to imagine our Lady appearing to one who was unacquainted with the story of Christ's nativity? If such cases exist, proven beyond suspicion, they would seem to settle the matter once and for all; but in their absence it would seem logical to conclude that the phenomena of mystical theology must take their origin from some image already in the mind.' *The Eagle and the Dove.* Michael Joseph, 1943.

for our immediate purpose, which is to get some preliminary notion of what mysticism in practice is. By beginning with comparatively ordinary men and women, who lived unremarkable lives and speak to us in a familiar idiom, I run the risk of being accused by specialists of confusing mysticism with mere romanticism or self-indulgent religiosity. But if it is uncritical to reject the testimony of illustrious 'God-intoxicated' souls on the ground that they were psychologically unbalanced—as they certainly were—it is surely no less uncritical, as well as supercilious, to disdain that of more normal people whose intoxication takes milder forms. A word of warning, however, is necessary. The mystical experience in its intensest form has never, so far as one may judge, been easily come by. Mental and spiritual (and sometimes physical) self-discipline, or the chastening discipline of dire events, has always preceded it. This is more conspicuously true of those whom William James, adopting F. W. Newman's categories, calls the 'twice-born', who, in contrast to their temperamentally sunny and sanguine 'once-born' brothers, are deeply and painfully aware of sin and death and judgment, and much exercised by the need (as they conceive it) of redemption and salvation. The untroubled innocence of Browning's Pippa ('God's in his heaven—all's right with the world!') and the guilt-neurosis of the self-condemned 'sinner' struggling for release from his own human nature, the ebullient life-enjoying optimism of a Whitman and the stern world-renouncing austerity of a St John of the Cross—these represent the south and the north pole of the human spirit: in the vast territory between them there is room for any number of different psychological types. Mysticism, it must be admitted, holds a specious attraction for shallow and sentimental as well as for religious minds; and certain phrases and notions associated with it, vulgarized by facile repetition, figure all too often in what Logan Pearsall Smith describes as 'mystical slipslop and dreadful musings in old-world gardens'.

It is not, however, difficult in practice to distinguish between mere sentimentality and genuine hard-won conviction; and we shall perhaps do well to remind ourselves that spiritual snobbery is at least no less reprehensible than bad literary taste.

Richard Jefferies (1848–1887) was born at Coate in Wiltshire, the son of a working farmer. All his boyhood was spent on or about the farm, and he differed from other boys of his class only in being endowed with sharper senses, a livelier curiosity, and a more implacable egoism. His father's fortunes rapidly declining, the family suffered increasingly from poverty. Except that he delighted in all rural things, Richard was a misfit, a stubborn and solitary spirit. Since he could not be persuaded to work on the farm, his idiosyncrasy was eventually accepted and a room set aside for him in which he could read and write to his heart's content. He became a reporter for a local newspaper, won some notoriety by writing a letter to *The Times* about the condition of Wiltshire labourers, and produced a number of quite worthless novels. He had no talent for making friends, possibly no wish to do so; but he was a close and sympathetic observer of men and women as well as of birds and beasts. The books by which he is now remembered were written during the last ten years of his life, and for six of those years he had to contend with the painful disease which killed him at the age of thirty-eight. With only one of those books are we here concerned, *The Story of My Heart*, a book which, whether one likes it or not, does bear witness to a fact, a cosmic emotion, a sense of communion with an immanent and transcendent reality, to which numberless others throughout human history— Christians, Moslems, Jews, Hindoos, Taoists, Buddhists, and Agnostics—have also testified.

Jefferies himself had no definite religious creed. He, like so many others in recent times, found his deepest ecstasy in the contemplation of natural beauty. His unrestrained emotionalism in this particular book, its occasional lushness of expression, must not blind us either to its patent sincerity or to its value as evidence. Make what you will of it, this is how one man felt; and many far greater men, in like circumstances, have felt much the same. 'I was utterly alone with the sun and the earth. Lying down on the grass, I spoke in my soul to the earth, the sun, the air, and the distant sea far beyond sight. I turned to the blue heaven over, gazing into its depth, inhaling its exquisite colour and sweetness. The rich blue of the unattainable flower of the sky drew my soul towards it, and there it rested, for pure colour is rest of heart. By all these I prayed; I felt an emotion of the soul beyond all definition; prayer is a puny thing to it, and the word is a rude sign to the feeling, but I know no other. Touching the crumble of earth, the blade of grass, the thyme flower, breathing the earth-encircling air, I prayed that I might touch to the unutterable existence infinitely higher than deity.' And so on and so on: my quotation is an abridgement of some pages from the first chapter. Tedious? Maybe. But we come very soon to the root of the matter, for a little later he speaks of how, losing his 'separateness', he 'came to seem like a part of the whole'; and how, 'listening to the sighing of the grass', he 'felt immortality' as he felt the beauty of the summer morning. 'And I thought beyond immortality, of other conditions, more beautiful than existence, higher than immortality.' Again: 'I cannot understand time. It is eternity now. I am in the midst of it. It is about me in the sunshine; I am in it, as the butterfly floats in the light-laden air. Nothing has to come; it is now. Now is eternity; now is the immortal life.' The thought is repeated and enlarged upon, but it sums itself up in one striking sentence: 'Haste not, be at rest, this Now is eternity.'

What is this, you may say, but mere words? But these words meant much to their author. In seventeen years there had been plenty of time for the event, whatever it was, to be inextricably mixed with thought, to be turned over and cogitated upon and translated into theory; but, unless we choose to dismiss the whole thing as a romantic fabrication, event of some kind there certainly was. 'Things that have been miscalled supernatural,' writes Jefferies in a reflective passage, 'appear to me simple, more natural than nature, than earth, than sea, or sun. It is beyond telling more natural that I should have a soul than not, that there should be immortality; I think that there is much more than immortality. It is matter which is the supernatural, and difficult of understanding. Why this clod of earth I hold in my hand? Why this water which drops sparkling from my fingers dipped in the brook? Why are they at all? When? How? What for? Matter is beyond understanding, mysterious, impenetrable; I touch it easily, comprehend it, no. Soul, mind—the thought, the idea—is easily understood, it understands itself and is conscious. . . . My naked mind confronts the unknown. I see as clearly as the noonday that this is not all; I see other and higher conditions than existence; I see not only the existence of the soul, immortality, but, in addition, I realize a soul-life illimitable; I realize the existence of a cosmos of thought; I realize the existence of an inexpressible entity infinitely higher than deity.' This is no doubt very ingenuous philosophizing. What, we may ask, can the so often repeated phrase 'infinitely higher than deity' mean, since nothing can be higher than that which is by definition the highest? Presumably it means higher than the particular conceptions of deity that Jefferies happened to have met with, whether the anthropomorphic personal God of popular evangelism, or the absentee potentate—disinterested First Cause of a clockwork universe—posited by Deism.

This answer is probably true so far as it goes; but there is possibly a deeper intuition struggling for expression in that phrase, and one which Jefferies unwittingly shared with minds more sensitive and subtle than his own. Unwittingly, for he was no dialectician, and it is extremely unlikely that he was acquainted with Plotinus's doctrine of the unconditioned One, or Absolute, which, through the writings of Proclus, Dionysius the Areopagite, and some others, was to flow into the main stream of Christian mystical thought, so that Johannes Scotus Erigena, in the ninth century, had recourse to the method of definition by negatives ('to call it super-essential is to say not what it is but what it is not'), as did Eckhart and others in later centuries ('No man can say or understand anything about God. If I say God is a being, it is not true: he is transcendent Being and superessential Nothingness'), and as the mystics of the East had done centuries before the Christian era. 'The Tao that can be spoken of,' says Lao-Tzu, 'is not the true Tao.' 'That which pervades the universe,' says the Krishna of the *Bhagavadgita*, echoing the still more ancient *Upanishads*, 'is imperishable . . . unshown, unthinkable, unalterable.' Coming back to Christian times: 'Of God himself can no man think,' writes the anonymous author of *The Cloud of Unknowing*; 'by love he may be gotten and holden, but by thought never.' It is possible, then, that Jefferies's 'higher than deity' represents his groping apprehension of an idea, a reality, which, while not denying or strictly speaking transcending deity, is nevertheless felt to be ludicrously *mis*represented in the language of a popular theology catering too exclusively for what are conceived to be the devotional needs of simpleminded people. In this he was perhaps more orthodox than he knew, for it is St Augustine who says, in paradoxical fashion: 'The best thing that man can say about God is to be able to be silent about him.' And Eckhart, quoting the paradox, adds roundly: 'Therefore be silent and prate not about God, for whenever thou dost prate about God, thou liest.'

§ 3

The loss of 'separateness', the consciousness of being 'part
of the whole', the beatific sense of a here-and-now 'eternity'
or 'immortality'—Richard Jefferies is only one among very
many who have experienced the condition which these phrases
struggle to describe. Their various accounts of the matter have
an almost monotonous similarity. In the year in which *The
Story of My Heart* was published, 1883, Edward Carpenter's
misleadingly-entitled *Towards Democracy* also appeared. That
long effusion of enthusiasm, a genuinely spontaneous out-
pouring notwithstanding that in literary method it owes so
much to the influence of Whitman, is no longer widely read;
but its author's account of how he came to write it is worth
recalling. In 1881, he says, 'no doubt as the culmination and
result of struggles and experiences that had been going on',
experiences which had involved much suffering and inward
tension, he became aware that a mass of material that impera-
tively demanded expression was forming within him. 'I
became for the time overwhelmingly conscious of the dis-
closure within of a region transcending in some sense the
ordinary bounds of personality, in the light of which region
my own idiosyncrasies of character—defects, accomplishments, limitations, or what not—appeared of no importance
whatever—an absolute freedom from mortality, accompanied
by an indescribable calm and joy.' Carpenter's was a religious
temperament, but he belonged to no Church, having moved
away from the Christianity in which he had been brought up.

The actual moment of 'revelation', mystical or otherwise,
is commonly preceded by a (voluntary or involuntary) 'one-
pointed meditation'. The habitual activity of the mind having
been stilled by concentration on one object, one image or
idea, there ensues what to the subject seems to be a luminous
and timeless moment. We can call it, if we choose, a form
of self-hypnosis; but no pathological diagnosis, no medical

label, can excuse us from examining the resultant event with an open mind: by their fruits, not by the biological process that produces them, can these things be known for what they are, whether good or evil, whether an enlargement of consciousness or an insane delusion. No reasonable mind will seek to evade the duty of discrimination either by a gushing credulous acceptance of everything put before it or by a dogmatic and equally uncritical denial of whatever does not tally with its preconceptions. Tennyson, in a letter, has left the following account of what more than once happened to him. 'I have never had any revelations through anaesthetics, but a kind of waking trance—this for lack of a better word— I have frequently had, quite up from boyhood, when I have been alone. This has come upon me through repeating my own name to myself silently, till all at once, as it were out of the intensity of the consciousness of individuality, individuality itself seemed to dissolve and fade away into boundless being, and this not a confused state but the clearest, the surest of the surest, the weirdest of the weirdest, utterly beyond words, where death was an almost laughable impossibility, the loss of personality (if so it were) seeming no extinction, but the only true life.' A word, a name, a physical object: the thing contemplated is a matter of indifference. Tennyson adds: 'I am ashamed of my feeble description. Have I not said the state is utterly beyond words?'

I borrow this example from William James's *The Varieties of Religious Experience*. But the experiences induced in this fashion are not necessarily religious at all: I call them mystical only when, as in Tennyson's case, they have a particular kind of religious quality or significance. From the same source comes an anonymous confession which speaks of a vivid sense of 'God's nearness', but goes on to explain: 'I say God, to describe what is indescribable. A presence, I might say, yet that is too suggestive of personality, and the moments of which I speak did not hold the consciousness of a personality, but something in myself made me feel myself a part of something bigger than I, that was controlling. I felt myself one with the grass, the trees, birds, insects, everything in Nature. I exulted in the mere fact of existence, of being a part of it all. In the years following, such moments continued to come, but I wanted them constantly. I knew so well the satisfaction of losing self in a perception of supreme power and love, that I was unhappy because that perception was not constant.'

This 'perception'—than which, to the person who enjoys it, nothing can be more utterly indubitable—is clearly the same in its essential features as the 'perceptions' of Carpenter and Jefferies and Whitman and many others. Something distantly approaching it is perhaps experienced at moments by nearly all sensitive people when they find themselves alone with

> *The silence that is in the starry sky,*
> *The sleep that is among the lonely hills.*

Its most perfect literary expression is in some other famous lines from Wordsworth, whose life and work will be fully considered in a later chapter.

§ 4

When we come to look more closely into the lives and writings (or sayings) of a few representative English mystics, two obvious but not always regarded facts must be borne in mind. The first is that the mystic, as such, has no moral or intellectual pre-eminence among men. He is as much subject as the rest of us to the determining influences of heredity and environment. His individual temperament, his education, his literary culture (if any), his acquired opinions and his habit of life, all contribute to the mode in which he expresses his intuition. However 'real' the experience that inspires him, its translation into doctrinal terms—always necessarily imperfect—affords infinite scope for variety and for error. The simple and vigorous personality of George Fox will express itself in one language, the highly cultivated intellect of William Law in another, the astonishing insight of Blake in yet a third; and by language is here meant not merely the vocabulary used but the idiom of the imagination, the forms in which thought and feeling naturally represent themselves in the mind. Jakob Boehme, seventeenth-century German cobbler and one of the greatest of illuminants, was misled into adopting a fantastic symbolism which renders much of his writing unintelligible; whereas that of William Law, his English interpreter, is (at its best) as full of light as of grace. Only by reason, in the fullest sense, reason which is not confined to formal logic but is a function of the whole human personality, can these things be judged.

The second and no less important point is that abnormal manifestations, visions and voices and spiritual 'ravishings', neither guarantee nor invalidate the truth of what they seem to reveal. They are no more miraculous, in the crude sense of that term, than any other psychological phenomena. In themselves they have no value and prove nothing: their value, if any, derives from their fruits in thought and action. Mr Bernard Shaw has summed up the matter with characteristic clarity and force in the preface to *Saint Joan*. 'Joan's voices and visions have played many tricks with her reputation. They have been held to prove that she was mad, that she was a liar and imposter, that she was a sorceress (she was burned for this), and finally that she was a saint. They do not prove any of these things; but the variety of the conclusions reached show how little our matter-of-fact historians know about other people's minds, or even about their own. There are people in the world whose imagination is so vivid that when they have an idea it comes to them as an audible voice, sometimes uttered by a visible figure. Criminal lunatic asylums are occupied largely by murderers who have obeyed voices. . . . But the seers of visions and the hearers of revelations are not always criminals. The inspirations and intuitions and unconsciously reasoned conclusions of genius sometimes assume similar illusions. Socrates, Luther, Swedenborg, Blake saw visions and heard voices just as Saint Francis and Saint Joan did. If Newton's imagination had been of the same vividly dramatic kind he might have seen the ghost of Pythagoras walk into the orchard and explain why the apples were falling. Such an illusion would have invalidated neither the theory of gravitation nor Newton's general sanity. What is more, the visionary method of making the discovery would not be a whit more miraculous than the normal method. *The test of sanity is not the normality of the method but the reasonableness of the discovery.*'

I italicize that last sentence because what it says is so exactly to our present purpose. Its implied converse is that a scrutiny of the method throws no light on the reasonableness or unreasonableness of the conclusion arrived at. In short the method is nothing, the quality of the supposed revelation everything. Reason, the highest intellectual endowment of the human spirit, has the last word. A mystical illumination may transfigure the subject's life, by giving him a new centre of gravity; but it cannot of itself transform his intelligence or endow him with a capacity for rational thought. It will in greater or less degree enlarge his spirit, purge him of self-centredness, and give him access to a peace that passes understanding, the peace of personal integration; but it will not transform an infantile mind, full of religious fairytales, into an adult reasoning one. The spiritual wisdom which the mystic acquires can very well co-exist with an extreme literal-minded credulity. Some, it is true, have had high intellectual as well as spiritual endowments; but no one has ever quite escaped from the limitations imposed by heredity and environment. That is why the personal history of the saints and mystics, as well as their teaching, is always in point. Palpably false notions of the nature of God are to be found in mystical literature as elsewhere, but they do not belong to mysticism as such. The crude dualism implied in mortification of the flesh and contempt for natural beauty, with all their accompaniments of pathological prudery, is happily repugnant to most modern minds. We shall meet it again and again, and recognize it for the psychological aberration it is, without incontinently dismissing as a meaningless hallucination the experience it misinterprets and disfigures. So too with the trivial conception of God as a person like ourselves who takes pleasure in bestowing 'favours'—in the form of visions, apparitions, and the like— on individuals that take his fancy: we can reject this pitiful absurdity without necessarily embracing atheism. The historical accidents of mysticism, and the residue of unreason and selfcomplacency in some mystics and accredited saints, do not invalidate its substance.

Asceticism is a much-debated question. Few will deny that some measure of austerity is more conducive to the life of the spirit than unbridled luxury: it is more conducive, moreover, to physical health and mental alertness, as every athlete knows. But the middle way is surely the way of wisdom. If to live only for the gratification of the senses is sub-human, to suppose that we can attain to 'pure' spirituality by despising and killing the senses is a dangerous and evil delusion. Sense is not the enemy of spirit but its instrument. To disdain the delight of visible and tangible beauty is a sign not of spiritual life but of spiritual death. Physical self-mortification, when practised for its own sake, is a disguised and degraded form of sensual indulgence. What theologians call 'sin' pertains not to the body as such but to the ego. Sin in its essence is self-assertion, the assertion of one's ego as a self-subsistent absolute and the centre of the universe. Its antithesis is love, the realization in thought and action of one's identity with the universal life, or, in the words of St Paul, that we are members one of another. The mystic believes that by a psychological process sometimes called the grace of God we can escape from the confinement of self into what seems like a region of boundless beatitude: something of the kind, indeed, may happen in any act of pure devotion or disinterested contemplation. But this spiritual enlargement can no more be achieved by mortification of the senses than a violinist can make music by destroying his violin.

The true asceticism, as Evelyn Underhill has said, is a gymnastic not of the body but of the mind. It is practised not only by the religious devotee but by every kind of artist and disinterested thinker. It may involve a severe mental discipline, a detachment, a withdrawal from the *distractions* of sense (not its annihilation), in order that the mind may attain to that state of stillness or inward poise which is the highest and deepest kind of prayer: not petitionary prayer addressed to an anthropomorphic deity, but the kind of prayer by which 'more things are wrought . . . than this world dreams of'. It does *not* involve bodily mortification, nor even 'the mischievous doctrine that the spiritual eye can only see when the eye of sense is closed' (Dean Inge). To the theologian Erigena the whole world was a theophany, or appearance of God. Whitman, the robustious American poet, saw in 'every blade of grass a miracle'. And Thomas Traherne, seventeenth-century country parson, declares: 'The whole world ministers to you as the theatre of your love. It sustains you and all objects that you may continue to love them.' This, the poet's vision, not 'otherworldliness', is the light that shines in all vital and vitalizing mysticism.

§ 5

The other world. The world of the unseen. The world beyond. These and similar expressions are always cropping

RICHARD JEFFERIES, BY WILLIAM STRANG, R.A.

up in religious literature; and it will be well to forestall
trouble by asking what, if anything, they can mean for us.
The answer, though it will still elude exact statement, can
be arrived at only by a process of elimination. If we cannot
say what they (legitimately) mean, we can at least get some
notion of it by saying what, for us, they do *not* mean. The
problem is highly complex, for meaning is in the last analysis
determined by the mind that entertains it: if you choose to
believe that there exists an actual unseen immaterial *world*
beyond or above the universe of sensual perception, there is
no gainsaying that that, for you, is what the phrase means.
But close scrutiny of such a belief will show, I suggest, that
the mind entertaining it is imprisoned in its own metaphors.

Human thought and language being ineradicably figura-
tive, a succession of images, and therefore inexact, we can
avoid deceiving ourselves only by recognizing the symbolic
or metaphorical character of the words we are forced to use.
There are no words by which the concept of a non-sensual
reality can be precisely and positively affirmed. Whether the
object contemplated be 'God' or 'the world of spirit', we are
obliged, like Erigena and Eckhart, to resort to description
by negatives or to the use of symbols drawn from sense-
experience. The term 'spirit' (*spiritus*, breath) is itself a
metaphor; 'unseen' and 'immaterial' are negative expressions;
'light' is a sense-derived symbol. Most insidious and deceiving of all, because we so easily slip into taking them literally,
are the ubiquitous spatial metaphors, such as 'beyond',
'above', 'higher', 'lower', and the rest. The 'world beyond'
—in what sense is it 'beyond'? Not, certainly, in any physical
sense. The mediaeval cosmography having been exploded,
belief in a localized heaven, somewhere beyond the sky, has
lost its basis. Mystical insight perceived the crude irrelevance
of that belief long before Copernicus (and Galileo after him)
made it untenable: it is a fourteenth-century writer who,
bidding us beware of the danger of taking metaphorical

expressions literally, declares (in *The Cloud of Unknowing*)
that heaven is as nigh down as up and up as down, and that
'the high and the next way thither is run by desires, and not
by paces of feet'. And had not Jesus himself said, simply and
profoundly, that the kingdom of heaven is within us?—
another metaphor, but an unmistakable one, in which is to
be found the key to the whole problem. God, spirit, heaven
—if that which these notions inadequately figure forth is
indeed within us, 'closer than breathing, nearer than hands
and feet', it cannot be other than the very light of our being:
boundless, immortal, inescapable. 'Look thou within,' wrote
the Emperor Marcus Aurelius, admonishing himself. 'Within
thee is the fountain of all good, whose waters shall never
cease to spring, so thou dig deep enough.' The qualification
is all-important; for clearly it is not by looking into the small
phenomenal self,* the busy chattering ego, that one finds 'the
fountain of all good'—but by digging deep, by *forgetting*
self, and so for a timeless moment breaking out of its narrow
confinement into a larger consciousness.

That the material universe may contain other inhabited
worlds beyond reach of our knowledge is not in question.
(Nor is there any good reason for assuming that we, mankind, represent the highest point that life in the universe has
so far reached: it may well be that our eminence is strictly
local, confined to this planet.) Other and better worlds there
may be; but let us recognize, and never forget, that 'the
spiritual world' is pure metaphor and—unlike 'The kingdom
of heaven is within you'—dangerously misleading. Unless

---

* Talk of 'two selves' can all too easily lead us into a morass of mythology.
But there is surely a valid distinction to be drawn between the unchanging *I*
which experiences experience and the empirical or historical *I* which is the
sum total, at any given moment, of my continuing experience in space-time.
The first is, so to speak, the faculty, the second the content, of consciousness.
The first is the perceiver, the second the perceiving. I do not 'exist pheno-
menally' apart from my actual personal history; but the *I* which gives to that
history a continuing identity by virtue of which I can call it mine is (in analysis,
not in fact) separable from it, an unchanging constant in a perpetual flux.

we are forewarned, the concreteness of 'world' looms so large
in the imagination as quite to exclude the significance of
'spirit', so that we dimly picture to ourselves a place, an
external 'kingdom of heaven', a celestial landscape. The same
illusion of concreteness attaches to Plato's ideal world where
dwell the essential forms (or 'ideas') of which, according to
him, the qualities we find in things of experience are the
imperfect and fleeting glimpses. Plato has been called 'the
father of European mysticism'—by Dean Inge, who quotes
Emerson's dictum that mysticism finds in Plato all its texts.
But in the incomparably rich mind of Plato not only are jewels
of truth to be found, but splinters of half-truth, and some
elements of insidious error. Plato himself seems to have
conceived his Ideal Forms, quite ingenuously, as celestial
patterns, which were also creative forces, existing in a real
though unseen world quite other than the world of human
experience.* It seems, to say the least, an unnecessary
hypothesis; and it has helped to perpetuate a sentimental
fiction and an artificial dualism. Literature's debt to Plato is
beyond calculation, but we owe him small thanks for teaching
philosophers the trick of hypostatizing pure ideas. The
Platonic Ideas, so called, were to Plato not ideas in our
modern sense—that is, things existing only in the mind—
but it is clear that the doctrine was arrived at by taking ideas,
in just that sense, and imaginatively endowing them with
external being. So a word or a thought becomes an independent entity, an imaginary power; and the cat of confusion
is among the pigeons of common sense.

How then, without embracing an illogical and incidentally
quite unspiritual fiction, can we conceive of this 'world of
spirit' of which we are to hear so much? By mentally deleting
'world' whenever it turns up in that context. The world of
politics is politicians. The world of cricket is cricketers. The
world of spirit is spirit. And spirit, says Dr Santayana, the

* See George Santayana, *Platonism and the Spiritual Life*. Constable, 1927.

most urbane of modern philosophers, is 'awareness'. It may be possible, but it is hardly necessary, to refine upon that definition. Talk of 'the unseen' is the source of much confusion of thought, because it suggests to our image-making minds something concrete that happens to be invisible or out of sight. But spirit is unseen in quite another sense and for quite another reason. It is unseen because it is the seer, and the seeing. We ourselves are spirit, and being so we are one with all spirit. The senses—'the chief inlets of Soul in this age' said Blake—are so many modes of spirit's operation. And the universe of material things, in all its unimaginable and fascinating complexity, is the outward form of an incidental part of spirit's experience. This, which is the ultimate philosophy of mysticism as I understand it, makes the world in which we find ourselves not less but more real: not an illusion, not a figment of fancy, not a solipsist dream, but an indubitable and significant experience in which we all share and to which by our infinite diversity we each contribute.

Chapter Two

THE MEDIAEVAL BACKGROUND

§ 1

I N any study of this kind we have to be constantly on our guard against literalism: not merely against literalism in the cruder sense, but against regarding as adequate, or truly definitive, the words and expressions we are obliged to use, for lack of any others. In any use of language that goes beyond simple statement of apparent fact ('There is a field. In the field is a cow. The cow has four legs.') we must resort either to metaphor, imagery, and a measure of symbolism, which is more or less the way of poetry, or to analysis, which is the way of the mathematician and the scientist. These modes of speech are seldom found in isolation: ordinary discourse is a blend of all three. The danger of building for ourselves a world of words and becoming immured in it, and so cut off from reality, is seen equally in the two extremes of materialistic monism and subjective idealism, as well as in all detailed theological systems. Never is the danger more acute than in the realm of religious philosophy. The life of religion is not in words, nor yet in ideas as such: it is when words are done with and disputation ended that the spirit flowers into grace. Religion is prayer, and the purest prayer is not only petitionless, but wordless.

In our first chapter the experience common to all mystics was described as a 'spiritual sensation'. It is a convenient phrase, but we shall do well to recognize its logical limitations. For is not all sensation spiritual, in the sense of involving spirit? Sensation cannot belong to the body alone, any more than to the spirit alone. The concepts 'body' and 'spirit' are in fact abstractions. They stand not for two independent realities, but for two aspects or appearances of that 'body-spirit' of which alone—not of either in isolation—we have actual and continuous experience. The duality is specious, not fundamental. We may indeed fairly describe it as a mere grammatical convenience, for it is no more fundamental than is that which is reflected in the terms *I* and *me*. I am spirit, the subject of my experience: *me* is that same spirit regarded objectively and known only by its behaviour. And my body *is* my behaviour, the temporal manifestation of *I*. In the 'absence' of its unifying principle it disintegrates, falls into multiplicity, and ceases to be in any meaningful sense 'mine'. The human body, in brief, like every other living thing, is a mode or form of spirit. That it *seems* to have a certain 'mechanical' automatism derives from two facts: the incidence of disease and the existence of physical appetites. But spirit, though for convenience we may equate it with 'awareness', that being its distinctive manifestation, does also operate at subconscious (and possibly at superconscious) levels, and, itself neutral, is the cause of evil effects no less than of good. As what theologians call 'sin' consists in unbridled self-assertion on the part of the individual ego, in denial of that human interdependence of which unity is the root and love the flower, so may bodily disorders be due to the self-assertion of infinitesimal constituent egos, at the expense of the unity of the whole organism. Love, on this showing, is simply the unifying principle of health, or wholeness, raised to the level of conscious volitional life.

The spiritual sensation enjoyed by mystics in their highest (that is, most self-forgetful) moments is something that seems to belong not to any one physical sense but to an unidentified faculty of the psyche in which perhaps all five senses are used, fused, and transcended. As the phrase implies, it is something felt rather than thought; and the great social value of mysticism is that being first an experience, and only afterwards an idea, it constitutes a perpetual challenge to

formal religion, which is for ever trying to strangle itself in
its own dogmas and institutions. But feeling cannot exist in
total isolation from thinking: so soon as one becomes aware
that one feels, or has felt, a sensation, of however diffused
and indefinable a character, the mind necessarily begins to
form some notion of it, whether true or fanciful. And if what
has happened seems to the subject to have been immensely
significant, he cannot but wish to make some record of it:
both for his own benefit, lest the memory lose its freshness,
and in the hope of sharing his blessedness with others. It is
not merely that something unusual has come his way. He is
not in the position of a man who has had an extraordinary
dream or visited a remote country. For the event is not
merely the strangest, it is (to his thinking and feeling) the
most real and the most blissful of events. It transfigures the
whole universe for him. The nearest parallel in normal human
life is that other spiritual sensation which we call 'falling in
love', in that early beatific stage of the process when all
beauty and all wonder seem to be concentrated in some one
other person. In those moments of pure adoration the lover
enjoys for the time being an essentially mystical rapture; as
does the poet, for whom 'beauty is truth, truth beauty', by
which oft-debated statement Keats meant, I suggest, not that
mere factual truth is necessarily beautiful, but that in beauty
we have direct sight of the eternal, the ultimately real.

The lover, the artist, and the illuminant, then, are all, in
their various modes, mystics. And they are all lovers, whether
the object of love be a single person, or all beautiful things,
or a reality beyond space and time of which beauty is (so
they say) the authentic sign. The lover's rapture and that
of the religious mystic are characterized not only by love and
wonder: they have a third feature in common, a sense of
recognition. Lovers recognize in each other the fulfilment of
their hearts' desire, even to the point of feeling that they
were 'made for each other' and did actually belong to each

other in some previous existence, so that their coming together is in effect a homecoming. We are free to dismiss
these fancies as nonsense, but we cannot deny that they are
part of the nonsense of being in love. And the religious
mystic, according to his own account of the matter, enjoys
precisely this same sensation of recognition and of coming
home. He falls in love with his vision of what he calls 'the
eternal' and he feels that he has unknowingly always belonged
to it. It is the paradise where once he was, and from which,
by some inexplicable cause and for some inscrutable purpose,
he is self-exiled. Plato's doctrine of *anamnesis*, which means
not memory merely but recollection, the recovery by memory
of something forgotten, must surely be the crystallization of
just that feeling, and may for all we know be the fruit of
a particular mystical experience. The doctrine's perennial
appeal to the imagination, exemplified in such poems as
Vaughan's *The Retreat* and Wordsworth's *Intimations of
Immortality*, would seem to suggest that the intuition which
it embodies, however we may choose to interpret it, is far
from uncommon.

The mystical vision, event, experience, call it what we will,
comes first; but the attempt to communicate it in words, to
clothe it in ideas, to translate it into doctrine, almost inevitably follows. That attempt may take the form of poetry,
narrative, exhortation, or philosophical treatise. Of these,
poetry, which at its highest is the perfect fusion of thought
with feeling and alone has the power to communicate a sense
of the ineffable, comes nearest to the heart of the matter;
but the spirit of poetry can and does animate other forms
than verse, and it is precisely in those moments when poetry
breaks in that the writings of mystics become luminous with
meaning for us. Expression, as we have seen, is necessarily
conditioned not only by the literary art but by the intellectual
environment of the writer. Though the experience is peculiarly his, and his alone, the interpretation he puts upon it

cannot but be coloured by his pre-existing beliefs and habits
of thought. It is therefore relevant to glance, however briefly,
at the philosophical antecedents of our earliest English
mystics.

During the third century, six hundred years after the death
of Plato, the doctrines of the Neoplatonist school found their
fullest statement in the *Enneads* of Plotinus, which were
compiled by a disciple from notes of his lectures. The
dialectical mythology which they embody is Platonic in spirit
and often in substance, as one would expect from a professed
follower of Plato; but Plotinus had assimilated other influences, and he refined upon and elaborated what he borrowed
from the master, as well as adding much of his own. His
power of meditative concentration, his biographer Porphyry
tells us, was such that he could suffer interruption without
annoyance, continue his private thinking undisturbed while
engaging in pleasant conversation, and, the moment the
visitor had departed, resume his writing instantly, without
so much as a glance at what had gone before. He was of a
kindly disposition, says the same witness, and always at the
service of his familiars. Many people of good family would,
at the approach of death, confide their children to his guardianship, so that his house became filled with young boys and
girls whose education and well-being were his special concern. A less agreeable feature in Porphyry's sketch of
Plotinus is indicated by the remark that he seemed to be
ashamed of living in a body: an aberration to which the more
extreme type of contemplative is lamentably prone. He
refused to sit for his portrait, saying: 'Isn't it enough that
one has to carry about this image with which Nature has
clothed one? Must one allow to be made of it another and
more lasting image, as though it were worth looking at?'
But as this incident may well have belonged to his last years,
when disease and disfigurement had hold of him, it would
be uncritical to make much of it. In the moment of death he

said to his friend Eustochius: 'I am striving to render back
that which is divine in me to that which is divine in the
universe.' An utterance that recalls the tranquil dignity of
Plato's Socrates in his last hour.

In those last words of Plotinus there is implied the animating idea of his system, that doctrine of Emanation which he
received from Plato and which Plato may (or may not) have
found in the philosophies of the East. All beings and things
come forth from the unconditioned One, or Absolute, and their
ultimate destiny is to return to their source: in other words,
the process of the universe is an eternal outflow of spirit into
matter, or form, and its return to the One. Plotinus chooses
to conceive the Divine Constitution as a triad or trinity, of
which the second proceeds from the first, and the third from
the second. They are the One or Absolute, the *Nous* (divine
Mind or Spirit), and the *Psyche* (the universal Life or Soul).
It is not clear (to me) whether he supposed his Triad to be
anything more than an intellectual convenience, a device for
bridging the logically impassable gap between the unknowable Absolute and the world we live in; but certainly it does
serve that purpose and does allow him without inconsistency
to rationalize his mystical apprehension of a divine life in
all things. For Plotinus was in spirit a poet as well as a
philosopher. The whole universe, for him, is alive at every
point. There is life, undiscerned by us, even in the things
we call inanimate. Each natural thing, moreover, has a life
proper to itself; for 'in saying that the *Psyche* is one we do
not say that plurality is excluded: we affirm it to be both one
and manifold'. Compare Wordsworth's:

> *To every natural form, rock, fruit, or flower,*
> *Even the loose stones that cover the highway,*
> *I gave a moral life: I saw them feel,*
> *Or linked them to some feeling: the great mass*
> *Lay bedded in a quickening soul . . .*

And again, in another well-known passage in *The Prelude*, describing the impact on his mind of a particular piece of landscape:

> The immeasurable height
> *Of woods decaying, never to be decayed,*
> *The stationary blasts of waterfalls,*
> *And in the narrow rent at every turn*
> *Winds thwarting winds, bewildered and forlorn,*
> *The torrents shooting from the clear blue sky,*
> *The rocks that muttered close upon our ears,*
> *Black drizzling crags that spake by the way-side*
> *As if a voice were in them, the sick sight*
> *And giddy prospect of the raving stream,*
> *The unfetter'd clouds and region of the heavens,*
> *Tumult and peace, the darkness and the light—*
> *Were all like workings of one mind, the features*
> *Of the same face, blossoms upon one tree;*
> *Characters of the great Apocalypse,*
> *The types and symbols of Eternity,*
> *Of first, and last, and midst, and without end.*

In these lines, as in so many others of Wordsworth's, Plotinus would have recognized an insight corroborating his own. The sense of a life peculiar to each thing is very strong in Wordsworth: he did not, any more than Plotinus did, allow his vision of the universal to blind him to the value and vitality of the particular. When he addresses the daisy as a 'sweet silent creature, that breath'st with me in sun and air', and asks to be given a share of its 'meek nature', he is indulging in no frigid poetical conceit: he is expressing, in anthropomorphic terms, his sense of the flower's aliveness.

§ 2

It is easy to see how, with a little ingenious modification, the Plotinian Triad could be assimilated in principle to the

Trinity of Christian dogma. Moreover, the three stages of the so-called Mystic Way recognized by mediaeval writers correspond closely to the purification, enlightenment, and ecstasy (or union), of the Neoplatonic system.* The first, sometimes called purgation, is a turning away from the sense-aspect of things to their animating soul; the second is the illumination that comes of communion with this 'eternal'; the third is an ultimate unimaginable beatitude of which no one who has not experienced it can properly speak and of which even those who believe they have experienced it can necessarily tell us very little. The three are separable only in analysis: they are stages in a continuing indivisible process, though in practice there may be an arrest at any point. Enlightenment, or illumination, can transform both the inward and the outward life of the individual; and it is to be supposed that very few can safely go further. Certain it is that a deliberate striving after ecstasy, for ecstasy's sake, can only defeat itself and lead us into fantasy and delusion, if nothing worse. Neoplatonism flowed into mediaeval thought through various channels, but mainly through the writings of the unknown sixth-century writer who chose to borrow the name of St Paul's Athenian convert, Dionysius the Areopagite.

The chief works of the pseudo-Dionysius were translated into Latin in the ninth century by Johannes Scotus Erigena. This John the Scot, said to have been (a) an Irishman and (b) born in Wales or (c) possibly Herefordshire, may with equal confidence be ranked as an English mystic. All that is positively known of him, apart from his writings, is that he spent some years in France at the court of Charles the Bald, by whom he was appointed head of the *schola palatina,* and with whom he seems to have been on terms of familiar

---

* See Evelyn Underhill's essay on Plotinus in *The Essentials of Mysticism,* Dent, 1920, to which I am indebted. For a full and detailed exposition—the *Enneads* being difficult of access—see Inge's *The Philosophy of Plotinus,* 2 vols.

friendship. The story is told that one day, seated at table with him, the king asked: 'Quid distat inter sottum et Scottum?' To which Erigena blandly replied: 'Mensa tantum.' It was at Charles's request that he undertook the translation of Dionysius: an enterprise displeasing to the Pope, Nicholas the First, who wrote to Charles demanding that the work should be sent to him for his approval. There is no evidence, however, that anything of the kind was done. Erigena differs from the later scholastics in that he exalts reason or philosophy to first place, and regards theology as something derived from it. For him the highest faculty of man is that intellectual vision (*Nous*) which sees all things as parts of the whole. Reason in this sense and at this level is God himself thinking in man, the second hypostasis of the Plotinian Triad. Though he was no rebel, the boldness and independence of his thought, and his tacit assumption that authority can be derived only from reason, made his orthodoxy suspect; and four centuries later his *De divisione naturae* was declared by Pope Honorius the Third to be 'swarming with worms of heretical perversity'. The story that in 882, four years after the defeat of the Danes at Ethandun, Alfred the Great invited him to England, and that he taught for many years at the Abbey of Malmesbury, is accepted by some authorities. Not so the fantastic sequel, that his pupils eventually stabbed him to death with their pens.

Erigena's *natura* stands, not for Nature in our limited sense, but for the totality of all things, both created and uncreated. The material universe is nothing more or less than the necessary self-manifestation of God. It is, as eighteenth-century Idealism was to declare in effect, part of God's thinking. Creation was not an act in (or before) time: it is an eternal fact, the *Genesis* account of the matter, and of Paradise and the Fall, being no more than an allegory faintly shadowing forth not local and temporal events but eternal truths concerning the constitution of God, Man, and the Universe. Erigena's system, like all systems that attempt to chart the unknowable, is highly vulnerable in some points of detail; but he was an acute thinker in the Neoplatonic tradition and seems to have had a considerable influence on later mystical thought. His monism has exposed him to the charge of being a 'mere' pantheist; but, as has been well said, it is either confusion of thought or abuse of language to call his philosophy pantheism and leave it at that. In official Christian theology 'the emphasis has always been more upon the distinctness of God from the world than upon the union of God with the world. Ecclesiastical religion has always been in more danger of Deism than of Pantheism, as, indeed, in respect of all other truth, it has been in more danger of the mechanical than of the mystical. It is certain that less than justice has been done to some great elements of New Testament doctrine.' * Erigena's doctrine is that the essence of God 'appears in the universe as multiple, visible, and accessible to human thought, but . . . is still single, invisible, and incommunicable in the Divine Nature. So the human spirit manifests itself in speech and writing, using audible syllables that are separated in time, and visible letters that are separated in space, and yet it remains itself undivided, unheard, unseen. . . . The whole view of Erigena is in the direction that the existence of the universe is a necessary moment in the life of God, a necessary fulfilment of the process of the Divine Nature'.†

§ 3

Moving on to the fourteenth century, the first full flowering-time of English mysticism properly so called, we find ourselves in a very different intellectual climate from that of the comparatively austere Plotinus and the school of

---

* Henry Bett, *Johannes Scotus Erigena*. Cambridge, 1925.   † *Ibid.*

thought that sprang from him. The key ideas of Neoplatonism are still traceable, but they are now modified, sometimes almost beyond recognition, by the Christology with which they are uneasily blended. Christian thought at its best has never disdained to enrich itself by borrowing and adapting to its own purposes whatever is congenial to itself in pre-Christian philosophies, and has always been more concerned to cater for imaginative needs than to formulate a logically impeccable system: in this flexibility, not in rigid adherence to the letter of a creed, has lain its chief strength. Heretics there have always been, but it is a commonplace that some of the most bitterly-resisted heresies of today, in so far as they embody aspects of truth that are relevant to our human situation, become part of the orthodoxy of tomorrow: a process known in ecclesiastical circles as 'progressive revelation'. Change and resistance to change are equally natural; and both are necessary, in that the tension between them is a necessary condition of vitality. Even in the Christian age of faith, when there was at least a large consensus of taken-for-granted belief, wide divergencies of interpretation and opinion existed, within as well as beyond the pale of the Church. With Richard Rolle, Walter Hilton, the Lady Julian of Norwich, and the author of *The Cloud of Unknowing*, however, we enter the realm not of theological controversy but of pure Christian devotion. Their orthodoxy, so far as I know, has never been questioned.

The particular kind of human experience which is the subject of this book finds expression in many diverse forms, ranging from a scarcely articulate stammering to the most elaborate and systematic philosophizing, and from artless ejaculations of wonder to the most luminous and highly wrought poetry. But its most important effect, conditioning all others, is a release of spirit and a transformation of life, an immense enlargement of sympathy and a rebirth of charity in the heart. In the traditional language of religion, by self-surrender to the inflowing tide the individual person becomes, in greater or less degree, a channel of Divine Grace. By self-surrender, self-oblivion: not by a self-indulgent emotionalism, not by concern for one's own salvation, not by seeking refuge from human responsibility in an exclusive otherworldliness, and not, above all, by that ambition for personal sanctity which is perhaps the most insidious of all spiritual dangers. All these things are merely so many snares set by the writhing, posturing, self-preening ego. And there are others. Human conduct can never be a matter of indifference; but the wisest of mankind have recognized that 'righteousness', over-zealously pursued, too easily becomes self-righteousness, and that all that is of value in righteousness (the word is a corruption of 'right-wiseness') proceeds from love. *Dilige et quod vis fac.* Without love, righteousness is 'filthy rags' and mysticism a dead letter, or, what is worse, a private luxury.

By way of recapitulation let us ask again what in essence the mystic's experience is. In the light of our various examples it is seen to be an intuition of something wonderful beyond one's imagining but to which nevertheless one intimately belongs. Its normal effect is to induce a sense of that unifying principle in things, of which love is the outward and visible sign. Love in this context is self-giving, a desire not for possession but for union—or should we not say reunion?—with that from which only the accident or illusion of time and space has divided us. We may call it 'cosmic emotion' or 'love of God', according to taste: neither phrase is anything more than a label. The mystic's vision is abortive unless it puts him 'in charity' with his fellow-creatures. But love cannot spend itself on metaphysical abstractions: even the most catholic love must in practice discriminate among particular things and persons. Still less can what is called 'worship' be content with the contemplation of a hypothetical Absolute: it can find expression in painting, poetry, music, and other

POEM AND DRAWING BY WILLIAM BLAKE

creative work, but, failing that outlet, it demands for its object a person or persons, either real or imagined. The personalization of 'God' is, in part at least, the product of this widespread, but not universal, psychological need. We need not pause to inquire in what sense God can be rightly conceived as personal; but it is obvious that that which by definition is present in all persons and things cannot be 'a' person, with the limitations which that term implies, and equally cannot be called non-personal, since persons are part of its manifestation.* For Christian believers this logically impassable gulf is bridged by the idea of a Divine Man, and personal devotion to Jesus plays necessarily a dominant part in the writings of Rolle, Hilton, and Julian. Jesus for them is the unique incarnation of that Divine Love which is their perennial theme. Richard Rolle, the hermit of Hampole, wrote a number of religious love-lyrics in the vernacular, as well as prose works in Latin:

> *My song is in sighing,*
> *My life is in longing*
> *Till I see [thee] my king,*
> *So fair in thy shining.*

In a poem on Christ's Passion beginning

> *My truest treasure so traitorly was taken,*
> *So bitterly bounden with biting bands,*
> *How soon of thy servants was thou forsaken,*
> *And loathly for my love hurled with their hands——*

* God cannot be either (*a*) a person separate from other persons, or (*b*) a mere aggregate of all persons. The English Prayer Book's use of the term 'person' in propounding the doctrine of the Trinity is indeed a most unfortunate historical accident. In that context the expression 'three persons' can only mean three aspects, appearances, or modes of being. To assert that God consists of three persons in the everyday modern sense of the term was surely not the intention of the Christian Fathers? It is significant that the Latin *persona*, from which our word is derived, meant the mask worn (and so, by natural extension, the part played) by an actor.

he entreats his 'dearworthy darling, so dolefully dight' not
to let him miss the meaning of the Passion:

> *But wind up my will to wone with thee ay,*
> *That thou be buried in my breast and bring me to bliss.*

And the same note of personal devotion is heard in the good
homely prose of Walter Hilton and in the dazzling 'revelations' recorded by Julian of Norwich.

Because they are so remote from us, and so near to each
other, in time and in habit of life and thought, these three
may at first glance look very much alike: the great difference
from ourselves tends to obscure the differences between one
and another. The resemblances are indeed obvious enough.
They were members of the same religious communion. They
all had a specifically religious vocation. Living at a time
when many men and women, for a variety of reasons, chose
personal sanctity for a career, as today they might choose
medicine or law, these three are remarkable for their candour
and sincerity and often for their searching common sense.
But, though they have qualities in common and agree in their
main doctrine, their writings reflect marked differences in
temperament. Evelyn Underhill in an essay on Rolle com-
pares him with Francis of Assisi, finding in both 'the same
engaging mixture of singleminded response to an interior
vocation, boyish romanticism, and personal courage'. They
both 'ran away to God, as other lads have run away to sea:
sure that their only happiness lay in total self-giving to the
one great adventure of life'. Walter Hilton, sometime Canon
of Thurgarten Priory, is a more quietly meditative spirit, less
lyrical in his mode of expression and of a more practical
turn of mind, though full, too, of sweetness and light. The
most startling and perhaps the most attractive of the three
is the anchoress Julian of Norwich.

Richard Rolle was born (*circa* 1290) in the village of
Thornton-le-Dale in Yorkshire. Nothing is known of his

parents except that his father, William Rolle, was acquainted
with the Sir John Dalton who afterwards befriended the boy.
In early adolescence Richard was sent to Oxford, where, we
are told, he showed a marked preference for theological above
secular studies and made great progress in them. At the age
of nineteen, returned from Oxford to his father's house, he
said one day to his sister that he greatly coveted two tunics
which she had, one white, the other grey, and begged that
she would bring them next day, together with their father's
rain-hood, to where he would be waiting for her in a near-by
wood. This she did, having no notion of what was in his mind.
Richard then, to her amazement, cut off the sleeves from the
grey tunic and the buttons from the white and dressed himself
up as a hermit, as nearly as might be, covering his head with
the hood. His sister cried out: 'My brother is mad! My
brother is mad!' Whereupon, the story says, he drove her
from him with threats, and ran off, afraid lest he should be
seen and seized by someone who knew him. On the eve of
the Feast of the Assumption he entered a church, probably
at Topcliffe near Thirsk, and by accident sat down in the
place reserved for the Daltons. Lady Dalton ordered her
servants not to disturb him, and her sons, who had been
fellow students of his at Oxford, recognized him as he rose
from his devotions. Next day he came to church again, and
without invitation put on a surplice and sang matins with the
others; and afterwards, having asked a blessing of the priest,
he went into the pulpit and preached 'a sermon of wonderful
edification' which moved the multitude to tears. After Mass
he was invited to dinner by the squire, Sir John Dalton; but
no sooner had he entered the house than he 'betook him to
a certain mean and old room' instead of going into the dining
hall with his hosts. He was quickly sought out and conducted
to a place of honour at table: much against his will, it seems,
for he sat in perfect silence throughout the meal and as soon as
he had eaten he got up to go. His host, however, said gently

that that was not customary, and prevailed on him to sit down again. Later on they had some private talk together, and the upshot of it was that Sir John provided him with a hermit's cell and dress and saw to it that his daily wants were supplied, so that he might live without hindrance a life of solitary contemplation. It is not known how long he stayed under the Daltons' protection. In later years he moved from place to place, finally settling at Hampole, where he ministered to the spiritual needs of the nuns of a Cistercian Priory which had been established there a hundred years earlier.

I have recited this story in what may seem unnecessary detail, for the sake of the light it throws on the mind and manners of the times. We have only to imagine what would happen today to a young man who behaved as Richard did, to see how great a gulf divides us from the fourteenth century. To us his assignation with his sister in the wood, and his assumption of a home-made hermit's garb, looks like a bit of boyish play-acting: as indeed it was. There is something touchingly ingenuous in the notion that in order to live the contemplative life one must wear a special uniform. Yet, as the result shows, granted his resolve to forsake the path of learning for that of religion it was an eminently sensible and practical thing to do; for in Richard's day hermits were part of the established social order, and he knew that to dress and behave like a hermit was the first step towards being accepted as such. And if we can more readily sympathize with his sister's startled cry, 'My brother is mad!', than we can understand the burning zeal that moved him to separate himself from his family, that perhaps implies some failure in imagination on our part rather than folly on his. Burning zeal, as it happens, is a singularly exact phrase; for his 'spiritual fire' seems sometimes to have produced in him an hallucination of actual physical heat. Psycho-physical phenomena of this kind do occur from time to time in the history of mysticism. They neither prove nor disprove anything whatever. Nor

are they, in general, regarded with favour by mystics themselves: Walter Hilton, for example, has some warning words
on the matter. Rolle records this purely subjective experience
in simple good faith, telling how, while in a chapel engaged
in prayer and meditation, he first felt within him a 'merry
and unknown heat', which, because it grew 'hotter and more
glad', he knew to be from God. This 'sensible and sweet-
smelling heat' remained with him, he says, for something
over three months, and then gave place to another sensory
illusion: he became aware above him of a 'heavenly and
ghostly sound . . . as it were of singers', so that presently,
'for plenteousness of inward sweetness', he burst out singing
what before he had been content to say.

He was by disposition a poet and a musician, and it is
natural that his mystical apprehensions should have reached
him in a form most congenial to his genius and be given by
him to the world in poetry and song. Both his singing and
his prose meditations are concerned always with love: love
which is above knowledge and without which knowledge of
God is impossible. Let us seek rather, he says, that the love
of Christ burn within us than that we pay heed to unprofitable
disputation. An old wife is more expert in God's love than
one who studies divinity that he may appear glorious and
get rents and dignities: 'the which is worthy to be held a
fool, and not wise'. He only knows God perfectly that knows
him to be beyond knowledge. It is enough for us to know
that God is: we cannot know, intellectually, *what* God is.
'Let it not irk thee that I say we are to know God perfectly
and yet deny that he may be known'; for we know him,
declares Rolle in effect, by loving him, loving him we sing
in him, singing we rest in him, and by inwardly resting in
him we come to the rest that is without end. Only by living
in perfect charity can we reach the heights of divine contemplation.

But here we run into danger; for it may well be objected

that to 'love God' is to love either a metaphysical idea, which
is impossible, or an imaginary personification of that which
is by definition unknowable. The language of devotion
inevitably exposes itself to this kind of criticism; and indeed
there is no language capable of expressing, without distortion, the innermost realities of human experience. Anthropomorphism offers us the grossest of all distortions, presenting
that which is at once the being of our being and the bond
of our union, a mystery which no words can compass and no
symbolism do more than dimly suggest, in the guise of a
large, vague, invisible man or superman, utterly separate
from ourselves. Every time we speak of God in third-personal
terms, as 'he' and 'him', we speak the language of primitive
mythology and perpetuate a crude fiction.* And by substituting
the impersonal pronoun 'it', or talking about a Life Force,
we merely avoid one error at the expense of embracing
another. The most luminous of all statements about God is
St John's 'God is love', which means, I suggest, not that God
is a loving person, but that God and love are interchangeable
terms, and that the living reality they represent is incarnate in
every loving act or impulse. This is implicit, too, in the
already-quoted saying of the great fourteenth-century mystic
who wrote *The Cloud of Unknowing*, that God may be gotten
and holden by love, but by thought never. What 'love' means
in this context may be difficult to define in precise terms; but
that does not matter, for no definition, however exact, can
tell us as much as we know by inward and inescapable
experience. To say that we 'love God', therefore, is only
another way of saying that the self-giving impulse within

* The unquestioning habitual use of such expressions in such a context has
inevitably obscured their mythological character. Here is a story that will help
us to recognize it. When the 'Votes for Women' agitation was at its height
(1912–14), a young suffragette confided to her leader that she was troubled
by religious doubts. 'Don't worry, my dear,' said that ardent feminist. 'Take
your troubles to God. She'll help you.' Now the comic force of that 'she' lies
in its unexpectedness, as well as in its ingenuous implications. The masculine
pronoun, if we were not so used to it, would be seen to be equally incongruous.

each of us responds to the self-giving impulse in others, that impulse being the sign of our essential unity as participators in the life of the one Divine Spirit. The 'love of God' is not a thought or a theological exercise. Nor does it animate only those who think in theistic terms. Whether or not we choose to make use of the expression, we 'love God' whenever we recognize and respond to what is lovable in nature, art, or behaviour. In other words we love God, as we love beauty (when we recognize it), not in the abstract, but as a seen, heard, felt, or apprehended harmony: whether in things apparent to the senses or in images conceived in the mind, and not least in human goodness, which is the full flower of love. And so we come back to love, the beginning and end, that without which life could have neither value nor meaning.

§ 4

The extraordinary document left by Julian of Norwich relates to an illness of which she nearly died at the age of thirty. Nothing positive is known of the outward circumstances of her life, except that she was born about 1342, dedicated herself to the religious life, and became an anchoress, or recluse, living (it is thought) in a cell built against the south wall of a Norwich church. She describes herself as a simple creature unskilled in letters at the time of the 'shewings'; but she was almost certainly of gentle birth, had received the education appropriate to that condition, and enjoyed, then or later, some acquaintance with religious literature. Her own writing is singularly fresh and apt: the story she tells, years after the event, has the brilliant clarity and power of an experience long meditated on. One conspicuous feature of it will perhaps offend the modern reader, if he fails to bear in mind the difference in mental climate between then and now. She herself tells us, with simple candour, that before receiving her revelations she had prayed

for three gifts from God. The first was that she might be
granted a 'bodily sight' of Christ on the Cross, in order that
she might suffer with him; the second was that she should
have a severe illness at the age of thirty; and the third that
she should receive of God 'three wounds', the wounds of
true contrition, of natural compassion, and of steadfast
longing. All these wishes were fulfilled: dropped into the
soil of the unconscious they flowered into fact. The first two
must seem morbid to many of us today, but would not have
seemed so to Julian's religious contemporaries. The suf-
ferings of the Crucified Christ were a favourite theme for
meditation, and the physical incidents of that agony, vividly
depicted in mediaeval art with an abundance of homely detail,
were dwelt upon with a particularity of which the best that
can be said is that it was ingenuous, innocent, childlike.
Illuminated missal and coloured crucifix must have powerfully
influenced Julian's visual imagination. As for the wish to be
ill, which the psychiatrist may be inclined to dismiss as pure
masochism, we shall do well to accept it as simply as Julian
records it, and without comment; for the clinical view can
tell us only of its psychological mechanism, in terms of wish
and wish-fulfilment, not of what, in the sequel, Julian herself
made of it. That disease should be deliberately self-induced
is alien to our notions of sanity. But, like it or not, that is
what happened. And it is not the first time, nor the last, that
dire physical suffering has been turned to good account.

When she was 'thirty years old and a half', Julian tells us,
God sent her the bodily sickness for which she had prayed
years before; and on the fourth night of the disorder she
took all 'my rites of Holy Church' and thought she could
not live till morning. After this she 'languored forth' for
two days and two nights, often thinking she was about to die,
as did those who were with her. 'And being in youth as yet,
I thought it great sorrow to die'; but convinced by her reason
and by her pain that it must be so, she assented fully, with

all the will of her heart. So she remained till morning, by which time the lower half of her body seemed already dead to her. A priest was sent for. He found her far gone and incapable of speech. Holding a crucifix before her eyes, he urged her to look upon it, which she did. 'After this my sight began to fail, and it was all dark about me in the chamber, as if it had been night, save in the Image of the Cross, whereon I beheld a common light.' The upper part of her body now began to lose the power of feeling, and she breathed with difficulty, and thought again that she must be dying; but in this moment, suddenly, 'all my pain was taken away from me, and I was as whole as ever I was before'. It came to her then to desire 'the second wound', the wound of 'kind compassion'. That other wish, of a 'bodily shewing' of Christ, was no longer in her conscious mind; but it had done its work unseen, and in the hypnotic trance induced by gazing at the crucifix she presently saw 'the red blood trickle down from the garland [of thorns] hot and freshly and right plenteously' and assumed, inevitably, that this 'shewing' was from Christ, not the projection of her own inner fantasy upon an object most congenial for its reception. Not that a crucifix was necessary: anything that drew the eyes, fixed the attention, held the mind still, would have done equally well.

If Julian's 'revelations' were all or mainly of this crude and conventional sort, they would not be worth bothering about. Happily it is not so. The visual hallucination is merely the outward form or accompaniment of an inward experience, the mind's dramatization of its intuitions. Julian herself treats the whole thing as a significant dream. She does not doubt that it is from God, but implicit in her account is a clear distinction between actually seeing God (or Christ) and being granted a 'shewing' or vision of God. Except that there is no conscious contrivance on her part, she is in the position of any poet in whom a work of creative imagination is being wrought. Moreover, as she was writing so long after the event, and had a natural predilection for vivid and concrete symbolism, we cannot always be quite sure where fantasy ends and allegory begins: they tend to shade off into each other. Whether, for example, she imagined that she had 'bodily sight' of the 'little thing the size of a hazel-nut' mentioned in the following passage is an open question. Nor does it in the least matter. 'In this same time,' she says, 'our Lord shewed me a ghostly [spiritual] sight of his homely loving. I saw that he is to us everything that is good and comfortable for us. He is our clothing that for love wrappeth us, claspeth us, and all becloseth us for tender love; being to us all-thing that is good, as to mine understanding. Also in this he shewed me a little thing the size of a hazel-nut, in the palm of my hand.' Looking upon this little thing with the eye of her understanding, she thought 'What may this be?' and the answering thought came: 'It is all that is made' —that is, a symbol of the whole creation. She marvelled how it could last, thinking that being so small and frail it might at any moment fall into nothingness. 'And I was answered in my understanding: It lasteth, and ever shall, because God loveth it.' By which she understands that nothing has being except by the love of God. 'In this little thing,' she goes on, 'I saw three properties. The first is that God made it, the second is that God loves it, the third that God keeps it. But what is to me verily the Maker, the Keeper, and the Lover, I cannot tell; for till I am substantially made one with him I may never have full rest nor true bliss: that is to say, till I be so fastened to him that there is right nought that is made betwixt my God and me. . . . No soul is rested till it is noughted of all things that are made. When, for love, it is willingly made nought, to have him that is all, then is it able to receive ghostly rest.'

Julian does not mean that created things are to be despised, or regarded as valueless, but only that their value is derived from the one life, or love, that sustains them. In the vision and contemplation of that, not in attachment to things as such, is our 'rest'. This is the ancient doctrine of non-attachment, purged of the insufferable disdain of natural and human things that too often infects it. For God, says Julian, 'hath no disdain of that which he hath made, nor any disdain to serve us at the simplest office that belongs in nature to our body. For as the body is clad in cloth, and the flesh in skin, and the bones in flesh, and the heart in the whole, so are we, soul and body, clad in the goodness of God and beclosed. Yea, and more homely; for all these may waste and wear away, but the goodness of God is ever whole, and more near to us.' She is quite explicit on this point: that the allegory of the hazel-nut does not imply a disdain of creatures and things. 'Well I wot that heaven and earth and all that is made is great and large, fair and good. The cause why it shewed so little to my sight was that I saw it in the presence of him that is the Maker of all things. For to a soul that seeth the Maker of all, all that is made seemeth full little.' But goodness can be in little things as easily as in great; for 'God is all that is good, as to my sight, and the goodness that each thing hath, it is he.' Julian's insight agrees with St Augustine's, that there is no health in those who find fault with any part of God's creation, and with Erigena's, that every creature, visible and invisible, is a theophany or appearance of God. 'In man is God, and God is in all,' she says, having already said, be it noted, that all is in God. In this luminous paradox is contained the whole doctrine of mysticism. 'After this I saw God in a point—by which sight I saw that God is in all things.'

From this she is led to consider the problem of sin. If God who is all-good is the soul of created things, how can sin, which is evil, occur? How escape the conclusion that God is the author of evil as well as of good? But if that be so, how can God be all-good? 'I saw truly that God doeth all-thing, be it never so little. And I saw truly that nothing is done by hap nor by adventure, but all things by the foreseeing wisdom of God. Wherefore me behoveth needs to grant that all-thing that is done, it is well done, for our Lord God doeth it. . . . He is in the mid-point of all-thing, and all he doeth. And I was certain he doeth no sin. And here I saw verily that sin is no deed.' Here, again, Julian is in line with other mystics: with Erigena, Dionysius, and Plotinus. As goodness is creative, unifying, so evil is uncreative, separative, and essentially negative. It arises from the delusion of self-isolation and is no more part of the Real which is the Whole than 'twice two are five' is a part of mathematics. Julian's way of disposing of sin will not silence the dialectician; but a logically watertight system of thought was not her aim. How to reconcile the existence of evil with that of a benevolent all-powerful and personal God is a question that cannot be answered because it does not make sense. The logical contradiction it embodies can only be resolved by denying or modifying one of its terms. Julian says that she had often wondered, in her folly, why by 'the great foreseeing wisdom of God' sin was not prevented from ever beginning. 'But Jesus, who in this vision informed me of all that is needful to me, answered by this word and said: Sin is behovable, but all shall be well, and all shall be well, and all manner of thing shall be well'—words used as a recurring refrain in Mr Eliot's *Little Gidding*.

Evil, according to Erigena, is parasitic, dependent for its very existence on the good which it feeds on. This is also St Augustine's view. All things are good in themselves, because created by God who is good. Good and being are identical. However small or of whatever kind the being in question may be, evil cannot destroy the good which constitutes that being without also destroying itself. Evil is not being but the privation of being, not real but a lapse from reality. 'Every being, therefore, is a good: a great good if it cannot be corrupted, a little good if it can; but in any event only the foolish or ignorant,' says Augustine roundly, 'will deny that it is a good. And if it be wholly consumed by corruption, then the corruption itself must cease to exist, since there is no being left in which it can dwell.'* As Julian herself puts it: 'I believe it [sin] hath no manner of substance nor no part of being, nor could it be known but by the pain it is cause of.' Pain is 'something for a time'. It purges us, and makes us know ourselves and ask mercy. But the Lord 'comforteth readily and sweetly, signifying thus: It is sooth that sin is cause of all this pain; but all shall be well, and all shall be well, and all manner of thing shall be well'. A 'kind soul', says Julian—and it is significant that her 'kind' means both *natural* and *loving*—'hath no hell but sin'. And true love 'teaches us that we should hate sin only for love'; for Christ would have us 'endlessly hate the sin and endlessly love the soul, as God loveth it'.

Sometimes she dramatizes her intuitions, by putting words into the mouth of Christ; sometimes she states them directly; but always they have for her the indubitable actuality of something seen or heard: not (for the most part) with the bodily senses but, as she is scrupulous to say more than once, 'in my understanding'. The Lord, she says in effect, 'shewed these words' to her mind: 'I am the Ground of thy beseeking. First, it is my will that thou have it. After, I make thee to will it. And after that, I make thee to beseek it and thou beseekest it. How should it then be that thou shouldst not have thy beseeking?' And so, 'prayer oneth the soul to God'. The unity of God and mankind is the very heart of her conviction. 'Truth seeth God, and Wisdom beholdeth God,

---

* *Enchiridion.* Quoted by Grace Warrack in her edition—indispensable to students—of Julian's *Revelations of Divine Love* (Methuen, 1901), page 57, footnote. My quotations from Julian, however, will be found to differ in minor points of diction, though not in meaning, from Miss Warrack's skilfully edited version of the *Sloane* text (British Museum MS 2499). The passages quoted below, on pages 62–63, I take direct from that manuscript, altering nothing except (here and there) the spelling.

and of these two cometh a holy marvelling delight in God, which delight is Love. God is endless sovereign Truth, endless sovereign Wisdom, endless sovereign Love, unmade; and man's Soul is a creature in God which hath the same properties made, and evermore it doeth that it was made for: it seeth God, it beholdeth God, and it loveth God. Whereof God enjoyeth in the creature, and the creature enjoyeth in God, endlessly marvelling.'

In God, who is Love, there is and can be no anger. 'Wrath is not else but a frowardness and a contrariness to peace and love.' It comes either of a failing of power, or a failing of wisdom, or a failing of goodness; and God cannot be subject to such failing. God 'may not forgive, for he may not be wroth: it were impossible. For this was shewed: that our life is all grounded and rooted in love, and without love we may not live. I saw no manner of wrath in God, neither for short time nor for long; for in sooth, as to my sight, if God might be wroth a touch [for an instant] we should never have life, ne stede, ne being. For verily as we have our being of the endless might of God and of the endless wisdom and of the endless goodness, so verily we have our keeping in the endless might of God, in the endless wisdom, and in the endless goodness. For though we feel (in us wretches) debates and strifes, yet are we all-mannerful beclosed in the mildhede of God and in his mekehede, in his benignity and in his buxomhede. For I saw full sekirly [surely] that all our endless friendship, our stede, our life and our being, is in God. Thus is God our stedfast ground.'

The pernicious notion that man's nature is evil in itself finds no warrant in the writings of this most Christian of mystics. To her mind, as to Augustine's, to say any such thing is to dishonour God. 'We have verily of kinde [nature] to haten sin, and we have verily of grace to haten sin. For kinde is all good and fair in itself, and grace was sent out to saven kinde and destroyen sin and bringen again fair kinde to the blessed point fro whence it came: that is God. For it shall be seen afore God, of all his holy in joye without end, that kinde hath ben assayed in the fire of tribulation and therein founden no lack, no default. Thus is kinde and grace of one accord: for grace is good as kind is good: he is two in manner or working and one in love. And neyther of them worketh without other, nor be departed [separated]. And when we, by mercy of God and with his helpe, accorden us to kinde and grace, we shall seen verily that sin is very viler and painfuller than helle, without likeness; for it is contrarious to our fair kinde.' When Julian asked the meaning of that saying, 'I am the Ground of thy beseeking', she was answered 'in ghostly understanding', thus: 'Wouldst thou witten thy Lord's meaning in this thing? Wete it well: love was his meaning. Who shewed it thee? Love. What shewed he thee? Love. Wherefore shewed it he? For love. Hold thee therein and thou shalt witten and knowen more in the same. But thou shalt never knowen ne witten therein other thing without end. Thus was I lerid [taught] that love was our Lord's meaning.'

§ 5

'For charity pray we all,' says Julian. She herself was filled with charity, and with that of which it is the flower, humility. Unlike some other ecstatics of her time, she is careful to point out that the revelations granted to her imply no merit on her part. She does not indulge in the sickly cant of supposing herself to be one of God's favourites. 'For truly it was not shewed me that God loved me better than the least soul that is in grace; for I am certain that there be many that never had shewing nor sight, but of the common teaching of Holy Church, that love God better than I.' Humility, or mekehede [meekness], is a word much out of favour. In recent centuries its original meaning has been overlaid by the notion of cringing servility or obsequiousness, which are things quite alien to it. 'As mickle as thou hast of meekness,' says Walter Hilton, in his *Scale of Perfection*, 'so mickle hast thou of charity, of patience, and of other virtues, though they be not shewed outward. Be then busy to get meekness, and hold it; for it is the first and last of all virtues.' In *The Cloud of Unknowing* we are told precisely what meekness is: it is self-knowledge. 'Meekness in itself is naught else but a true knowing and feeling of a man's self as he is. For surely whoso might verily see and feel himself as he is, he should verily be meek. And therefore, in all that thou canst and mayest, swink and sweat for to get thee a true knowing and a feeling of thyself as thou art . . .' There is a distinction, however, to be made between the self (the empirical self) and the soul, which is of one substance with God. For it is readier to us, says Julian, 'to come to the knowing of God than to know our own soul.' For our soul 'sitteth in God in very rest, and standeth in God in very strength, and is kindly [naturally] rooted in God in endless love. And therefore if we will have knowledge of our soul, and communing and dalliance therewith, it behoveth to seek unto our Lord God in whom it is beclosed.'

Chapter Three

GEORGE FOX

§ 1

EVERY man is a man of his times, even though he be a stern critic of his times. Whatever singularity he possesses or may acquire, he is still in large measure the product of his environment. He is not indeed the passive effect of antecedent causes; for there is something in him, or of him, which discriminates, which selects, making him as impervious to some influences as he is receptive to others; but this process, unlike the artistic process which in principle it resembles, is in earliest formative years beyond his conscious control; it is something that happens to him rather than something that he does, or, more exactly, it is something to which he, being himself a cause as well as an effect, contributes unwittingly. We cannot form a true judgment of any man unless we see him in his historical context. Even so, since every human soul is a mystery penetrable only by omniscience, we cannot pretend to a full understanding or a final judgment.

In George Fox, as in all powerful personalities that have left a mark on the world, there is much to exasperate us as well as much to admire. He was a simple man, yet with a character full of apparent contradictions. He was gentle and contentious, humble and militant, noisy and serene, self-educated, uncultured, dominating, unselfseeking, and—after the religious crisis of his young manhood—utterly persuaded of being always right in everything he said and did. The Puritans of his time bitterly opposed and persecuted him; yet he himself, by the accident of birth and upbringing, was in practice, and partly in theory too, the sternest puritan of them

E

all. He affirmed the presence in all men of a divine Inward Light and exalted the spirit above the letter; yet sought to prove the unrighteousness of swearing oaths by an appeal to the letter of Scripture, and was zealous to reprove those whose inward light allowed them to indulge in the innocent game of bowls. He was a pigheaded and opinionated fellow; and he was also, incontestably, a great and good man.

The first thing to remember about him is that he lived and died (1624–1691) in a period of unparalleled religious ferment. Charles the First began his lamentable reign during Fox's first year of life and died on the scaffold when Fox was twenty-five. Thenceforward, until the Restoration, Fox and his followers had to endure savage if sporadic persecution from the 'saints' of the Commonwealth; and after the Restoration, till easygoing Charles the Second found time from his pleasures to intervene, the same persecution was carried on by authorities too stupid, too idle, or too fearful, to see that Quakers were the last people in the world to plot against king and constitution.

In the seventeenth century religion and politics were inextricably mixed. To a degree which we of today find it difficult to imagine, the name of God was in every man's mouth as a sanction for whatever conscience self-interest or expediency prompted him to do. The indefatigable William Laud (nicknamed *parva Laus* by his Oxford contemporaries) had come near to establishing theocratic rule in England; the Royalists, when the conflict between Crown and Parliament began, held fast by the comparatively novel doctrine of Divine Right; the Parliamentarians opposed the Royalists for equally godly reasons; and almost all public speeches were plentifully larded with pious unction, more especially of course those of the so-called 'lecturers' or licensed preachers (not priests) who frequented market-places and discoursed on Sunday afternoons—an institution dating from Elizabethan times. The nation was divided into warring religious factions, each of which, by an entertaining coincidence, was the sole repository of God's truth. Speciously composing these differences was the legal fiction that the whole population of England, estimated at something under five millions, belonged to the established Anglican Church, though obvious exceptions were confessed Papists (or Recusants) at one extreme and Puritan Separatists (or Dissenters) at the other. Inside the Church, among the clergy themselves, there were two main parties of opinion: (i) the non-separatist Puritans, eager for further reforms, alert to exclude all rites and ceremonies that might seem to savour of Popery, and in doctrine strongly inclined towards Calvinism; and (ii) the Prelatists or Episcopalians, who in the main detested Calvinism and were zealous defenders of the divine right of bishops, as well as of the king.

These are live issues for only a tiny minority of our countrymen today: to the rest of us it must seem that there was right and wrong on both sides, as in nearly all party disputes. If the Puritans' excessive fear of Romanism looks like a neurosis, it must be conceded that there was some historical basis for it, and that they had excellent reason to distrust the king and his cronies; and if the Prelatists were too eager in their pursuit of temporal power, it is at least to their credit that so many of them repudiated that central doctrine of John Calvin's which, in the words of Johann Kollmann, a Dutch opponent of the system, made God 'both a tyrant and an executioner'. The most formidable single opponent of Calvinism was the more celebrated Dutch theologian, Arminius, who died some fifteen years before Charles's accession but whose teaching survived to be an influence in seventeenth-century English theology. *Arminian* and *Popish* seem to have been used as interchangeable terms of opprobrium by the English and Scottish Puritans of the time, though Arminius himself was far from being an adherent of Rome. The Synod of Dort (1619), in which English as well as Continental ecclesiastics took part, came down heavily on

the side of the Calvinists; but, so far from silencing controversy, its effect in England was rather to widen the breach
between the two parties. We are not concerned with the
details of this historic quarrel, but we cannot begin to understand George Fox's position, still less the cruel hostility he
encountered, without some notion of the main points in
dispute.

Calvin (1509–1564) is one of the most influential and
disastrous figures in religious history. He owed much to the
earlier Reformer, Luther; but he excelled his master in
dialectical skill, in personal austerity, and in the intolerant
zeal with which he propagated his opinions and established
in Geneva his theocratic tyranny. He and his followers took
upon themselves the power of excommunication; required
every citizen to subscribe publicly, on oath, to the twenty-one
articles of what he was pleased to call Christian doctrine;
and conducted a vigilant and punitive inquisition into private
morals. It is said that the men he trained at Geneva carried
his principles into almost every country in Europe; and this
is incontestable. But the further statement that these principles 'did much for the cause of civil liberty' is difficult to
reconcile with the fact that the only liberty he allowed was
the liberty to do and believe as he ordained. Everything he
did, whether good or evil, was done conscientiously and for
the glory of God—for the glory, however, of a God made
in Calvin's own image. Though one can admire his courage,
sincerity, and perseverance, and applaud at least some part
of his considerable achievement, it is difficult not to see him
as a man sadly self-deceived about his own motives.

The doctrine of Predestination, by which Calvin is chiefly
remembered today, differs from Atheistic Determinism only
in being infinitely more horrible, because it affirms the
immortality of the soul and the existence of an implacable
Deity. His mind was dominated by two ideas: the transcendent sovereignty of God and the utter depravity of Man.

God, the creator of men, had by an absolute and immutable decree predestined some of them to salvation and the rest to eternal punishment. Those that were to be saved were 'called' to salvation and could not by any misbehaviour forfeit their title. One can see how, at a time when life-after-death loomed large in men's minds, the persuasion of being among 'the elect' must have been a prime source of confidence and power to those fortunate enough to have it. By ridding them of fear and uncertainty it would effect a great release of energy. Nor, though theoretically they could sin with comparative impunity, would they be likely to take advantage of that freedom: as God's elect they would feel it incumbent upon them to live a life of rectitude. But what of the others? What of those earnest believers who were unsure of their salvation and who knew that if in fact they were among the damned nothing they did could avert the ultimate doom? Such a one, in a later century, was the gentle-hearted Cowper.

Calvin was inexorably logical: more so indeed than most of his opponents. His doctrine of Predestination follows inescapably from assumptions which he and they had in common: it is logically implied in the notion that God the creator is an almighty omniscient person entirely separate from his creatures. He detested mysticism, as well he might; for the mystical intuition that identifies God with Love makes nonsense of his system. The God of Calvin's fancy has all the disadvantages of anthropomorphism with none of its compensations. He is personal but remote; transcendent, all-powerful, inscrutable; arbitrary in his acts and utterly indifferent to considerations of justice. Atheism is infinitely more reasonable than such a theology. 'It were better to have no opinion of God at all,' said Bacon, 'than such an opinion as is unworthy of him: for the one is unbelief, the other is contumely.' To know God was for Calvin 'the supreme end of human endeavour', though it is difficult to see what profit or satisfaction there could be in knowing a God who created men with the deliberate intention of tormenting for ever all but an arbitrarily selected few of them. The position of a believer in doubt of his own 'election' was indeed pitiable. God alone knew what fate God had decreed for him, and what God had decreed had been decreed before the beginning of time. Do what he might he was already destined for either salvation or damnation. Good works could not avert the one, nor works of wickedness impede the other. Even faith, though necessary to salvation, was no guarantee of it. Arguing so, many a harassed soul must have been driven to the verge of madness, and beyond it, by the hideous prospect of immortality.

Robert Barclay, the first apologist of Quakerism, says of the doctrine of Absolute Reprobation (of which he finds some traces, prior to Calvin, in Augustine and Dominicus) that 'it is highly injurious to God because it makes him the author of sin, which of all things is most contrary to his nature'. The point is sufficiently obvious, but Barclay's words are worth quoting. 'If God has decreed that the reprobated ones shall perish, without all respect to their evil deeds but only of his own pleasure, and if he hath also decreed long before they were in being or in a capacity to do good or evil that they should walk in those wicked ways by which, as by a secondary means, they are led to that end; who, I pray, is the first author and cause thereof but God, who so willed and decreed? This is as natural a consequence as can be: and therefore, although many of the preachers of this doctrine have sought out various strange, strained, and intricate distinctions to defend their opinion and avoid this horrid consequence, yet some, and that of the most eminent of them, have been so plain in the matter as they have put it beyond all doubt.' He quotes Calvin himself in support of this statement. 'I say,' says Calvin, 'that by the ordination and will of God, Adam fell. God would have man to fall. Man is blinded by the will and commandment of God. We refer the causes of hardening us to God. The highest or remote cause of hardening is the will of God. It followeth that the hidden counsel of God is the cause of hardening.' There follows a citation from Calvin's friend Theodore Beza: 'God hath predestinated not only unto damnation, but also unto the causes of it, whomsoever he saw meet. The decree of God cannot be excluded from the causes of corruption.' In speaking of the 'causes' of damnation Beza means the secondary causes, the first and sufficient cause being God's decree. The matter is prettily summed up by the last author whom Barclay quotes in this connexion: 'Reprobate persons are absolutely ordained to this twofold end, to undergo everlasting punishment, and necessarily to sin; and, therefore, to sin that they may be justly punished.' The cream of the jest is in that word 'justly'.

Whatever may be the truth about God, it is clearly not here. Nor is it to be found in any intellectual formula. All that is said and written about God reveals to us, not God, but only, for good or ill, the minds and hearts of men. By their gods ye shall know them. We cannot positively assert that the full rigour of the Calvinistic logic was accepted by all the Puritan parsons to whom Fox resorted, first to seek their counsel and afterwards to controvert and exhort them; but undoubtedly the disease was widespread. It is of the essence of his historical situation that he found himself spiritually homeless, an exile among worldlings on the one hand, and on the other among men whose religion was (in his view) either empty or evil. The child of 'godly' parents, in matters of conduct he was by training and inclination puritanical: this at least he had in common with the chief of his enemies. But in all else he was a protestant against the protestantism of his day. He was not, like his young apostle Robert Barclay, a student of theology. The whole point of his mission or ministry was to insist on the primacy of experience, to exalt spiritual 'light' above mere 'notions'. He became, once he had found himself, a great disputer, a

man of many words; but all his words amounted to little
more than the assertion that religion, God, is nothing if not
an inward experience: which is the testimony of the mystic
in all ages. In seventeenth-century protestantism he found,
and hotly repudiated, two stupidities which survive in an
attenuated form even today: bibliolatry, the fetishistic worship of the Old and New Testaments, and that doctrine of
total human depravity which implies the utter separation of
man from God. Against these traditional tenets of protestantism he affirmed the inwardness of authority and the
presence of God in every human soul. His opponents 'could
not endure to hear of purity [of conscience] and of victory
over sin'. Again and again he tells us of how the 'professors'
—by which he means professed believers in religion—
'pleaded for sin'. He found among these men no one who
in the crisis of his young manhood could 'speak to his condition'. They seemed to him to be eaten up with 'notions',
concerned only with a mechanical observance of ceremonies
and with preaching doctrines that were either plainly untrue
or spiritually null and void.

It was probably his disgust with this state of affairs that
led him to out-puritan the Puritans and with characteristic
indiscrimination denounce sacramental ritual and refuse the
name of 'churches' to the buildings in which they preached.
Notwithstanding his dislike of bibliolatry he could bandy
texts as well as the next man and was always ready to cap
quotation with quotation and beat the 'professors' at their
own game. He was quick, and shrewd, and deeply sincere;
but being unschooled in things of the intellect, and having
nothing but mother wit to guide him, he made no distinction
between the essentials and the inessentials of his teaching
and was as stubborn in trivial matters as in great. He put
himself and others to much trouble by refusing to doff his
hat in court; and would quote chapter and verse to justify
the refusal, for he was always ready to argue your head off.

The men he had to deal with were more incensed by this kind of intransigence than their successors in high places today would be, because, being men of their time, they took it seriously. Though they were resolved to subdue his turbulent spirit, and very ready to turn his scruples into a weapon against him, there is a sense in which they understood them better than we can; for they lived in the same mental world as he, a world of zealous opinionativeness and hairsplitting literalism in which the notion of mutual toleration had no part. In Charles the First's England a man was either right or wrong in his opinions; if wrong he must be corrected; if resolute in error he must be persecuted as a matter of course. That was taken for granted by all parties, just as today it is taken for granted by totalitarian governments. The same rule held during the period of the Commonwealth, despite Cromwell's promise of religious liberty; and it persisted after the Restoration despite Charles the Second's wish to be amiable; because neither Protector nor King proved able to control the persecuting lust of the dominant religio-political party, though it is true that each of them did, on occasion, intervene on Fox's behalf. Fox and his enemies understood each other because, in our slang sense of the phrase, they spoke the same language. To us, living three centuries later and in an utterly different intellectual climate, it is almost a foreign language.

§ 2

He was born in 1624, 'in the month called July', at Fenny Drayton in Leicestershire. His father, Christopher Fox, was by profession a weaver: an honest man, says George, with 'a seed of God in him'. The neighbours called him Righteous Christer, the latter being, I suppose, a contraction of Christopher and therefore pronounced with a short vowel. George's mother is described by her son as an upright woman, and of the stock of the martyrs, whatever that may mean. He was, in short, the godly son of godly parents. They seem also to have been exceptionally prosperous for their social station and to have supplied his wants freely; for there is no hint of his having earned any money after the age of nineteen or so, yet on his numerous missionary journeys up and down the country he never lacked for means: 'I had wherewith both to keep myself from being chargeable to others and to administer something to the necessities of others.' In the light of this fact his indignation with the clergy for receiving payment for their services (though the tithe system was admittedly unjust and extortionate) may seem to be a little out of place. We have Fox's own word for it that in infancy he had a staidness of mind and spirit not usual in children; that he was taught how to walk to be kept pure; that the Lord showed him that his words should be few and savoury, seasoned with grace; that he was abstemious in eating and drinking, 'being brought up into the covenant, as sanctified by the Word which was in the beginning, by which all things are upheld, wherein is unity with the creation'. With the frankness that knows nothing of humour he gives himself a handsome testimonial, saying that when boys and rude people would laugh at him, in his sober teens, he let them alone and went his way; 'but people had generally a love to me for my innocency and honesty'.

His parents had thought to make a priest of him, but other counsels prevailed and he was apprenticed to a shoemaker who dealt also in wool and cattle. He learnt something of all three trades, but most, it would seem, of the care of sheep. A great deal, he says, went through his hands; and it is a safe guess that shepherding, with the abundant opportunity it afforded for quiet meditation, was the most congenial of his duties. His master, while Fox was with him, was 'blessed'; but after Fox left him he 'broke, and came to nothing'. Is there a hint here of cause and effect? One would rather not think so, but the suspicion cannot be altogether allayed; for time and again we read in his autobiography how the judgment of the Lord fell upon this person or that, and Fox, gentle and forgiving though he genuinely was on many occasions, cannot quite conceal his satisfaction in these disasters. The beginning of his religious crisis came when one day, being (as he says) upon business at a fair, he fell in with some 'professors' and agreed to share a jug of beer with them. When they had all drunk a glass each, his companions called for more and proposed to drink healths, on the understanding that whoever should refuse to join in should pay for all; whereupon Fox, much grieved that professedly religious persons should so behave, laid a groat on the table before them and went his way. This trifling incident so much affected him that he could not sleep that night. He spent the hours of darkness walking up and down, and praying, and crying 'to the Lord', who said to him—and this was the first of a series of very precise injunctions from the Lord—'Thou seest how young people go together into vanity, and old people into the earth. Thou must forsake all, both young and old, and keep out of all, and be as a stranger unto all.' And so, on the 9th of September 1643, he left home, broke off all fellowship with old and young, and set out on the first of his travels.

There followed a long period of darkness and distress of spirit. For something like four years of wandering he was racked by doubts and questions and unspecified temptations. At intervals he visited his parents, but soon left them again when he found that they could no more help him in his extremity than could the accredited ministers of religion in the various parishes whom, going to them for instruction, he always stayed to instruct, until by their obduracy (*i.e.* disagreement) he was driven away. For at intervals, too, he had 'openings from the Lord' which revealed to him at least some part of the 'truth' he was seeking. He 'heard a voice' which said: 'There is one, even Christ Jesus, that can speak

to thy condition'—and held fast to that faith while much else
was still in doubt.

Even during this time of perplexity, when his wretchedness
was 'great and heavy upon him' beyond description, he was
a very positive person. If he knew nothing else he knew that
these mentors of his—sometimes patient and longsuffering,
sometimes angry and hostile—were wrong. He was always
clamouring for the bread of life and being given a stone of
unpalatable doctrine. His parents urged marriage. His neighbours advised him to go for a soldier. The parsons disputed
with him, commended him, derided him, tried to win him
by flattery or subdue him by authority. The better-disposed
were content to refer him to a Bible which he knew better
than they did and interpreted much more sensibly; the
malicious stirred up the people to violence against him;
and all in authority, except the few who were 'convinced',
regarded him as a nuisance. A nuisance, from their point
of view, he certainly was: to trouble the still waters of
religious complacency was his life's mission. Among his early
'openings' was (i) that 'being bred at Oxford or Cambridge
was not enough to fit and qualify men to be ministers of
Christ', a thought which came as a great surprise to him
because it contradicted the common belief, and (ii) that
'God, who made the world, did not dwell in temples made
with hands', for which reason Fox vigorously objected to
a 'steeple-house' being called the House of God. Fox was
in the tradition of the Old Testament prophets, as indeed
were the Puritans themselves, in that not only his opinions,
but every practical decision of his life, seemed to him to be
enjoined upon him by God. He was always 'moved of the
Lord' to go here or there, to do this or that. Not infrequently
he was moved to go into a church and argue with the preacher
either during or after the sermon. This seems to have been
in accordance with a custom of the times and not necessarily
to have constituted a breach of the peace. His first followers

were won in this fashion, and his first persecutions provoked; for the more he seemed to gain ground in the argument the readier were his adversaries to have him manhandled and beaten out of the town.

The first of his numerous imprisonments resulted from an episode which is typical of many. One Sunday morning, going with some others towards Nottingham, to a meeting of Friends there, he came to the top of a hill and espied, as he says, the great steeple-house. And the Lord said to him: 'Thou must go cry against yonder great idol, and against the worshippers therein.' He said nothing of this to his companions, but went on with them to the meeting, 'where the mighty power of the Lord was amongst us'. Leaving them there, he then made his way to the church alone. When he entered the church 'all the people looked like fallow ground, and the priest, like a great lump of earth, stood in his pulpit above'. The text was from Peter's Epistle: 'We have also a more sure word of prophecy, whereunto ye do well that ye take heed, as unto a light that shineth in a dark place, until the day dawn, and the daystar arise in your hearts.' These words, said the priest, referred to the Scriptures, by which all doctrines religions and opinions were to be tried. 'No,' cried Fox, 'it is not the Scriptures. It is the Holy Spirit, by which the holy men of God gave forth the Scriptures.' It was by the Holy Spirit that all opinions religions and judgments were to be tried. The Jews, he argued, had the Scriptures, yet persecuted Christ and the apostles, and took upon them to try their doctrines by the Scriptures, but erred in judgment and did not try them aright, because they tried without the Holy Ghost. 'As I spake thus amongst them, the officers came and took me away, and put me into a nasty, stinking prison, the smell whereof got so into my nose and throat that it very much annoyed me'—that is, was very noisome and harassing to him. But his preaching had made a great impression on the people; he was evidently a man of great personal magnetism and commanding power. At night he was taken before the mayor, aldermen, and sheriffs of the town, and examined at large. The mayor was in a peevish, fretful temper; and Fox was sent back to prison; but 'some time after'—whether hours or days he does not indicate—the head sheriff, John Reckless by name, had the prisoner brought to his house, where he was greeted by the sheriff's wife with the words: 'Salvation is come to our house.' She took him by the hand, and, says Fox, 'was much wrought upon by the power of the Lord God; and her husband and children and servants were much changed, for the power of the Lord wrought upon them. I lodged at the sheriff's, and great meetings we had in his house. Some persons of considerable condition in the world came to them, and the Lord's power appeared eminently amongst them. This sheriff sent for the other sheriff, and for a woman they had had dealings with in the way of trade; and he told her before the other sheriff that they had wronged her in their dealings with her . . . and made restitution to the woman and exhorted the other sheriff to do the like.' The next day this friendly sheriff went into the market and preached repentance to the people; others were moved to offer the same unpalatable advice to the mayor and magistrates, who thereupon 'grew very angry' and had Fox sent back to the common prison.

A full account of Fox's trials and imprisonments is beyond the scope of this essay. They occurred at intervals throughout his life, and many of his adherents suffered with him. He is not always as explicit about the legal points at issue as we could wish, but it is clear that there was plenty of legal machinery for laying him by the heels whenever local authorities thought it worth while to do so. The Blasphemy Law, passed by the two Houses of Parliament in 1648, made it possible to impose the death penalty on anyone who, without benefit of clergy, should call in question the orthodoxy of the day. He was indicted at least twice under this statute, but on the first occasion suffered nothing worse than imprisonment, and on the second was acquitted, the evidence against him being plainly perjured. Efforts were made to entrap him into uttering obviously blasphemous claims. A sort of 'third degree' inquisition was practised upon him. They put him, he says, in and out of the room often, hurrying him backward and forward, and asking questions of him for eight hours at a time. This was at Derby, in 1650. They asked him if he was sanctified, and how he and his followers knew that Christ abode in them. He answered: 'By his Spirit, that he has given us.' They then, hoping to ensnare him, asked if any of them were Christ. He answered: 'Nay, we are nothing, Christ is all.' They asked: 'If a man steal, is it no sin?' He answered: 'All unrighteousness is sin.' When they had 'wearied themselves' in examining him—and one suspects that they were more quickly wearied than he was, for he had a shrewd answer for every question—they committed him and one other man to the House of Correction for six months as blasphemers. True, no blasphemy had been proved; but what matter? Another attempt to discredit him in the eyes of the common people, among whom his fame and following grew, was a carefully circulated rumour that he was a necromancer who could bewitch folk and be in two places at once. It was no doubt hoped that the occasional sudden conversions to his cause of jailers, parsons, judges, and others who had close dealings with him, might lend colour to this accusation; but it seems to have gained no general credit.

Fox and his Friends held apart from all other religious parties: not only from the 'Common-Prayer-men and Presbyters', but from the separatists (Baptists, Independents, and minor sects) as well, even from 'those called the most experienced people'. The monstrous Blasphemy Law, though mainly an instrument of persecuting zeal, was perhaps in part an honest attempt to discourage the wilder and more mischievous kinds of religious fanaticism, such as that of the Ranters. During one of his periods of freedom Fox visited some of this sect who were in prison at Coventry. 'I was ravished with the sense of the love of God, and greatly strengthened in my inward man. But when I came into the jail where the prisoners were, a great power of darkness struck at me, and I sate still, having my spirit gathered into the love of God. At last these prisoners began to rant, and vapour, and blaspheme, at which my soul was greatly grieved. They said they were God.' When presently they grew calmer Fox began to reason with them, in a style well suited to their limited intelligences. 'Seeing they said they were God, I asked them if they knew whether it would rain tomorrow. They said they could not tell. I told them God could tell.' And more to the same purpose. 'After I had reproved them for their blasphemous expressions, I went away; for I perceived they were Ranters. I had met with none before; and I admired'—that is, marvelled at—'the goodness of the Lord in appearing so to me before I went amongst them. Not long after this, one of these Ranters, whose name was Joseph Salmon, put forth a paper or book of recantation; upon which they were set at liberty.'

Fox was no friend to extravagance or self-glorification. If we are sometimes tempted to smile at his persuasion that everything he preached was put into his mouth by God, we must remember how careful he always was to 'give God the glory' and to claim nothing for himself. Years later a follower of his own, James Nayler, suffered rebuke from him for 'running into imaginations'. Nayler allowed himself to become spiritually intoxicated by the adoration of a group of women disciples, who persuaded him to ride into Bristol in a manner closely imitative of Christ's Palm Sunday entry into Jerusalem: for which offence he was punished with un-speakable savagery by order of Cromwell's Parliament. As the Quaker movement gathered numbers and strength, Fox

GEORGE FOX, BY ALFRED TURNER

must have had his work cut out to defend it from the fanaticism that attends all religious revival; and that he did succeed in doing so, and in establishing a tradition of what may be called sober illuminism, proved that he possessed the qualities of a statesman as well as the enthusiasm of the mystic. If, by his own account, he seems to have been often ungracious and overbearing in his dealings with the unfortunate 'professors', who suffered from the initial disadvantage of being always in the wrong, that was, after all, in perfect harmony with the controversial manners of the day. 'Come down, thou deceiver!' may seem to us not the likeliest way to persuade an erring parson to abandon his pulpit, but probably no one but the parson himself took much offence at it. 'The black earthly spirit of the priests,' writes Fox, 'wounded my life; and when I heard the bell toll to call people together to the steeple-house, it struck at my life; for it was just like a market-bell, to gather people together that the priest might set forth his ware to sale.'

The *Journal* is written in a plain robust style and rises to moments of power and splendour; but its general tone imperfectly reflects those kindlier human virtues to which men who knew Fox intimately have testified. At Ulverston, where he had incurred the enmity of Parson Lampitt and Justice Sawrey by winning over the influential Justice Fell and his wife Margaret, of Swarthmoor Hall, he was first beaten by police officers and then thrust among a 'rude multitude, who, having furnished themselves, some with staves, some with hedge-stakes, and others with holm-bushes, fell upon me and beat me on my head, arms, and shoulders, till they had mazed me, so that I fell down upon the wet common. When I recovered again, and saw myself lying in a watery common, and the people standing about me, I lay still a little while; and the power of the Lord sprang through me, and the eternal refreshings refreshed me, so that I stood up again in the strengthening power of the Eternal God.' What

F

followed is difficult to reconcile with Fox's assertion that
he was 'in the love of God' towards his persecutors. Stretching
out his arms he said in a loud voice: 'Strike again! Here are
my arms, my head, and my cheeks.' Whereupon one of the
bystanders, a mason and a professing Christian, 'with his
walking rule-staff gave me a blow with all his might over
the back of my hand as it was stretched out: with which
blow my hand was so bruised, and my arm so numbed, that
I could not draw it unto me again . . . but I looked at it in
the love of God, and after a while . . . I recovered strength
in my hand and arm in the sight of them all'. Now it is
obvious that Fox's 'Strike again!' was anything but loving,
and the reverse of meek. Such words, in such circumstances,
are either defiant, or taunting, or both: they are calculated
rather to provoke violence than rebuke it. Unless we are to
suppose that Fox was perversely enjoying his suffering, or
was deliberately tempting the mob to further cruelty in order
that they might sicken of it and become ashamed, his words
are clearly those of a brave undaunted man very conscious
of the cowardliness of his assailants, so many against one,
and very willing that they should be conscious of it too. That
is human and natural enough. What is puzzling, what suggests that Fox's 'enormous sacred self-confidence' (in
Carlyle's phrase) sometimes involved an element of self-
deception, is his evidently sincere persuasion, years after the
event, that all was said and done on his part 'in the love of
God' to those who were persecuting him.

A militant spirit, however, is not inconsistent with
humility; and true humility does not take the form of
sanctimonious self-depreciation, a vice of which Fox had no
tincture. And with all his self-confidence he was as little
corrupted by the power which came to him as it is possible
for a man to be. William Penn's testimony, among that of
others, is decisive on this point. 'Though God,' says Penn,
'had visibly clothed him with a divine preference and

authority, and indeed his very presence expressed a religious majesty, yet he never abused it; but held his place in the Church of God with great meekness, and a most engaging humility and moderation. . . . I write by knowledge and not report, and my witness is true, having been with him for weeks and months together on divers occasions, and those of the nearest and most exercising nature, and that by night and by day, by sea and by land, in this and in foreign countries; and I can say I never saw him out of his place, or not a match for every service or occasion. For in all things he acquitted himself like a man, yea, a strong man, a new and heavenly-minded man. . . .'

Of this heavenly mind the *Journal* gives at least some glimpses. The experience that changed Fox's life is wonderfully true to type, and is described in language astonishingly similar to that of other illuminants of various times and places: astonishingly, because Fox can have had no book-knowledge except of the Bible. 'Now was I come up in spirit through the flaming sword, into the paradise of God. All things were new; and all the creation gave another smell unto me than before, beyond what words can utter. I knew nothing but pureness, and innocency, and righteousness, being renewed up into the image of God by Christ Jesus, to the state of Adam, which he was in before he fell . . . in which the admirable works of the creation, and the virtues thereof, may be known through the openings of that divine Word of wisdom and power by which they were made. Great things did the Lord lead me into, and wonderful depths were opened unto me beyond what can by words be declared; but as people come into subjection to the Spirit of God, and grow up in the image and power of the Almighty, they may receive the word of wisdom that opens all things, and come to know the hidden unity in the Eternal Being.'

§ 3

Fox's imprisonments varied in severity as in duration. At Derby in 1650 he was much visited by well-meaning persons who came to 'plead for sin'—that is, for the doctrine of human depravity. They said they could not believe, as Fox did, that any one could be free from sin on this side the grave. At which he bade them 'give over babbling about the Scriptures, which were holy men's words, whilst they pleaded for unholiness'. The 'keeper' of this prison was greatly incensed against Fox on religious grounds; but 'it pleased the Lord' to strike terror into him, so that he came to Fox trembling and full of repentance, saying: 'I have been as a lion against you, but now I come like a lamb.' Next morning this man went to one of the magistrates, who agreed with him that plagues were upon them for keeping a good man in jail. Fox was given leave to walk as far as a mile from the prison, the hope being that he would take himself off and ease them of their misgivings. But he saw through this strategem and kept strictly within the assigned limit.

At Launceston, on the other hand, six years later, the vilest humiliations were put upon him. The chief charge against him, of conspiring 'to raise forty thousand men, and bring in King Charles, and involve the nation in blood', was too palpably mendacious to carry weight even with magistrates prejudiced against all he stood for; but pretexts were never lacking for putting him away to await further trial, which trial seems often to have been indefinitely postponed. Finding on this occasion that they were not likely to be soon released, Fox and his companion in misfortune stopped all that payment to the jailer, seven shillings a week each for themselves and another seven for their horses, by which that gentleman had till then been kept in an accommodating mood. A rash proceeding, for prisoners in those days were utterly at the mercy of the jailers, who were in effect the lessees of the jails and ran them for personal profit, extorting 'fortunes for themselves out of their victims, under penalty of blows, starvation, and foul lodging'; and 'when one of these bad men retired, he often sold his lucrative post to another wretch equally prepared to speculate in the woes of mankind'.* Deprived of his emoluments, Fox's jailer 'grew very wicked and devilish, and put us down into Doomsdale, a nasty stinking place where they used to put witches and murderers after they were condemned to die. The place was so noisome that it was said few that went in ever came out again alive. There was no house of office in it, and the excrements of the prisoners that from time to time had been put there had not been carried out (as we were told) for many years. . . . At night some friendly people of the town brought us a candle and a little straw, and we burnt a little of our straw to take away the stink. The thieves lay over our heads, and the head jailer in a room by them, over us also. Now it seems the smoke went up into the jailer's room, which put him into such a rage that he took the pots of excrements of the thieves and poured them through a hole upon our heads in Dooms- dale; whereby we were so bespattered that we could not touch ourselves or one another. And the stink increased upon us so that . . . we had nearly been choked and smothered.' They were forced to stand up all night, being unable to sit down for the filth, while the jailer railed at them 'most hideously', calling them hatchet-faced dogs and the like. This jailer, an ex-thief, branded in the hand and shoulder, had been appointed to his office by the owner of the jail, Colonel Bennet, a Baptist teacher, who had acquired it by purchase: a notable triumph of private enterprise. 'The prisoners, and some wild people,' says Fox, 'talked of spirits that haunted Doomsdale, and how many had died in it; thinking perhaps to terrify us therewith.' But Fox was not the man to be terrified, either by talk or ill-usage. 'I told them that if all

* G. M. Trevelyan, *England under the Stuarts*. Longmans, 1904.

the spirits and devils in hell were there, I was over them in the power of God, and feared no such thing.'

When other persecuting devices failed, Fox's peculiar scruples provided a pretext for locking him up. His refusal to do 'the honour of the hat' could always be regarded as contempt of court, if the magistrate were so minded; and nothing was easier than to put to him the oaths of abjuration and allegiance, the swearing of oaths being forbidden him by his conscience. He was always ready to affirm his loyalty as a subject, and did so in explicit terms both to Cromwell and to Charles the Second. Those potentates recognized his good faith and had him set free; but having other things to attend to they could not, or did not, until Charles's Toleration Act two years before Fox's death, prevent the sporadic persecution going on. The Conventicle Act of 1664, which forbad the meeting of more than five persons in addition to members of a family for any religious purpose not in conformity with the Church of England, was a most useful stick to beat the Quakers with. Fox's last imprisonment, of three years, was under a statute passed in James the First's reign against Roman Catholics, whereby it was enacted that if any person above eighteen, being not noble, should refuse the oath of allegiance when tendered by a bishop or by the Justices of the Peace at their Quarter Sessions, such persons should be liable to the penalties of a *praemunire:* namely, confiscation of all property both personal and real, loss of the king's protection, and perpetual imprisonment during the king's pleasure. The prosecution was shockingly bungled; Fox, finding flaw after legal flaw in the indictment, had by far the best of the argument; but he was imprisoned none the less, and it took his friends three years to get him set free. With the stubborn adherence to principle that was so characteristic of him, he refused a royal pardon, and persisting in his refusal was eventually released without such an implied admission of guilt. The officers and soldiers of the garrison which had charge of him in the last period of his incarceration learnt to respect him, as did so many others in like circumstances. When his name was mentioned in after times they would say: 'He is as stiff as a tree, and as pure as a bell, for we could never move him.'

It is obvious that Fox's mysticism had no taint of otherworldliness. He was a practical reformer, with ideas far in advance of his times, as may be seen in his attitude to slavery, his impassioned denunciation of the death penalty for stealing, his recognition of a basic human equality despite all differences of rank, his view of the status of women, his belief in religious freedom, and his repudiation of violence as a means of settling disputes. Under this last head there is, I think, an important distinction to be made. Fox's 'testimony against war' has been carried on to this day, often heroically, by the Society of Friends which he founded; but present-day pacifism, which refuses to fight in any cause whatsoever and recognizes no distinction between aggression and self-defence or the defence of others, is far more absolute and arbitrary than Fox's ever had occasion to be. True, his language on the subject was absolute enough; but then it always was, no matter what the subject; he saw only what was to his immediate purpose and knew better than to blunt the sharp edge of his tongue with refinements and qualifications. But here, applying our rule, we must look at his action in its historical context. He was invited to take part in a civil war, a political war, a war against his own countrymen, and for a cause which, even if he understood it (which is doubtful), was none of his. He saw himself as a man with a mission, a chosen instrument of God. He was not concerned with forms of government: he was concerned only with spreading knowledge of 'the light' in an age which certainly had need of it. That was his business and he minded his business and saw to it that his adherents did likewise.

I do not suggest that his repudiation of war, as such, was

accidental or a matter of mere expediency. To his contemporaries, to whom violence and bloodshed were as natural
as breathing, even to question the lawfulness of fighting must
have seemed the quaintest of heresies. What I do suggest
is that in other circumstances even the absolute Fox might
have found it necessary to distinguish between aggressive
and defensive warfare. In the present century many a man
as gentle and Christian as he, has willingly, though with
infinite distaste, taken up arms in defence of people and things
dear to him. Fox, refusing to fight against Charles, justified
his refusal by a denunciation of all soldiering. But what would
he have done if he had seen England invaded and English
homes desolated by a foreign army? We do not and cannot
know. We cannot know either that he would, or would not,
have lent a hand in repelling the invader. It is true that in
personal encounters he never returned violence with violence:
he disarmed his assailants (when he did not the more
infuriate them) by passively submitting to their assaults and
even asking for more. But in this matter of war, which is a
very different thing, his absolutism was never tested.
Denouncing war in general is as easy as denouncing measles,
and as useful: it is the *particular* war that presents a moral
problem, a problem such as George Fox, standing aloof from
the conflict that then divided England, never had to face.
Therefore, though his *words* may be cited in support of an
unqualified refusal to take up arms in any circumstances or
for any cause, just as other words of his may be held to
establish the wickedness of playing bowls or of taking off
one's hat in a court of justice, his personal conduct in this
particular matter has little or no relevance for the world
today.

§ 4

Certain questions suggest themselves. Was Fox 'original'?
Is there any radical difference between his Inward Light and

the light of Reason exalted by his contemporaries the so-called
Cambridge Platonists and by Richard Hooker before them?
In refusing absolute authority to the letter of the Bible, again
as Hooker had done in opposition to the Puritan party in the
Elizabethan Church, was he doing any more than assert that
principle of private judgment which was so dear to Puritan
sects as a stick to beat Catholicism with and so obnoxious
when used against themselves? Since there is clearly a harmony among the three conceptions, is the difference one of
statement rather than of essence, or, more precisely, is one
an intellectualization of the other?

Fox arrived at his position by a process in which reflection
and reason played a vital but an all but unconscious part.
During his spiritual wrestling with himself he had been
unaware of even an inkling of the conclusions to which he
was being led. His final convictions—few, simple, dynamic—
astonished him. They emerged suddenly into consciousness
with all the appearance of revelations or 'openings', which
indeed is what they were, none the less so because a psychological process was involved—how could it not be? What was
not involved in Fox's mystical intuition was that process of
calculated reasoning, or ratiocination, by which the more
intellectualist type of mind seeks to arrive at truth. This is
not to say that a mind trained in dialectic is necessarily
impervious to sudden (or seemingly sudden) illumination,
or that an intuitional mind is incapable of sober reasoning.
Both capacities must exist potentially in all sane human
beings; and they are seen conspicuously (if not always
harmoniously) coexisting in some great poets, such as Milton
and Dante. Fox himself was a man of great natural sagacity:
no mere inspired simpleton could have constructed, as he did
in the Society of Friends, a system or order which to so
large an extent safeguards itself against the dangers inherent
in systematization. And if in Fox, the unlettered God-
possessed mystic, there was any amount of practical common

sense and no discord between the deliverances of revelation and those of reason, so in the learned, humane, equable mind of Richard Hooker, in whom (as Dowden well says) 'the liberal spirit of the Renaissance, which does honour to every human faculty, reacts against the narrower spirit of the Reformation', there was a strong vein of mysticism.

Hooker's *Ecclesiastical Polity* contains passages which are among the glories of our literature. 'Dangerous it were for the feeble brain of man to wade far into the doings of the Most High; whom although to know be life, and joy to make mention of his name, yet our soundest knowledge is to know that we know him not as indeed he is, neither can know him, and our safest eloquence concerning him is our silence, when we confess that his glory is inexplicable, his greatness above our capacity and reach. He is above, and we upon earth, therefore it behoveth our words to be wary and few. Our God is one, or rather very Oneness, and mere unity, having nothing but itself in itself, and not consisting (as all things do besides God) of many things.' To be united with God, says Hooker, is the necessary end of man's desire. Nothing short of that union can satisfy him, for only the infinite can appease an infinite hunger. Our desire is natural, since all men have it; and it is axiomatic that no natural desire can be, of its own nature, frustrate. Therefore, Hooker argues, the divine fullness of joy which we desire, and which the joys of our life in this world at best imperfectly hint of, cannot be beyond our eventual attainment. 'Nothing,' he says, 'may be infinitely desired but that good which indeed is infinite; for the better the more desirable; that therefore most desirable wherein there is infinity of goodness: so that if anything desirable may be infinite, that must needs be the highest of all things that are desired. No good is infinite but only God; therefore [is] he our felicity and bliss. Moreover, desire tendeth unto union with that it desireth. If then in him we be blessed, it is by force of participation and conjunction

with him. Again, it is not the possession of any good thing
can make them happy which have it unless they enjoy the
thing wherewith they are possessed. Then are we happy
therefore when fully we enjoy God, as an object wherein the
powers of our souls are satisfied even with everlasting
delight; so that although we be men, yet by being unto God
united we live as it were the life of God. . . . Complete union
with him must be according unto every power and faculty
of our minds to receive so glorious an object. Capable we
are of God both by understanding and will: by understanding,
as he is that sovereign Truth which comprehendeth the rich
treasures of all wisdom; by will, as he is that sea of Goodness
whereof whoso tasteth shall thirst no more. As the will doth
now work upon that object by desire, which is as it were a
motion towards the end as yet unobtained, so likewise upon
the same hereafter received it shall work also by love. . . .
Whereas we now love the thing that is good, but good
especially in respect of benefit to us, we shall then love the
thing that is good only or principally for the goodness of
beauty in itself. The soul, being in this sort, as it is active,
perfected by love of that infinite good, shall, as it is receptive,
be also perfected with those supernatural passions of joy,
peace, and delight. All this is endless and everlasting.'

So Hooker, the greatest of Elizabethan divines. The men
of the Cambridge school of liberal theology which sprang
up a generation after his death, with Benjamin Whichcote
of Emmanuel as its fountain-head, were at one with him, and
with their humble contemporary George Fox did they but
know it, in rejecting the doctrine (or superstition) of the
Infallible Book, incontinently set up by Puritanism in place
of the Infallible Church which it repudiated, and in refusing
to allow that there exists disharmony, still less an opposition,
between reason and revelation. Reason was for them, as we
shall see in a later chapter, an inward light, a God-given
faculty of apprehension; whereas Fox's inward light was to

Fox an actual divine presence in the soul, which presence the Cambridge theologians also affirmed. Indeed the distinction is almost too fine to be accurately stated: in this central doctrine of inwardness the Quakers and the Cambridge Platonists (or Latitude-men) were in closer agreement than perhaps either party, had they been confronted, would have been ready to recognize. But they were never confronted. Robert Barclay, it is true, in his *Apology for the True Christian Divinity*, quotes a pertinent passage from John Smith, Fellow of Queens', in support of the Quaker doctrine; but Barclay's book was a late flower of the movement, and it is as certain that Fox knew nothing of Smith as that Smith learned nothing from Fox. 'To seek our divinity merely in books and writings,' declares Smith, 'is to seek the living among the dead; we do but in vain many times seek God in these, where his truth is too often not so much enshrined as entombed. *Intra te quaere Deum:* seek God within thine own soul. He is best discerned (as Plotinus phraseth it) by an intellectual touch of him. . . . The soul itself hath its sense, as well as the body. And therefore David, when he would teach us to know what the divine goodness is, calls not for speculation, but sensation: *Taste and see how good the Lord is.* That is not the best and truest knowledge of God which is wrought out by the labour and sweat of the brain, but that which is kindled within us by a heavenly warmth in our hearts.' In another context he says, voicing a favourite thought of Whichcote's and anticipating a saying of eighteenth-century William Law: 'Hell is rather a nature than a place, and Heaven cannot be so truly defined by anything without us as by something that is within us.' Whatever their points of difference, the spiritual affinity of these men with Fox is clear enough, though temperamentally they were worlds apart.

We come back, then, to our question. Was Fox original? The answer can scarcely be in doubt. If the question means did he contribute to human thought an idea that had never before been entertained, quite clearly he did not. But original he was, in two senses. He was original in the minor sense of owing nothing to the writings and teachings of other men; for the only book with which he was intimately acquainted was the Bible. And, far more important, he was original as every true 'saint' is original, in that he found his truth experimentally, in his own person, and lived the truth he had found. There was a fire within him, from which, by precept and example, he was able to kindle, within and beyond the borders of England, a flame that should burn up the dry stubble of a dead religion in the hearts of men.

Chapter Four

SOME SEVENTEENTH-CENTURY POETS

§ 1

AMONG the miscalled 'metaphysical' poets of the seventeenth century, the man of most startling and original genius is John Donne: sensual, passionate, melancholy, learned, subtle, inexhaustibly curious, and, in his later years, deeply devout. He was a poet always, whether in verse or prose, with a raging appetite for experience and a restless probing wit that sought to penetrate to its inmost reality and was quick to discern correspondences analogies and identities in the most unexpected contexts. His audacious metaphors and far-fetched comparisons set a fashion in such things. Sometimes they seem merely wilful, both in him and in those who learnt the trick from him; but more often they are the indispensable vehicle of his thought: that subtle, passionate thought under whose weight his verse, with its numerous parentheses and qualifying clauses, seems sometimes to stagger and stumble. It would be idle to deny the name of mystic to a poet so deeply and continuously aware of the interpenetration of spirit and flesh as the author of *The Ecstasy*:

> *This ecstasy doth unperplex*
>   *(We said) and tell us what we love.*
> *We see by this it was not sex,*
>   *We see we saw not what did move:*
>
> *But, as all several things contain*
>   *Mixture of things, they know not what,*
> *Love these mixt souls doth mix again,*
>   *And makes both one, each this and that.*

A single violet transplant,
  The strength, the colour, and the size
(All which before was poor and scant)
  Redoubles still, and multiplies.

When love with one another so
  Interinanimates two souls,
That abler soul, which thence doth flow,
  Defects of loneliness controls.

We then, who are this new soul, know
  Of what we are composed and made,
For the atomies of which we grow
  Are souls whom no change can invade.

But O alas, so long, so far
  Our bodies why do we forbear?
They are ours, tho' they are not we: we are
  The intelligences, they the sphere. . . .

As our blood labours to beget
  Spirits as like souls as it can,
Because such fingers need to knit
  That subtle knot which makes us man:

So must pure lovers' souls descend
  To affections and to faculties
Which sense may reach and apprehend:
  Else a great prince in prison lies.

To our bodies turn we then, that so
  Weak men on love reveal'd may look:
Love's mysteries in souls do grow,
  But yet the body is his book.

But, though we cannot but call Donne mystical, it is clear, when we look at his work as a whole, that with his feverish intellect and unquiet spirit he does not belong in the same category with such illuminants as Rolle, Julian of Norwich, George Fox, and some of his own literary contemporaries. That he was forever a stranger to the deep peace and abiding joy to which they won is more than we can confidently assert, but there is little trace of either in his writings. True, he is at one with them in their sense of a universal mystery. 'There is not so poor a creature but may be thy glass to see God in. All things that are, are equally removed from being nothing; and whatsoever hath any being, is by that very being a glass in which we see God, who is the root and the fountain of all being. The whole frame of nature is the theatre; the whole volume of creatures is the glass; and the light of nature, reason, is our light.' He is at one with them, too, in recognizing that in essence that mystery is beyond the utmost reach of knowledge or imagination. 'In my third day, when my mortality shall put on immortality, he shall give me the light of glory by which I shall see himself. To this light of glory, the light of honour is but a glow-worm, and majesty itself but a twilight; the cherubims and seraphims are but candles; and that Gospel itself which the apostle calls the glorious Gospel, but a star of the least magnitude. And if I cannot tell what to call this light by which I see it, what shall I call that which I shall see by it, the essence of God himself?' But he differs markedly from these others in temperament and personal quality. In his sermons as in his religious poems Donne dwells with more conviction and imaginative power on sin and suffering, on death and corruption, than on heavenly things.

These dark themes inspire him to high eloquence. Take this, of mortality: 'We have a winding sheet in our mother's womb which grows with us from our conception, and we come into the world wound up in that winding sheet, for we come to seek a grave . . . we celebrate our own funerals with cries even at our birth, as though our threescore-and-ten-years life were spent in our mother's labour, and our circle made up in the first point thereof . . . This whole world is but an universal churchyard, but our common grave, and the life and motion that the greatest persons have in it is but as the shaking of buried bodies in their grave by an earthquake.' And again, this so justly celebrated passage: 'It [death] comes equally to us all, and makes us all equal when it comes. The ashes of the oak in the chimney are no epitaph of that oak, to tell me how high or how large that was: it tells me not what flocks it sheltered while it stood, nor what men it hurt when it fell. The dust of great persons' graves is speechless too: it says nothing, it distinguishes nothing. As soon the dust of a wretch whom thou wouldest not as of a prince whom thou couldest not look upon will trouble thine eyes if the wind blow it thither; and when a whirlwind hath blown the dust of the churchyard into the church, and the man sweeps out the dust of the church into the churchyard, who will undertake to sift those dusts again, and to pronounce, This is the patrician, this is the noble flower, and this the yeomanly, this the plebeian bran.' It is something more than fine prose that makes the heart lift, sombrely exulting in the bleak truth of its transient condition, when we read that. It speaks a humility prouder than pride, and securely based, as pride is so conspicuously not, in the ultimate nature of things. Not to desire the impossible is the beginning of wisdom and the way of inward peace, and nothing is more plainly impossible than that any one of us, by wishing or fearing, by trembling or crying out, should escape the common lot.

Donne was born in London in 1573, the son of a prosperous merchant. His parents were Roman Catholics, and he had therefore his 'first breeding and conversation', as he tells us, 'with men of a suppressed and afflicted religion, accustomed to the despite of death, and hungry of an imagined martyrdom'.

G

He was sent to Hart Hall (now Hertford College), Oxford, at the age of eleven, having already, says Walton, 'a good command both of the French and Latin tongue'; three years later he was transplanted to Trinity, Cambridge; and in his seventeenth year he was admitted to Lincoln's Inn as a law student. In spite of his much learning, he took no degree at either university, because the oath that would have been required of him was against his secret religion. Nor did he ever practise law. The next ten years were crammed with a diversity of experience: amorous adventures, foreign service under the Earl of Essex, visits to Italy and Spain. During these years, too, he is believed to have written many of the 'secular' poems of which he afterwards so bitterly repented but which, luckily on the whole, had been too widely circulated in manuscript to be overtaken and destroyed. Soon after his return to England he became secretary to Sir Thomas Egerton, afterwards Lord Chancellor. He remained with Egerton for four or five years, and was then dismissed at the request of Sir George More, whose daughter Ann he had secretly married. There followed a time of anxiety, privation, and sickness. Both Donne and his young wife had been used to easy and comfortable living: they now had to make do with a small damp house (at Mitcham) and suffer the indignity of being in part dependent on the charity of friends. Their family, moreover, grew apace. Happily the two were deeply in love. He had already broken away from his allegiance to Rome, though without attaching himself elsewhere. It is customary to regard his decision to take orders in the Church of England as the turning-point, or true beginning, of his spiritual life; but it was almost certainly his marriage, his passionate devotion to Ann, that purged away the harshness and cynicism from his mind and heart.

Urged in 1607 to take holy orders, by his friend Thomas Morton, afterwards Bishop of Durham, he refused on the grounds that God's glory, not worldly maintenance, should be the first motive for such a step, and that public memory of his former irregularities might bring dishonour on a sacred calling. Mixed with these excellent reasons was perhaps a personal disinclination, and a hope that something more to his liking might turn up. It is suggested by Edmund Gosse that Ann's death in 1617, which was a shattering grief to him, 'brought about the final process of sanctification and illumination'. It may be so, but Donne himself dated his religious life from the time, two years earlier, when (in January 1615) he yielded to the advice of his friends and of the King and accepted ordination at the hands of the Bishop of London. He became Dean of St Paul's six years later, and died at the age of fifty-seven the most illustrious cleric of his day. The first of the *Holy Sonnets* provides a magnificent example of his later mind and art:

> *Thou hast made me, and shall thy work decay?*
> *Repair me now, for now mine end doth haste.*
> *I run to death, and death meets me as fast,*
> *And all my pleasures are like yesterday.*
> *I dare not move my dim eyes any way,*
> *Despair behind, and death before, doth cast*
> *Such terror, and my feeble flesh doth waste*
> *By sin in it which it towards hell doth weigh.*
> *Only thou art above, and when towards thee*
> *By thy leave I can look, I rise again;*
> *But our old subtle foe so tempteth me*
> *That not one hour myself I can sustain;*
> *Thy grace may wing me to prevent his art,*
> *And thou like adamant draw mine iron heart.*

Death, it would seem, was seldom absent from his imagination; but before the end came he found release from all terrors, as the poem written during his last illness makes clear: a poem as characteristic, in its blend of inspiration and ingenuity, as anything he wrote.

Since I am coming to that holy room
 Where with thy choir of saints for evermore
I shall be made thy music, as I come
 I tune the instrument here at the door,
 And what I must do then, think here before.

Whilst my physicians by their love are grown
 Cosmographers, and I their map, who lie
Flat on this bed, that by them may be shown
 That this is my south-west discovery
 Per fretum febris, by these straits to die,

I joy, that in these straits I see my West;
 For though their currents yield return to none,
What shall my West hurt me? As West and East
 In all flat maps (and I am one) are one,
 So death doth touch the Resurrection.

Is the Pacific Sea my home? Or are
 The Eastern riches? Is Jerusalem?
Anyan, and Magellan, and Gibraltare,
 All straits, and none but straits, are ways to them,
 Whether where Japhet dwelt, or Cham, or Sem.

We think that Paradise and Calvary,
 Christ's cross and Adam's tree, stood in one place.
Look, Lord, and find both Adams met in me:
 As the first Adam's sweat surrounds my face,
 May the last Adam's blood my soul embrace.

So, in his purple wrapt, receive me, Lord;
 By these his thorns give me his other crown;
And as to others' souls I preach'd thy word,
 Be this my text, my sermon, to mine own:
 Therefore, that he may raise, the Lord throws down.

§ 2

Among Donne's most valued friends were the Lady
Magdalen Herbert and her son George Herbert. With her
he enjoyed 'an amity made up of a chain of suitable inclina-
tions and virtues . . . begun in a happy time for him, he being
then near to the fortieth year of his age; a time when his
necessities needed a daily supply for the support of his wife,
seven children, and a family; and in this time she proved one
of his most bountiful benefactors, and he as grateful an
acknowledger of it'. George Herbert was then about nineteen,
already showing promise of scholarship but hardly, it would
seem, of exceptional piety. Descended on his father's side
from the Earls of Pembroke, he was born (1593) in a castle
and died (forty years later) in his country parsonage at
Bemerton. In 1614 he was elected a Fellow of Trinity College,
Cambridge, and in 1619 was appointed Public Orator, in
which capacity he won, and studied to keep, the favour of
King James. Great learning, high fancy, a civil and sharp
wit, and a natural elegance: these were his conspicuous
qualities at this time. If, says Walton, he expressed any
error, 'it was that he kept himself too much retired, and at
too great a distance with all his inferiors; and his clothes
seemed to prove, that he put too great a value on his parts
and parentage'. He 'enjoyed his genteel humour for clothes
and court-like company, and seldom looked towards Cambridge unless the King were there; but then, he never failed'.
James Stuart however, and other powerful friends, died before
Herbert's ambitions could be realized. Thereupon he retired
to the seclusion of the country, and 'at last God inclined him
to put on a resolution to serve at his altar'. The course of
his life resembles Donne's in this: that not until all ways to
worldly advancement seemed blocked did he turn to the
Church. That step once taken however, he was a changed man.

The very best of George Herbert's poems, hardly more

perhaps than a dozen in all, are exquisite both in temper and workmanship; but there is nothing distinctively mystical about them. No one who has read the 'sacred poems and private ejaculations' posthumously published under the title of *The Temple* can question his sincerity and saintliness. They are very unequal in merit, pious conceits and trivialities mingling or alternating with things of a freshness and beauty that silence criticism, such as this:

> *Love bade me welcome: yet my soul drew back,*
> > *Guilty of dust and sin.*
> *But quick-ey'd Love, observing me grow slack*
> > *From my first entrance in,*
> *Drew nearer to me, sweetly questioning*
> > *If I lack'd any thing.*
>
> *A guest, I answer'd, worthy to be here:*
> > *Love said, 'You shall be he.'*
> *'I the unkind, ungrateful? Ah my dear,*
> > *I cannot look on thee.'*
> *Love took my hand, and smiling did reply,*
> > *'Who made the eyes but I?'*
>
> *'Truth, Lord, but I have marr'd them: let my shame*
> > *Go where it doth deserve.'*
> *'And know you not,' says Love, 'who bore the blame?'*
> > *'My dear, then will I serve.'*
> *'You must sit down,' says Love, 'and taste my meat.'*
> > *So I did sit and eat.*

But he belongs to our story not by virtue of any specific mysticism, for that is lacking, but because his example, in life and in verse, stimulated the more intense and soaring imagination of Henry Vaughan, who was eleven years old when Herbert died. For the completest contrast in religious poetry to the manner of George Herbert one must turn to another near-contemporary, Richard Crashaw. Where, even in his most rapturous moments, Herbert is quiet and gentle, Crashaw writes at white heat, yet too often softens and over-sweetens his effect by a surfeit of amorous fancies and metaphors. At his best, however, as in the invocation which ends his poem 'upon the book and picture of the seraphical Saint Teresa', he is magnificent:

> *O thou undaunted daughter of desires!*
> *By all thy dower of lights and fires,*
> *By all the eagle in thee, all the dove,*
> *By all thy lives and deaths of love,*
> *By thy large draughts of intellectual day,*
> *And by thy thirsts of love more large than they . . .*

One could almost wish that he had ended there, and indeed that he had begun with this passage. For the poem contains nothing to equal that last couplet.

The quality we find in Vaughan, at *his* rare best, is not heat but light. He can be diffuse; he seldom wrote a technically quite perfect poem; but his greatest and simplest things bear the mark of an unearthly inspiration.

§ 3

Henry Vaughan (1622–1695), the elder of twin-brothers, was born at Newton near Skethrog, in the green valley of the Usk, the river whose bright waters wind through his verses, and of which in a moment of unwonted self-confidence he wrote:

> *When I am laid to rest hard by thy streams,*
> *And my sun sets where first it sprang in beams,*
> *I'll leave behind me such a large kind light*
> *As shall redeem thee from oblivious night . . .*

He was of gentle lineage, and, like all his family, ardently royalist. Both he and his brother Thomas bore arms for Charles Stuart during the First Civil War, and afterwards suffered imprisonment and deprivation. Both were students at Jesus College, Oxford. After publishing, at the age of twenty-four, his first poems, Henry took a degree in medicine, which he practised first at Brecon and then in his native place. For the greater part of his life he lived in the house where he was born. Though it would be absurd to call him a 'nature poet', for any poet worthy of the name is more than that, nature for Vaughan was evidently a presence, a power, a symbol of divine things. His verses are saturated in sunlight and sweetened with rainfall. Heaven may be their theme, but the scent and savour of green earth is in them. He lives by virtue of a few poems, and these all contained in the volume called *Silex Scintillans* ('The Sparkling Flint'):

> *Lord, thou didst put a soul here. If I must*
> *Be broke again, for flints will give no fire*
> *Without a steel, O let thy power clear*
> *Thy gift once more, and grind this flint to dust.*

Like Wordsworth a century and a half later, he looked back to his childhood, as to a lost Eden:

> *I cannot reach it; and my striving eye*
> *Dazzles at it, as at eternity.*
> *Were now that chronicle alive,*
> *Those white designs which children drive,*
> *And the thoughts of each harmless hour,*
> *With their content too in my power,*
> *Quickly would I make my path even*
> *And by mere playing go to heaven . . .*

and again, in *The Retreat*:

> *Happy those early days, when I*
> *Shined in my angel-infancy,*

> *Before I understood this place*
> *Appointed for my second race,*
> *Or taught my soul to fancy aught*
> *But a white, celestial thought . . .*

This *white* is a recurring idea which holds much more than blankness. We are safe in relating Vaughan's fondness for it, says his latest biographer,* 'to the rich connotations of the Welsh word *gwyn*, which signifies not only white, but fair, happy, holy, blessed. There is no more frequent epithet in Welsh poetry: it is the word which introduces each of the Beatitudes in the Sermon on the Mount, and a Welsh word for Paradise is *gwynfyd*, the white world.' And, 'next after white, his special fondness is for green', the colour of leaves and grass.

Though his versification rarely if ever attains to the neatness and finish of George Herbert's, the influence of the older poet is very evident both in thought and style. A dozen examples could be found. *The Pursuit* embodies the same idea as Herbert's *The Pulley;* Vaughan's *Praise* ('King of comforts, King of life') strikingly resembles, in mood and metre, Herbert's poem of the same title ('King of glory, King of peace'); and the poem that begins

> *How rich, O Lord, how fresh thy visits are!*

is palpably an echo, in part, of one of the most exquisitely beautiful of Herbert's:

> *How fresh, O Lord, how sweet and clean*
> *Are thy returns, even as the flowers in spring;*
> *To which, besides their own demean,*
> *The late-past frosts tributes of pleasure bring.*
> > *Grief melts away,*
> > *Like snow in May,*
> *As if there were no such cold thing.*

* F. E. Hutchinson, *Henry Vaughan*. Oxford, 1947.

> *Who would have thought my shrivel'd heart*
> *Could have recover'd greenness? It was gone*
> *   Quite under ground, as flowers depart*
> *To see their mother-root when they have blown;*
> *   Where they together*
> *   All the hard weather,*
> *   Dead to the world, keep house unknown . . .*
>
> *   And now in age I bud again,*
> *After so many deaths I live and write;*
> *   I once more smell the dew and rain,*
> *And relish versing. O my only light,*
> *   It cannot be*
> *   That I am he*
> *On whom thy tempests fell all night.*

There is indeed much else in Vaughan that reads like an amplification of Herbert's more economical, more epigrammatic utterance. Not everything he learnt from Herbert was good: like his master he can be tiresomely ingenious. Sometimes one comes upon a passage which might have been written by either poet. This (the Soul is addressing the Body)—

> *Ah go, thou 'rt weak and sleepy. Heaven*
> *Is a plain watch, and without figures winds*
> *All ages up. Who drew this circle, even*
> *   He, fills it. Days and hours are blinds.*
> *Yet this take with thee: the last gasp of Time*
> *Is thy first breath, and man's eternal prime—*

this might be Herbert's or Vaughan's, equally. But Vaughan's higher flights, such as

> *I saw Eternity the other night*
> *Like a great Ring of pure and endless light,*
> *   All calm as it was bright,*

are beyond Herbert's imaginative compass.

If white and green are Vaughan's recurring colours, it is *quickness* that informs them, making him feel

> *through all this fleshy dress*
> *Bright shoots of everlastingness.*

Quick, with all its derivatives, is a favourite word:

> *Nothing that is, or lives,*
> *But hath his quicknings, and reprieves,*
> *As thy hand opens or shuts.*
> *Healings and cuts,*
> *Darkness and daylight, life and death,*
> *Are but mere leaves turn'd by thy breath.*

Life, he says, is 'a fixt, discerning light, a knowing joy'; and, contrasting false life with true:

> *Thou art a toilsome mole, or, less,*
> *A moving mist.*
> *But life is, what none can express,*
> *A quickness, which my God hath kist.*

Vaughan's verse is pictorial as well as musical, a delight to the mind's eye as well as the ear. His best poems have a brilliant clarity and a sustained, colloquial, delicately weaving rhythm. Their diction is at once homely and exact. But the quality in which his verse is rivalled by no other poet of his time, except perhaps Andrew Marvell, is translucency. The ancient sundial motto, *lux umbra Dei*, might well have been the text of his mystical poems. 'With what deep murmurs,' he says, apostrophizing a waterfall in his beloved Usk:

> *With what deep murmurs through time's silent stealth*
> *Doth thy transparent, cool, and watery wealth*

> *Here flowing fall,*
> *And chide, and call,*
> *As if his liquid loose retinue stay'd*
> *Lingering, and were of this steep place afraid,*
> *The common pass*
> *Where, clear as glass,*
> *All must descend*
> *Not to an end,*
> *But, quicken'd by this deep and rocky grave,*
> *Rise to a longer course more bright and brave.*

He sees in this waterfall, this river, a symbol or microcosm of the outflowing of the One into the Many, and of the Many back into the One:

> *Dear stream, dear bank, where often I*
> *Have sat and pleased my pensive eye,*
> *Why, since each drop of thy quick store*
> *Runs thither, whence it flow'd before,*
> *Should poor souls fear a shade or night,*
> *Who came (sure) from a sea of light?*
> *Or, since those drops are all sent back*
> *So sure to thee, that none doth lack,*
> *Why should frail flesh doubt any more*
> *That what God takes he'll not restore?*

He might well have left it at that, but he goes on for another nine couplets which add little or nothing to what he has already said. It was Vaughan's weakness that he did not always know when to stop.

The *Ascension Hymn* ('They are all gone into the world of light'), like *The Retreat* itself, is too well known to need quoting. But *The Night*, which of all Vaughan's poems is perhaps the one we could least bear to lose, is less frequently found in anthologies. It begins with a reference to Nicodemus, who visited Jesus by night; asks

What hallow'd solitary ground did bear
          So rare a flower
     Within whose sacred leaves did lie
     The fullness of the Deity;

and ends with five lovely stanzas:

     Dear night, this world's defeat;
The stop to busy fools; care's check and curb;
The day of spirits; my soul's calm retreat
          Which none disturb;
     Christ's progress, and his prayer-time;
     The hours to which high Heaven doth chime;

     God's silent, searching flight,
When my Lord's head is fill'd with dew, and all
His locks are wet with the clear drops of night;
          His still, soft call;
     His knocking time; the soul's dumb watch,
     When spirits their fair kindred catch.

     Were all my loud, evil days
Calm and unhaunted as is thy dark Tent,
Whose peace but by some angel's wing or voice
          Is seldom rent:
     Then I in Heaven all the long year
     Would keep, and never wander here.

     But living where the sun
Doth all things wake, and where all mix and tire
Themselves and others, I consent and run
          To every mire;
     And by this world's ill-guiding light
     Err more than I can do by night.

There is in God (some say)
A deep but dazzling darkness, as men here
Say it is late and dusky because they
See not all clear.
O for that night! where I in him
Might live invisible and dim.

§ 4

For a pendant to this chapter we have the shining and searching simplicity of Thomas Traherne, a humble contemporary of Vaughan's, and born, like him, somewhere on the Welsh border. Traherne, the son of a shoemaker, was entered at Brasenose College, Oxford; took degrees in Arts and Divinity; and became vicar of a parish in Herefordshire. He was a better poet in prose than in verse: it is his prose *Centuries of Meditations** that gives him his high place in seventeenth-century literature. For sheer radiance of apprehension and sustained felicity of heart there is nothing that can compare with it. Because he retained the unclouded vision that sees heaven in everything and everything as for the first time, the note of wonder and delight never falters; and if after a while it tends to cloy, that is surely rather our fault than his. The book is at once a spiritual autobiography and a lyrical discourse on the beauty and blessedness of all creation.

Love is the first law of our being: nothing else, therefore, is so natural to us. 'You are as prone to love as the sun is to shine, it being the most delightful and natural employment of the Soul of Man: without which you are dark and miserable. The whole world ministers to you as the theatre of your Love. It sustains you and all objects that you may continue to love them. When we dote upon the perfections and beauties of some one creature, we do not love that too

* First printed in 1908 from a newly discovered MS. See Bibliography.

much, but other things too little. Never was anything in this world loved too much, but many things have been loved in a false way, and all in too short a measure.' The way to become rich and blessed, he finds, is to see more clearly the beauties and glories of the natural world. And not only to see them but to be united with them, realizing oneself as part of the universal being. 'You never enjoy the world aright, till the sea itself floweth in your veins, till you are clothed with the heavens and crowned with the stars, and perceive yourself to be the sole heir of the whole world: and more than so, because men are in it who are every one sole heirs as well as you.' For the world, *this* world, 'is a mirror of infinite beauty, yet no man sees it. It is a temple of majesty, yet no man regards it. It is a region of light and peace, did not men disquiet it. It is the Paradise of God.'

But Traherne is a psychologist as well as a rhapsodist. In the love he so ardently commends is included, as a necessary basis, 'self-love', but in a sense which he is careful to define. Love of self is dishonourable, or evil, only when it *ends* with self. 'It is more glorious to love others, and more desirable, but by natural means to be attained. That pool must first be filled that shall be made to overflow.' In other words, we cannot be in charity with others unless we are in charity with ourselves. And this is demonstrably true; for we have only to look within us and around us to see that all vice and cruelty, all 'man's inhumanity to man', has its root not in this innocent self-enjoyment which Traherne chooses to call 'self-love', but in its very opposite, self-hatred. It is the unhappy man, the man frustrated of joy whether by his own fault or another's, who plunges into gross sensuality, or becomes possessed by an insatiable lust for power, or—the more insidious danger—uses his own moral rectitude as a rod for his brother's back.

'In the Soul of Man,' says Traherne, 'there are innumerable infinities. One soul in the immensity of its intelligence is greater and more excellent than the whole world. The ocean is but the drop of a bucket to it, the heavens but a centre, the sun obscurity, and all ages but as one day; it being by its understanding a temple of eternity, and God's omni-presence, between which and the whole world there is no proportion.' But no one human soul is sufficient to itself: it needs others, with whose beauty it may be crowned and entertained. 'As in many mirrors we are so many other selves, so are we spiritually multiplied when we meet ourselves more sweetly, and live again, in other persons.'

Chapter Five

THE CAMBRIDGE PLATONISTS

§ 1

MANY extravagances have been committed in the name of mysticism; but if, with such things in mind, we are still tempted to regard that too ambiguous word as a synonym for frenzy and irrationalism, a visit to the University of Cambridge any time during the middle and late years of this same seventeenth century should finally dispose of the idea. Whichcote's use of 'mystical' in the pejorative sense, when he declares the Christian religion to be 'not mystical, symbolical, enigmatical, emblematical', is by no means inconsistent with the fact that there is a strong vein of what we now call mysticism running through the thought of the so-called Cambridge Platonists, whose spiritual father he was. This becomes crystal clear when he goes on to say what religion, in his judgment, is. It is 'unclothed, unbodied, intellectual, rational, spiritual'. What this passage amounts to, translated into present-day language, is that religion is not fanciful, fantastical, and theoretical, but an actual spiritual experience susceptible of rational interpretation.

Whichcote subscribed heartily to the cardinal points of Christian doctrine, and defended them stoutly; but his emphasis is always on the spirit of religion, and the sweetness and light that are its fruits, rather than on theological niceties and abstractions. He wrote nothing for publication, and the sermons as we have them, though no doubt faithfully recording his line of thought, almost certainly do not give a true idea of his actual preaching. He was a teacher and preacher first and last, not a writer; and his best, his most telling

H

phrases would be struck off suddenly, the inspiration of the moment, minted in the genial warmth of personal contact. 'He was a born teacher—one whose highest qualities were stimulated by contact with young minds, and that play of speech which seems to be necessary to the finest development of certain intellectual natures, from Socrates downwards. Such men are teachers divinely called. Their proper place is in the academic chair or the pulpit. Surrounded by questioning spirits and eager looks, there they are great, as the life and thought grows warm within them and overflows in copious and impressive utterance.' * The least ambitious of men, the most unegoistical and self-effacing, he was well content that his work should prosper and himself be forgotten. And, as Tulloch finely says, the obscurity which has overtaken him is not without relation to his very greatness. For 'there are some kinds of influence which perish in their very fruitfulness, as the seed dies and wastes away at the root of the ripening grain. Whichcote's influence was of this kind. He was careless of his own name, providing the higher thoughts for which he cared were found bearing fruit. He possessed that highest magnanimity of all—a magnanimity extremely rare—of forgetting himself in the cause which he loved, and rejoicing that others entered into the results for which he laboured.'† In point of style and eloquence he was excelled by some of those who learnt from him, and in his humility would rejoice in the fact; but it was his personal quality, his robust common sense, his eye for essentials, his liberality of mind and spirit, that inspired in academic and ecclesiastical circles a dynamic movement which, mediating between the two extremes of Prelatism and Puritanism, and therefore angrily opposed by both, sought to bring the English Church back to what a pamphleteer of the time calls 'her old loving nurse the Platonick philosophy'. The Cambridge Platonists did not call

---

* John Tulloch, *Rational Theology and Christian Philosophy in England in the Seventeenth Century*. Edinburgh & London, 1874.   † Tulloch, *op. cit.*

themselves so. The name was first given them reproachfully, by their opponents; and it is broadly true to say that the Platonism that colours and illumines their thought was derived rather through Plotinus and his Christian expositors than direct from Plato himself. Nor did they organize themselves as a party or confront the world with a systematized philosophy. They do form, nevertheless, a compact school of liberal religious thought. Its chief members were all Anglican clergymen, of high academic standing; they were nearly all associated with a particular Cambridge college, Emmanuel; and Whichcote was their fountain-head.

Their lives ran concurrently with those glanced at in our two previous chapters, and in the same spiritual world, though in retrospect the three social circles in question, that of Fox, that of the predominantly Royalist 'metaphysical' poets, and that of academic Cambridge, seem, and probably were, quite separate and self-contained. Henry Vaughan was four years old, and George Fox minus two, when Benjamin Whichcote, the son of a Shropshire squire, entered Emmanuel College in 1626 at the age of fifteen or sixteen. His tutor was Antony Tuckney, a man ten years his senior, of eminent scholarship, stern integrity, and strict theological opinions, who was later to admonish him, in a series of letters, for precisely those elements in his preaching and teaching which are now seen to be of the highest value—his liberality of mind and his emphasis on the inwardness of authority. He was too fond, Tuckney complained, of quoting (from the Book of Proverbs): 'The spirit of man is the candle of the Lord.' It was indeed a favourite text with him. The idea it embodies is central to his thought. Man's reason, 'a seed of deiform nature', is for him the ultimate seat of authority in religion. 'The Law externally given,' he says, in a sermon on Divine Truth, 'was to revive, awaken Man, after his apostacy and sin, and to call him to remembrance, advertency, and consideration. And, indeed, had there not been a Law written in the Heart of Man, a Law without [outside] him could be to no purpose.' Religion, then, is 'the introduction of the Divine Life into the Soul of Man, and men cannot possibly be really happy in the separate state' except by 'having a Divine Love ruling in their hearts, by self-resignation and submission to the Divine Will, and by being like unto God'. The implication of that phrase 'the separate state' is worth unravelling. It might be stated in the pregnant words of St Paul: 'The temple of God is holy: which temple ye are.' The separateness Whichcote refers to is the effect of that artificial, or accidental, separation of Man from his Divine Source which culminates in the illusion of a self-subsistent ego. God is defined by Whichcote as 'the Original of Man's being, the centre of his soul, his ultimate end'.

This kind of thing seemed to Tuckney dangerously tendentious stuff, and especially lamentable when coming from a man taught by himself at a college founded (in 1584) as a Puritan seminary and designed for the teaching and advancement of Calvinist theology. It is as natural for a man, says Whichcote, to live in love and to carry himself well in God's family, as for a beast to be guided by his senses, or for the sun to give light. 'Nothing is more certainly true than that all Vice is unnatural, and contrary to the Nature of Man. All that we call Sin, that which is naught, and contrary to the Reason of Things, is destructive of Human Nature, and a man forceth himself when he doeth it; so that to comply with those principles of natural Light and Knowledge which God did implant in us in the moment of our creation, and exactly to be obedient to the ducture of Reason, is connatural to Man, in respect of the state of God's creation.' Natural religion was 'the very temper and complexion of Man's Soul in the moment of his creation'; and sin, being against reason and nature, is an aberration. No wonder Dr Tuckney was alarmed: his old pupil had travelled a long way from the prescribed dogmatics of the Westminster Confession. Whichcote was even audacious enough to declare: 'It is a matter of very fair belief, that the Original of all Beings, the Father of all our Spirits, the Fountain of all Good, will, one way or another, pardon sin, and do what behoves him for the recovery of his laps'd Creation.' And again: 'We are in the hands of him that is primarily and originally good; and he will certainly commiserate every case so far as it is compassionable. Now the case of a sinner is compassionable if he be penitent, because he was never better than finite and fallible. Nothing is more credible than that the first and chiefest Goodness will save to the utmost extent of disposition in the Subject.' But this would never do. It smacked dangerously of Arminianism to suggest that a man's ultimate salvation might depend on himself, as well as on the grace of God. No true Calvinist could tolerate such heresy.

At the time when this correspondence was taking place between Whichcote and Tuckney, the elder man was Master of Emmanuel and Whichcote Provost of King's. The dispute, conducted on both sides with a firmness that did not impair their mutual affection and high esteem, arose from a sermon preached by Whichcote, in 1851, in his capacity of Vice-Chancellor, but it concerned, no less, the general colour of his religious thought. The situation was the more alarming to such men as Tuckney, sincerely zealous for the truth as they saw it, because Whichcote, by virtue both of his office and (far more) his personal magnetism, was evidently, willy nilly, the leader and inspirer of a new school of thought in the university. All free, generous, forward-looking minds among the younger generation eagerly flocked to him. He had graduated in 1629 and become a Fellow of Emmanuel in 1633. Three years later he was ordained by the Bishop of Lincoln, and in 1643 was presented by his college with a living in Somersetshire: whence, however, having married and begun to settle down, he was recalled in the following year to succeed Dr Collins, who had been ejected by Par-

liament from the provostship of King's. Whichcote was much
exercised in his mind by this totally unexpected offer of
preferment. He respected Dr Collins and believed him to
have been unjustly treated. The idea of superseding him was
therefore doubly odious to him. After anxiously weighing
pros and cons he at last consented to accept office, but only
on the condition that half his salary should go to Collins.
This gesture, so characteristic of him, was remembered
against him at the Restoration, when he himself was ejected.
We learn from Tillotson, who preached his funeral sermon,
that Whichcote 'never took the Covenant' and that 'he
prevailed [with the authorities] to have the greatest part
of the Fellows of King's College exempted from that
imposition, and preserved them in their places'.

To Tuckney's accusation that he had been influenced by
the Dutch Arminians he answered with a flat denial, adding:
'Truly I shame myself to tell you how little I have been
acquainted with books, but for your satisfaction I do. While
Fellow at Emmanuel College, employment with pupils took
my time from me. I have not read many books, but I have
studied a few. Meditation and invention hath been rather my
life than reading.' Another charge brought against him,
apropos perhaps of his readiness to find truth in pre-Christian
philosophers, was that he was too much addicted to the use
of school language. This is not borne out by the clear simple
prose of his sermons and aphorisms, but there is an amusing
story (probably invented) that one day, seeing two boys
fighting in the street, he exclaimed, as he parted them:
'What!—moral entities, and yet pugnacious!' But Tuckney's
chief point of grievance, to which he returns when his other
complaints have been rebutted or whittled away, was Whichcote's exaltation of Reason and Nature. Reason, for
Whichcote, is a natural light. 'Sir,' he says in reply to his
mentor, 'I oppose not rational to spiritual—for spiritual is
most rational. But I contradistinguish rational to conceited,

DR BENJAMIN WHICHCOTE, BY MARY BEALE, 1682

impotent, affected canting, as I may call it, when the ear
receives words which offer no matter to the understanding,
make no impression on the inward sense.' In one of his
sermons he declares it, *pace* his critics, to be 'a very profitable
work to call upon men to answer the principles of their
creation, to fulfil natural light, to answer natural conscience,
to be throughout rational in what they do; for these things
have a divine foundation. The spirit in man is the candle of
the Lord, lighted by God, and lighting man to God'. And,
in an aphorism, one of many: 'Reason is the divine governor
of man's life. It is the very voice of God.' The real quarrel,
it is clear, was between two radically opposed notions of God.
Is God to be conceived as an almighty potentate and judge,
utterly separate from man; or as the very being of man's
being, his source and end, the beat of his blood and the light
in his mind? The first, with whatever refinements, was the
view of theological dogmatism in Whichcote's time. The
second is implicit in all true mystical religion, and the core
of all wholesome mystical experience.

   Though in this controversy Whichcote defended his position with spirit (as well as with singular gentleness and
courtesy), he had no taste for polemics. Witnesses agree that
he was of a serene meditative temper, and kindly in all his
dealings. Particularly, says Tillotson, 'he excelled in the
virtues of conversation, humanity, gentleness and humility,
a prudent and peaceable and reconciling temper'. And these
were the virtues he enjoined upon others, as a joy in themselves and a pre-condition of the religious life. 'The breakings-
in of God upon us,' he says, 'require a mind that is not
subject to passion, but [is] in a serene and quiet posture,
where there is no tumult of imagination. There is no genuine
and proper effect of religion where the mind of man is not
composed, sedate, and calm.' He warns his hearers, too,
against enslavement in the life of sense. 'They who sit loosely
to earthly things which obstruct the mind do easily receive

the Divine Light.' Serenity, humility, patience, and forbearance, these are his recurring theme. True religion, he
says, by setting a man free from black melancholy, from
exorbitant appetites, from empty joys, from anxious self-
devouring cares, from swelling pride and ambition, from a
gnawing aching conscience, from an arbitrary presumption,
from rigid sourness and severity of spirit, keeps the mind
in a good frame and temper and establishes a healthful
complexion of soul. 'The soul of man to God is as a flower
to the sun: it opens at its approach, and shuts when it with-
draws. Religion in the mind is as a bias upon the spirit,
inclines it in all its motions. Though sometimes it be jogg'd
and interrupted, yet it comes to itself. It is a Rule within,
a Law written in Man's heart. It is the Government of his
spirit. . . . Religion puts the soul in a right posture towards
God, for we are thereby renew'd in the spirit of our minds.'

§ 2

A detailed account of the movement of thought set going
by Whichcote would take us too far from our subject.
Tulloch devotes to it the whole second volume of his masterly
work already cited. The impulse behind the movement was
twofold. In its beginnings it was very largely a reaction from
the bitterly contending bigotries of the time, a revolt against
that arid scholasticism which regarded Christianity as
primarily a set of theological opinions. Only as it developed
did the Neoplatonic element, implicit from the first, become
conspicuous. In John Smith, the most brilliant of Whichcote's
pupils, a man of high literary gifts, the part played by ancient
writers is indeed a little too conspicuous: again and again
the luminous flow of his discourse is interrupted by learned
quotations from the Greek. The same is true in varying
measure of all the later Cambridge Platonists, but not of
Whichcote. It is true of Ralph Cudworth, of Henry More,

and of Nathanael Culverwel. Whichcote may be said to have had a more immediately practical end in view than his successors: to combat intolerance, to preach charity and humility, to revitalize the whole notion of religion by presenting it as a life to be lived not a mere creed to be accepted, and to commend natural reason as the light of the mind, the 'candle of the Lord', the 'very voice of God'. These aims, it is true, were never lost sight of; the teaching of Whichcote was assimilated by the men who followed him and never superseded; but as the movement expanded and advanced, its philosophical or speculative character became more pronounced. To these two motivating causes, the revolt against prevalent bigotries and the inspiration derived from Platonism, must be added a third, though it should go without saying, for it is the most vital of all: namely, the personal experience, the living 'sense of God', which these men unquestionably had. Though they dealt much in 'notions', and would thereby have incurred the disapproval of George Fox, it was not a notion, but something actually experienced, a 'spiritual sensation' (Smith uses this very phrase), that quickened and sustained their labours.

John Smith, the son of a small farmer, was born at Achurch, Northamptonshire, in the year 1618. At the age of eighteen he was entered at Emmanuel, and Whichcote, then a Fellow of that college, became his tutor and good friend, not only directing his studies but making 'seasonable provision for his support and maintenance when he was a young scholar'. In 1644 he was elected a Fellow of Queens' College, where, as a tutor, a lecturer in mathematics, and a man always at the service of such as resorted to him, he found full scope for his genius as a teacher. 'For,' says his friend Simon Patrick (afterwards Bishop of Ely), 'he was not a library locked up, nor a book clasped, but stood open for any to converse withal that had a mind to learn. He had such a plenty of words, and those so full, pregnant, and significant, joined with such an active fancy as is very rarely found in the company of such a deep understanding and judgment as dwelt in him.' Very little is known of his personal life, but this same witness tells us that he 'insouled' all principles of justice and righteousness, and so made them one with himself. He was 'dipped into justice as it were over head and ears; he had not a slight superficial tincture, but was dyed and coloured quite through with it'. And what, exclaims Patrick, later in this eulogy, 'what shall I say of his *love?* None that knew him well but might see in him love bubbling and springing up in his soul, and flowing out to all; and that love unfeigned, without guile, hypocrisy, or dissimulation. I cannot tell you how his soul universalized, how tenderly he embraced all God's creatures in his arms'.

With all allowances made for the rhetorical grandiloquence of a funeral oration, it is difficult to resist the impression that Smith was indeed a man in whom the flame of the spirit burned with a singular power and clarity, and this judgment is amply borne out by the *Select Discourses*, his only published work, in which learning and poetry, a soaring imagination and a fine critical intelligence, are luminously blended. A few quotations will suffice to give an idea of his quality. Very apt to our present purpose is the opening argument of his *True Way of Attaining Divine Knowledge*. 'Were I indeed to define divinity, I should rather call it a divine life than a divine science, it being something rather to be understood by a spiritual sensation than by any verbal description, as all things of sense and life are best known by sentient and vital qualities. . . . He that is most practical in divine things hath the purest and sincerest knowledge of them, and not he that is most dogmatical. Divinity indeed is a true efflux from the eternal light, which, like the sunbeams, does not only enlighten, but heat and enliven; and therefore our Saviour hath, in his beatitudes, connected purity of heart with the beatifical vision. And as the eye cannot behold the sun unless it be sunlike and hath the form and resemblance of the sun drawn in it, so neither can the soul of man behold God unless it be Godlike, hath God formed in it, and be made partaker of the divine nature.'

This doctrine, the primacy of spiritual sensation and the relative unimportance of intellectual notions, is common to all the Cambridge Platonists, and to all mystics of whatever school. It is the defining feature of mystical philosophy. Ralph Cudworth (also of Emmanuel) has a passage to very much the same purpose: 'Words and syllables, which are but dead things, cannot possibly convey the living notions of heavenly truths to us. The secret mysteries of a divine life, of a new nature, of Christ formed in our hearts, they cannot be written or spoken; language and expressions cannot reach them; neither can they be ever truly understood except the soul itself be kindled from within and awakened into the life of them. A painter that would draw a rose, though he may flourish some likeness of it in figure and colour, yet he can never paint the scent and fragrancy; or, if he would draw a flame, he cannot put a constant heat into his colours. All the skill of cunning artisans and mechanicks cannot put a principle of life into a statue of their own making; neither are we able to enclose in words and letters the life, soul, and essence of any spiritual truths.' In the same sermon, delivered before the House of Commons on the 31st of March 1647, Cudworth strongly deprecates the arrogance of pretending to an intellectual knowledge of God. Excellent medicine, this, for an audience of men many of whom, bred in an atmosphere of bitter religious contention, had been willing to shed blood, and lose their own, in defence of this or that theological opinion. 'The best assurance that anyone can have of his interest in God,' Cudworth told them, 'is the conformity of his soul to him. Those divine purposes, whatsoever they be, are altogether unsearchable and unknowable by us; they lie wrapt up in everlasting darkness and covered in a deep abyss.

Who is able to fathom the bottom of them? Let us not, therefore, make this our first attempt towards God and religion, to persuade ourselves strongly of these everlasting decrees; for if at our first flight we aim so high, we shall haply but scorch our wings, and be struck back with lightning, as those giants of old were that would needs attempt to assault heaven. And it is indeed a most gigantick essay to thrust ourselves so boldly into the lap of heaven; it is a prank of Nimrod, of a mighty hunter, thus rudely to deal with God, and to force heaven and happiness before his face, whether he will or no.' How then are we to attain to knowledge of divine things, if not by theological dogmatism? Cudworth's answer goes to the root of the matter: 'The way to obtain a good assurance of our title to heaven is, not to clamber up to it by a ladder of our own ungrounded persuasions, but to dig as low as hell by humility and self-denial in our own hearts. And though this may seem to be the farthest way about, yet it is indeed the nearest and safest way to it. We must, as the Greek epigram speaks, *ascend downward* and *descend upward*, if we would indeed come to heaven, or get any true persuasion of our title to it.' Which is surely only another way of saying that the Kingdom of Heaven is within us.

Cudworth, greatly gifted though he was, in his more elaborate works is an author whom only the most resolute reader could persevere with to the end; but John Smith is still eminently readable and rewarding. Two of Smith's shorter pieces are concerned, the one with Superstition, the other with Atheism. These two things are closely related: they spring from the same cause. The true cause and rise of superstition, he says, is simply a false opinion of God, which represents God as dreadful, rigorous, imperious, apt to anger; yet easily appeased by 'some flattering devotions, especially if performed with sanctimonious shows and a solemn sadness of mind'; and though he quotes ancient writers in support of this remark he makes it very clear that what he has in mind is 'that picture of God which some Christians have drawn of him, wherein sourness and arbitrariness appear so much'. And, as superstition is engendered by a base opinion of the Deity as cruel and tyrannical (and 'comprehends not the true divine good that ariseth to the souls of men from an internal frame of religion'), so also is atheism; for 'that sour and ghastly apprehension of God, when it meets with more stout and surly natures, is apt to enrage them, and, cankering them with malice against the Deity they so little brook, provokes them to fight against it and undermine the notion of it'.

This kind of plain speaking could not have given unmixed pleasure to Smith's Calvinist brethren. But he was not in general a polemical writer. He was far less concerned to controvert what he held to be error than to translate into terms of religious philosophy his own deep sense of a divine life within and beyond him. He did not live to be old, but he was endowed with a mellow wisdom, a charitable spirit, an acute understanding of the hearts of men; and the richness of his mind is reflected in every page of his writing. In a long discourse concerning the existence and nature of God there is a passage implying that 'God' and 'happiness', rightly understood, are virtually synonymous terms. 'The whole work of this world is nothing but a perpetual contention for true happiness, and men are scattered up and down the world, moving to and fro therein, to seek it. Happiness is that pearl of price which all adventure for, though few find it. It is not gold or silver that the earthlings of this world seek after, but some satisfying good which they think is there treasured up. Neither is it a little empty breath that ambition and popularity soars after, but some kind of happiness that it thinks to catch and suck in with it. And thus, indeed, when men most of all fly from God, they still seek after him.' What, then, is the quality of this happiness which God is?

In other words, what are we to understand by this term 'God'? God, says Smith, 'is not better defined to us by our understandings than by our wills and affections. He is not only the eternal Reason, that almighty Mind and Wisdom which our understandings converse with; but he is also that unstained beauty and supreme good to which our wills are perpetually aspiring. And wheresoever we find true beauty, love, and goodness, we may say [that] here or there is God. And, as we cannot understand any thing of an intelligible nature but by some primitive idea we have of God whereby we are able to guess at the elevation of its being and the pitch of its perfection, so neither do our wills embrace any thing without some latent sense of him, whereby they can taste and discern how near any thing comes to that self-sufficient good they seek after. And, indeed, without such an internal sensating faculty as this is, we should never know when our souls are in conjunction with the Deity, or be able to relish the ineffable sweetness of true happiness.'

The emphasis, once again, is upon the 'internal sensating faculty'. All genuine mystical philosophy has its root, not in a theory, but in an actual inward experience.

§ 3

Henry More, though in his day much read and admired, lives rather as a character than as a writer. With the possible exception of Smith, who died at the early age of thirty-four as brilliant in promise as in achievement, he was perhaps the most unworldly, the most 'heavenly minded', of all the Cambridge school. There was indeed no tincture of world-liness in him, no spark of ambition except the noble ambition of spreading the light that was in him. To that end he devoted many volumes, of prose and of verse. The verse scarcely ever rises to poetry, and the prose is no longer read. He was singleminded and simplehearted, with a personal

radiance that was visible to all who came near him. The son
of 'a gentleman of fair estate and fortune', of whom he speaks
in terms of the highest love and respect, up to the age of
nearly fourteen he was carefully indoctrinated with a strict
and pious Calvinism, but, of his own accord, without prompt-
ing from outside, soon broke away from that system. Even
in early childhood he enjoyed a strong 'inward sense of the
divine presence' and could never swallow 'that hard doctrine
concerning fate' which his Calvinist father and uncle commended to him. At Cambridge (Christ's) he became possessed
of 'a mighty and almost immoderate thirst after knowledge',
but after four years' study of certain ancient philosophers he
found himself in a state of doubt and misgiving. He did not
question the existence of God or the value of human goodness, but was greatly exercised about first and last things,
the perennial problem of meaning and purpose. He then
encountered the Neoplatonic writers, including Plotinus himself. These, together with the *Theologia Germanica*, that
'golden little book', opened up new worlds of airy speculation
to his eagerly aspiring mind. From the German mystics, in
particular, he learnt the discipline of self-renunciation and
so came to believe that 'the *divine seed* alone is that which
is acceptable to God, and the sole invincible basis of all true
religion'. He became 'solicitous about nothing so much as
a more full union with the divine and celestial principle, the
inward flowing wellspring of life eternal'. He was indeed, of
all the Cambridge Platonists, the most conspicuously mystical
type, and with all his learning remained singularly ingenuous
and guileless, living from day to day, from year to year,
happily excited and astonished by his own radiant thoughts
But he seems to have lacked intellectual ballast, for in his
latter years he became childishly credulous and lost himself
among theosophical daydreams.

He became a Fellow of his college, but stubbornly declined
any further promotion, despite the earnest solicitations of

friends who felt that so great and influential a man should occupy a more exalted office. He refused not only the Mastership, offered him in 1654 (when Cudworth was appointed instead), but also a deanery and two bishoprics. The story is told that one day his friends managed to get him as far from Cambridge as Whitehall, that he might kiss the king's hand; but when he discovered that this ceremony would imply his acceptance of a bishopric 'he was not on any account to be persuaded to it'. One preferment he did accept, a prebend in Gloucester Cathedral, but only in order to resign it almost at once in favour of another man. He was more than content to live quietly, and as obscurely as might be, in his college, teaching and lecturing and enjoying his meditations and visions. In the *Divine Dialogues*, under the transparent disguise of fiction, he has recorded a dream-experience of his own: how he was approached by a 'very grave and venerable person' who gave him 'the two keys of Providence, that thou mayest thereby be able to open the treasure of that wisdom thou so anxiously and yet so piously seekest after'. Each key was found to contain a scroll inscribed with a maxim. The first key, of silver, carried the words: *Claude fenestras ut luceat domus*. The second, of gold: *Amor Dei lux animae*. But while he was meditating on these things, suddenly a loud noise assaulted his ears; the vision vanished; and he awoke to find himself sitting at the foot of an oak tree, with a braying ass on each side of him.

Chapter Six

WILLIAM LAW

§ 1

To present William Law as a man who by contact with the mystical teaching of Jakob Boehme was changed from a severe legalist into an illuminated spirit and an embodiment of all-embracing charity would be to over-simplify the story. The seed that eventually flowered into mysticism was almost certainly sown in him long before he encountered Boehme's writings, and the severity of aspect and behaviour so conspicuous in early and middle life stayed with him till the end. Moreover he remained rigid in the High Church orthodoxy in which he began; he continued to be punctilious in all outward observances; and he never recanted—though it seems scarcely possible that he did not in some degree modify—the extravagant puritanism of his moral opinions. Nevertheless, that a great change took place in him is evident and incontestable. The balance of his qualities was shifted. He attained to a new spiritual orientation, a new inwardness; so that what he had formerly received as an item of belief, one among many, became intimately realized as the cardinal fact of his religious life. The fervours of a Julian of Norwich were alien to his austere temperament; visions and voices and emotional raptures he distrusted and disapproved of; and this contrast of personalities makes it the more significant that the central point of his later theology—'God is love, yea all love, and so all love that nothing but love can come from him'—was the same as Julian's. At this distance of time, with only cold print to represent him, he must seem in his earlier phase a somewhat forbidding figure. Yet he was revered and loved, as well as (possibly) a little feared, by all who came within his personal orbit; and even his bitterest opponents in religious controversy recognized the saintliness of his life.

He was born at King's Cliffe, Northamptonshire, in 1686, during James the Second's reign, the son of a prosperous grocer and chandler descended from a 'good family'. He had seven brothers and three sisters, but for reasons unknown to us it was William alone who was sent by his father to a university, being entered as a sizar of Emmanuel College, Cambridge, in the year 1705. After graduating he was elected a Fellow of his college and a year or two afterwards took holy orders. By then Queen Anne was occupying the throne, and his prospects were bright; but he asked for trouble, and got it, by making a Jacobitical speech in which he inquired of his audience, with an irony that foreshadowed his later controversial method, 'whether, when the children of Israel had made the golden calf the object of their worship, they ought to keep to their God *de facto* or return to their God *de jure*'. This is the secondhand account of the matter confided by John Byrom to his journal. Byrom, who was afterwards to become an ardent disciple and fast friend of Law, adds: 'He is much blamed by some and defended by others; has the character of a vain, conceited fellow.' Another version of this 'Tripos Speech' cites 'whether the sun shines when it is in an eclipse' and 'whether a dubious successor be not in danger of being set aside' as among the tendentious queries put by Law. At the instance of Dr Adams, Provost of King's, disciplinary action was taken against him, though what form it took is not clear. He remained a Fellow of Emmanuel, and in that capacity, on a day appointed 'for Public Thanksgiving for Her Majesty's General Peace', he preached a sermon warmly defending the Peace of Utrecht· which the Tory Government had lately concluded, arguing 'that every good Christian and loyal subject must have a care of examining too nicely the affairs of his Prince', deprecating public criticism of the governing body, and fulsomely praising, as the fashion was, 'the best of Queens . . . dear offspring of great Charles'. As the fashion was, but with a significant difference; for the sermon ends by commending 'those good old principles of our religion, concerning the Divinity of our Sovereign's authority and the absolute passive obedience we owe to her'.

If any among his audience were so guileless as to regard this curious oration as an attempt to make amends for past indiscretions they were soon undeceived; for during the next year Queen Anne died, to be succeeded by George the First, and in 1716 Law was faced with the necessity of deciding whether he would or would not take the oaths of allegiance to the new monarch and abjuration of the Pretender. Every consideration of self-interest, had he not been deaf to such things, would have urged compliance. So, too, one might have thought, would ordinary common sense; for Jacobitism, though it was to prove itself capable of disturbing the peace, was already an anachronism. For William Law, however, the decision was never in doubt. Now, as always, he was a man of inflexible principles, obedient to nothing but his own conscience. It was an article of his religion that the Stuarts had been divinely appointed to reign over us, and there was an end of it. In a letter to his brother George announcing his resolve to refuse the oaths required of him he says: 'I have sent my mother such news as I am afraid she will be too much concerned at, which is the only trouble for what I have done. I beg of you, therefore, to relieve her from such thoughts, and contribute what you can to satisfy her about my affairs. My prospect, indeed, is melancholy enough, but had I done what was required of me to avoid it, I should have thought my condition much worse. . . . I expected to have had a greater share of worldly advantages than what I am now likely to enjoy; but am fully persuaded that if I am not happier for this trial it will be my own fault. . . . I shall conclude as I began, with desiring you to say as many comfortable things as you can to my mother, and persuade her to think with satisfaction upon that condition, which upon my account gives me no uneasiness, which will much oblige your affectionate brother, W. Law.'

If ever he had entertained personal ambition he now turned his back upon it for ever. As a nonjuror he was deprived both of his Fellowship and of all hope of ecclesiastical preferment. His worldly prospects were dreary in the extreme. Nor were there any compensating satisfactions, except the comfort, all-sufficient to him, of being at peace with his own conscience in at least one point. For his action was purely disinterested. Holding himself aloof from the world of affairs, he had not the least inclination to meddle in politics and never did so. He did not set himself up in opposition to the governing authority or in any way conspire against it. Abjuration of his allegiance to the Pretender would have made not a pennyworth of difference in his behaviour as a citizen; nor can it have much interested him personally whether this man or that occupied the throne of England. But, though he does seem to have cherished a romantic attachment to the Stuarts, his allegiance was not to the Pretender as an individual, but rather to the source of that individual's 'divine right', as he conceived it; and he could not—the point needed no arguing—make formal profession of what to him would have been a lie. Many others did so, and he seems to have harboured no rancour against them; but for him it was simply impossible, he being what he was.

During his residence at Cambridge, probably in undergraduate days, he drew up eighteen rules for his future conduct. Here are some of them. 'To avoid all concerns with the world, or the ways of it, but where religion and charity oblige me to act. To remember frequently, and impress it upon my mind deeply, that no condition of this life is for enjoyment, but for trial; and that every power, ability, or advantage we have, are all so many talents to be accounted for, to the Judge of all the World. To avoid all excess in eating and drinking. To avoid all idleness. To think humbly of myself, and with great charity of all others. To forbear from evil speaking.' And, last of all: 'To spend some time in giving an account of the day, previous to Evening Prayer: how have I spent this day? what sin have I committed? what temptations have I withstood? Have I performed all my duty?' This document constitutes perhaps the best portrait of him in early manhood that we have. It is an impressive but hardly an attractive one, except in its emphasis on humility and charity. 'I think I could turn and live with animals,' said Whitman. 'They do not sweat and whine about their condition. They do not lie awake in the dark and weep for their sins. They do not make me sick discussing their duty to God.' Nor, indeed, did William Law do these things; but he had undeniably, at this time, a singularly joyless conception of what religion is.

His first published writings were controversial. Though done with much skill and spirit they make tedious reading today. A glance at *The Absolute Unlawfulness of the Stage-Entertainment fully demonstrated* (1726) will give us the measure of his unbridled puritanism. No doubt the condition of the stage in 1726 was such as to give great offence to a serious-minded churchman, but it strikes one as odd that a mind normally so acute as Law's could fail to distinguish between the art of the theatre as such and the particular examples that excited his displeasure. That word 'absolute' in the title of his pamphlet underlines this elementary error. And in the text itself it is as if he were at pains to show how utterly unreasonable he can be when he sets his mind to it. 'The Stage is not here condemned, as some other diversions, because they are dangerous and likely to be occasions of sin . . . it is condemned, as drunkenness and lewdness, as lying and profaneness are to be condemned, not as things that may only be the occasion of sin, but such as are in their own nature grossly sinful.' Nothing could be plainer than that. 'I may venture to challenge anyone to show me that the business of the player is a more Christian employment than that of robbers. For he must know very little of the nature of religion that can look upon lust, profaneness, and disorderly passions, to be less contrary to religion than the taking money from the right owner. And a person who devotes himself to this employment, to get his bread by gratifying the corrupt taste of the world with wanton, wild, profane discourses, may be justly supposed to have a more corrupt heart himself than many a man who has taken unlawful ways of relieving his wants.' But what if the discourses should be *not* wanton, wild, and profane? It is a question that seems never to occur to the zealous author.

Later on, we find him disputing against the sufficiency of natural reason and, later still, controverting a series of four sermons on *The Nature, Folly, Sin, and Danger of being Righteous Overmuch*. The author of these sermons, Dr Joseph Trapp, is tilting against what he considered to be the extravagances of Methodism and kindred movements: he begins by admitting that there can be no such thing, properly speaking, as being righteous overmuch, and that he uses the phrase for lack of a better. Its meaning must have been plain enough to most people, and his plea not unreasonable; but Law would have none of it; it stood, in his eyes, for just that comfortable eighteenth-century compromise between godliness and worldliness which he was for ever striving to extirpate. For him there was no golden mean in Christian behaviour. His piety knows no measure. And it cannot be denied that he practised what he preached. Undeviating in his pursuit of Christian perfection, he commended nothing to his fellow Christians that he did not require of himself. In controversy he could hit hard. In conversation with admiring friends like the simplehearted Byrom he could be occasionally abrupt and even snubbing. But there was no radical unkindness or arrogance in him; and in his spiritual maturity, to which the mystical insight of Jakob Boehme contributed so much, he came near to embodying that spirit of love which was the theme of his last and best writings. In the beginning of his answer to Trapp (1739) he declares, with manifest sincerity, that 'under the real influence and full belief of this great mystery of Divine Love there seems to be no room left for anything else amongst Christians but return of love to God and flowings out of love towards one another'. This is a far cry from the asperity of the three open letters which he had addressed to Bishop Hoadly of Bangor some twenty-two years earlier.

§ 2

Earlier still, just after leaving Cambridge, he is said to have been for a while a curate at St Mary's in the Strand. Then came the Bangor controversy, in which he won some reputation by entering the lists against latitudinarianism. It was not until 1726, however, with the publication of *Christian Perfection*, that he began to be regarded by kindred spirits as a kind of oracle. The popularity of this 'practical treatise', like the still greater popularity of the *Serious Call to a Devout and Holy Life* three years later, can hardly be understood today except as evidence of a reaction against the spirit of the age, a hunger for a more strenuous conception of the religious life than was commonly preached from eighteenth-century pulpits. We have seen in our own day how a call to desperate adventure, 'blood and tears and sweat', can fire a people whom the promise of easy victory would have left cold and slack. So it was, perhaps, with those ardent souls who responded to Law's grimly serious call to Christian perfection: the difficulty of the Christian life as he so narrowly conceived it was the secret of its attraction for them. Grim

and narrow, at this time, his notions certainly were. He is
at pains to tell his readers that he calls no one to a cloister,
but only to a right and full performance of the duties that
are necessary for all Christians; but it is clear that he wished
to shut up the human *mind* in a cloister. We are to confine
our reading to godly and edifying books. We are to shun the
theatre. We are to avoid the horrible sin of reading plays.
We are to cultivate a contempt for human learning. For, as
he failed to distinguish between the legitimate art of the
stage and its prostitution to vicious ends, so he chose to
equate all academic scholarship with vain and arid pedantry:
a preposterous position for one whose scholarly breeding is
apparent in every page he wrote and who in fact had a very
imperfect understanding of simple untutored minds. Add
renunciation of the world, systematic mortification of the
natural appetites, and imitation of the life of Christ, and you
have Law's 1726 recipe for the soul's salvation. It is odd that
a self-respecting man should even wish to propitiate the kind
of God that Law then believed in. He never, so far as I
know, repudiated this book; but if in his last years he ever
opened a copy of it he must have been painfully aware of
its gross errors in emphasis if not in doctrine.

When next we hear of him he is established as private
tutor to Edward Gibbon, the young man, then in his teens,
who was destined to be the father of the great historian.
Law became an honoured member of the Gibbon household
at Putney and in due time accompanied his pupil to Emmanuel,
Law's former college. This Edward Gibbon's illustrious son
of the same name says of Law in his autobiography that he
left behind him in the family 'the reputation of a worthy and
pious man, who believed all that he professed, and practised
all that he enjoined'. This tribute from the arch-sceptic would
be pretty conclusive, even if there were not abundant other
evidence to the same effect. It was probably at Putney and
at Cambridge that the *Serious Call* was written: his best-

known work, still readable in parts for its vigour and racy characterization, but infinitely inferior to his comparatively unknown later writings. It was at Putney, too, that John Byrom, who had been Law's contemporary at Cambridge but had not met him there, made his first timid approaches. Byrom had, as well as talent, an engaging simplicity and a total incapacity to distinguish, in his own work, between good workmanlike verse and rank doggerel. His attempts to versify some of Law's most excellent prose produced ludicrous results, which Law himself, however, warmly applauded. He is the author of a famous epigram:

> *God bless the king, God bless the Faith's defender,*
> *God bless—no harm in blessing—the Pretender.*
> *But who Pretender is, and who is king,*
> *God bless us all, that's quite another thing!*

—a sentiment that must have helped to endear him to Law— and he sums up his own character very neatly in some verses written in the Elizabethan manner:

> *With good and gentle-humoured hearts*
> *I choose to chat where'er I come,*
> *Whate'er the subject be that starts;*
> *But if I get among the glum,*
> *I hold my tongue to tell the troth,*
> *And keep my breath to cool my broth.*

In Law's company, one would have thought, he must often have found himself 'among the glum'. There can hardly be imagined a greater contrast than between Law's ultra-seriousness and Byrom's cheerful and sanguine temper. But the fact of their undoubted friendship should give pause to snap judgments and modify our notions of both men. They met as mentor and disciple; but it throws a new light on Law, and a new light on Byrom, if we have seen them only in their writings, to know that a real and lasting affection grew up between them. Law had as little vanity, and Byrom as little self-conceit, as any man alive: no such friendship as theirs, however it may have begun, could have subsisted on a diet of mere mutual flattery.

Law cannot have been an easy man to get on terms with. He was abrupt and outspoken, had no patience with anything that savoured of idleness or affectation, and pretended to none. Moreover, he was indissolubly attached to his own opinions and very ready to instruct the uninitiated. Had it not been for his genuine Christian virtues he must have been, as he clearly was not, an insufferable person. Spiritual pride, the deadliest of sins, was the pitfall that beset his path; and that he always avoided it, if in his heart he *did* always avoid it, is little short of a miracle; for being a man of few personal friends, and none his intellectual equal, he was at the disadvantage all his life long of being king of his company. He was treated as an oracle by all who came near him. Did he ever, for a moment, regard himself so? The question is ultimately unanswerable, but all the evidence goes to show that the spirit of humility he enjoined upon others, the counting of self as naught, was signally exemplified in his own person. Forthright and dogmatic he was; but adulation he would have none of. Yet his mind, if not his character, must surely have been the poorer for lack of companions of his own mettle, in conversation with whom he might have been a learner as well as a teacher. The thrust and parry of argument among equals is something which he seems never to have experienced, and the want of it can only have retarded his intellectual and spiritual growth. His mind was powerful but, in its earlier phase, narrow to the point of bigotry. Humility alone saved him, the humility that kept him essentially sweet for all his sternness and made him happy to receive new enlightenment from the writings of a German shoemaker.

Byrom earned guineas by teaching a shorthand of his own invention, and among his pupils, eventually, was Law's pupil,

Edward Gibbon. Law, at the beginning of their acquaintance, had gratified Byrom by taking a kindly interest in the system, even going so far as to express a 'curiosity to learn'. In February 1729 John writes to his sister Phebe: 'I find the young folk of my acquaintance think Mr Law an impracticable, strange, whimsical writer, but I am not convinced by their reasons.' And in his journal, three days later, he mentions a Mr Green of Emmanuel, a clergyman living at Putney, who told him that Mr Law was at Putney, was going to wear his own hair, and was thought half crazy. 'But I could find that Mr Green must own that he was a very good Christian; we had much talk about such matters.' He was for ever talking about Law with his friends, and one of his first exploits after reading the *Serious Call* was to turn into verse Law's illustrative anecdote of the man who spent years of his life filling a pond with water from various sources and then drowned himself in it. This effusion he recited to Law. 'I repeated the verses about *The Pond* to him and Mildmay, and they laughed, and Mr Law said he must have a copy of them, and desired I would not put the whole book into verse, for then it would not sell in prose—so the good man can joke.'

Most of their conversation, however, was of a more serious kind. Byrom was already much interested in mystical literature and eagerly sought the master's opinion of Antoinette Bourignon and Jeanne Marie Guyon, whose extravagant visionary pretensions had made a great stir in the previous century, and of the Cartesian philosopher Nicolas Malebranche whose influence on Law, in the opinion of Law's nineteenth-century biographer Canon Overton, was second only to that of Boehme. Byrom gives in his journal the text of a letter about Madame Bourignon written by Law to a common acquaintance which is valuable for the light it throws on Law's attitude—at once discriminating, charitable, and cautious—to the more unbridled manifestations of pietism. 'Though I have not ventured to recommend her books to any persons, because of certain uncommon sayings and passages which I was apprehensive might be made an ill use of, yet I have and do often read her works with great admiration of an extraordinary spirit in them. Neither would I upon any account presume to say that she was not guided by the Holy Spirit in that manner which she asserts. When I meet with some things in her writings that I can't account for either from reason or scripture, as they don't concern the substance of religion I pass them by. They do me no hurt if I let them alone. I don't immediately conclude that either she is in such things illuminated by the Holy Spirit, or carried away by some evil one. For as I am myself a stranger to, and utterly unworthy of, that divine illumination which she pretends to, so I neither dare nor ought to pretend to say how it is or how it must be with persons in that extraordinary state which she ascribes to herself. . . . Look at nothing but humility, charity, and penitence in any outward form of life, and only choose or renounce for the better exercise of these virtues; and then, I think, you will be best secured of the divine assistance and direction.' To Byrom himself he had said 'that the first time a man was touched by the reading of any book, that was the time to fall in with grace; that it passed into mere reading instead of practice else; [and] that if we received benefit from reading a book, the last person we ought to say so to should be the author, who might receive harm from it and be tempted to take a satisfaction in it which he ought not'.

Other and greater mystics in whose writings Law was well versed before his acquaintance with Jakob Boehme's were those of the fourteenth-century German school. Eckhart, now generally accounted the greatest of them, he seldom mentions. Tauler, it would seem, was more to his mind; for Tauler, even in his boldest mystical flights, never loses touch with the earth of common sense and practical piety. 'The ground or centre of the soul,' says Tauler (in a passage quoted by Overton), 'is so high and glorious a thing that it cannot properly be named, even as no adequate name can be found for the Infinite and Almighty God. God pours himself out into our spirit as the sun rays forth its natural light into the air and fills it with sunshine, so that no eye can tell the difference between the sunshine and the air—how far less this divine union of the created and uncreated spirit. Our spirit is received and utterly swallowed up in the abyss which is its source. Then the spirit transcends itself and all its powers, and mounts higher and higher towards the Divine Dark. Yet,' he warningly adds, 'let no man in his littleness and nothingness think of himself to approach that surpassing darkness: rather let him draw nigh to the darkness of his ignorance of God, let him simply yield himself to God, ask nothing, desire nothing, love and mean only God, yea, and such an unknown God! . . . Moreover'—and here Tauler's practical good sense shines forth—'if while busy in this lofty inward work a man were called by some duty in the providence of God to cease therefrom and cook a broth for some sick person, or any other such service, he should do so willingly and with great joy.'

Another who resorted to Law at Putney for spiritual direction was young John Wesley, who had been deeply impressed by *Christian Perfection* and the *Serious Call*. 'I was at one time,' wrote Law years afterwards, 'a kind of oracle with Mr Wesley.' This association led to Law's being accused by some opponents, quite falsely, of being the true *fons et origo* of Methodism. It came to an end when Wesley, having found at last a form of belief that gave him satisfaction and inward peace, wrote to reprove his former mentor for the inadequacy of his teaching. He writes, he says, in obedience to what he thinks the call of God. 'If you are born of God, you will approve of the design; if not, I shall grieve for you, not for myself.' Neither tact nor humour was Wesley's strong suit; and his letter, for all its Christian protestations, exhibits something of that spiritual arrogance which lies in wait for all who fancy themselves to be in possession of the whole truth of God. 'For two years I have been preaching after the model of your two practical treatises, and all who heard allowed that the law was great, wonderful, and holy; but when they attempted to fulfil it they found that it was too high for man, and that by doing the works of the law should no flesh be justified.' That the rule of life set forth in *Christian Perfection* is too high for man—if 'high' is not too flattering a description—was sound criticism; but it should not have taken Wesley two years to perceive that, nor would if he had listened to his own common sense. 'I then exhorted them,' Wesley's letter continues, 'to pray earnestly for grace, and use all those other means of obtaining which God hath appointed. Still I and my hearers were more and more convinced that by this law man cannot live; and under this heavy yoke I might have groaned till death, had not a holy man to whom God has lately directed me answered my complaint at once by saying, *Believe, and thou shalt be saved*. Now, Sir, suffer me to ask, how will you justify it to our common Lord that you never gave me this advice? Why did I scarcely ever hear you name the name of Christ? —never so as to ground anything upon faith in His blood? If you say you advised other things as preparatory to this, what is this but laying a foundation below the foundation? Is not Christ the First as the Last?' Wesley ends by warning Law that his state was a very dangerous one, and asking whether his 'extreme roughness', and 'morose and sour behaviour', could possibly be the fruit of a living faith in Christ.

Law's reply, the more so for being temperately phrased, is crushing. He reminds Wesley that he himself, Wesley, had two years ago published a new translation of Thomas à Kempis, 'an author that of all others leads us the most directly to a real, living faith in Jesus Christ'. How then could he have been supposed ignorant of that faith? And, if ignorant he was, how could Law be chargeable with his ignorance?—quite apart from the fact that during their many conversations together 'I dare say you never was with me half an hour without my being large upon that very doctrine . . .' Finally, if Wesley has received this faith only a few weeks ago, Law advises him not to be hasty in believing that because he has changed his language and expressions he has also changed his faith. 'The head can as easily amuse itself with a living and justifying faith in the blood of Jesus as with any other notion; and the heart, which you suppose to be the place of security, as being the seat of self-love is more deceitful than the head. Your last paragraph, concerning my sour, rough behaviour, I leave in its full force; whatever you can say of that kind without hurting yourself will be always well received by me.' The break in their personal friendship was final; but they continued to speak of each other, privately and publicly, with charity and esteem.

§ 3

Law could hardly have stayed so long with the Gibbons at Putney had he been no more than a tutor to the son of the house. When that young man had no further need of his tuition he was presumably retained as a kind of private chaplain or spiritual director, as were many other nonjuring priests by prosperous gentlemen with Jacobite sympathies. But in 1739 Gibbon senior died; the family dispersed; and Law, finding himself with no fixed occupation, during the next year left London and settled down in his native village of King's Cliffe, where his eldest brother still lived and where he himself owned a house. He was now fifty-four, but still vigorous, and with the best years of his life still to live.

By this time, though we do not know the precise date, he had begun his study of Boehme's works and was meditating upon the doctrines which were to change so radically the spirit of his own writings. Thirteen years earlier he had founded at King's Cliffe a school for the education and clothing of fourteen poor girls, using for that purpose, it is surmised, a sum of money (£1000) handed to him in the street one day by an unknown admirer of his *Christian Perfection*. He lived alone in his native village for some three years, busying himself with this and other works of charity, as well as with his books. *An Appeal to All that Doubt* (1740) marks the beginning of the change in his thought. 'Thinking and willing are eternal, they never began to be. Nothing can think or will *now*, in which there was not Will and Thought from all eternity. For it is as impossible for thought in general to begin to be, as for 'That which thinks in a particular creature to *begin* to be of a thinking nature. Therefore the soul, which is a thinking willing being, is come forth or created out of That which hath willed and thought in God from all eternity. The *created* soul is a creature of time . . . but the *essences* of the soul . . . had been in God from all eternity, or they could not have been breathed forth from God into the form of a living creature.' Herein, he continues, 'appears the high dignity and never-ceasing perpetuity of our nature. The *essences* of our souls can never cease to be, because they never began to be; and nothing can live eternally but that which hath lived from all eternity'.

The doctrine is so important to him that he cannot refrain from repeating it again and again. 'The essences of our soul were a breath in God before they became a living soul, and therefore the soul is a partaker of the eternity of God. . . . Thou begannest as time began, but as time was in eternity before it became days and years, so thou wast in God before thou wast brought into the creation. And as time is neither a part of eternity nor broken off from it, yet come out of it, so thou art not a part of God, nor broken off from him, yet born out of him. Thou shouldst only will that which God willeth, only love that which he loveth, co-operate and unite with him in the whole form of thy life; because all that thou art, all that thou hast, is only a spark of his own life and spirit derived into thee. If thou desirest, inclinest, and turnest towards God, as the flowers of the field turn towards the sun, all the blessings of the Deity will spring up in thee; Father, Son, and Holy Ghost will make their abode with thee.' All this, and more, is implicit in the statement with which Law begins this treatise: that the soul of man, so far from being created by God out of nothing (which would condemn man to absolute and eternal separation from the Divine Spirit), is 'an effluence from God, and so must have the nature and likeness of God in it, and is and can be nothing else but something or so much of the Divine Nature become creaturely existing'. This is a far cry indeed from the arid legalism of Law's earlier discourses.

In 1744 he received into his house two women disciples, and the three remained together, full of good works, till his death. One of them was a Mrs Hutcheson, the widow of a man who in his last illness had received comfort from Law's ministrations and who had confided both to Law and to his wife the wish that after his death she should live in religious retirement. The other was Hester Gibbon, sister of his former pupil. The joint income of the three, of which Mrs Hutcheson's was by far the largest part, is said to have amounted to three thousand a year. Only a tenth of this sum was spent upon themselves, the whole of the rest—for it was against Law's principles to accumulate money—being devoted to the relief of distress in the neighbourhood and the financing of their various charitable enterprises. Mrs Hutcheson founded a school for the accommodation of twenty boys, similar to the one provided by Law for girls, and 'directed that every boy who should have stayed out his full time in the school, with good behaviour, should be put to some trade'. Good behaviour was also enjoined upon the masters

K

and mistresses of the schools, provision being made for their instant removal in the event of any breach of it, and was laid down as an indispensable qualification in the 'ancient maidens and widows' who were to be admitted to the almshouses which Law and Mrs Hutcheson built for them. Of the schools, the Rector of King's Cliffe for the time being was to be always a trustee. No other person of the neighbourhood was to be so: 'be he who he will, or of what degree soever, he is utterly incapable of being admitted or chosen into any share of this trust'. The holidays were to be only at the times of the Church festivals—Christmas, Easter, and Whitsun—'but in harvest time the children are allowed to glean in the fields for their parents, after having said each of them one lesson early in the morning'.

Law's rules and regulations for the conduct of the children combine common sense with a powerful emphasis on Christian piety. Prayers to be said daily and passages from the Bible to be learnt by heart are conspicuous features of the curriculum: his main purpose, it would seem, was to make good churchmen and churchwomen of his boys and girls, and he set about it systematically. His more casual charities, however, were marked by no such good sense. They were indiscriminate and in effect mischievous. He refused help to no one who asked for it and was constantly being imposed on, with the inevitable result that King's Cliffe became before long a resort for professional beggars. The more enterprising among them, having been fed and clothed and provided with money by Law, would change into rags behind the projecting buttress of the neighbouring church and present themselves thus disguised with a new tale of destitution. This state of affairs provoked the Rector of the parish, Wilfred Piemont, to make a series of protests from the pulpit and with others of the neighbourhood to lay an information with the local justices praying for judgment against the almsgivers. They replied with an open letter in which, after speaking of the 'unchristian behaviour' of the Rector, they declare: 'We will immediately put a stop to everything that we have set on foot, and stay no longer here than till we can conveniently remove'. This threat was not carried out, and the charities were continued, but probably with more discrimination; for we hear of no more trouble between Law and the longsuffering Mr Piemont.

Law's daily routine at King's Cliffe is described by Christopher Walton in his voluminous notes for a biography. * He rose early each morning, probably about five o'clock. After some time spent in devotion he breakfasted, generally on a cup of chocolate in his bedroom. He then began study. He kept four cows, whose milk, except for what was required in his own household, he distributed every morning among the poor with his own hands. At nine o'clock a bell called the family to prayers; after which he retired to his room, to spend what remained of the morning in reading and meditation. His window, however, overlooked a courtyard, and he was frequently interrupted by poor people wanting his help. These 'never failed to secure his immediate attention'. He would inquire into the particular needs of all who came to him and see them supplied with whatever they wanted, whether money, food, or clothing. If he discovered that no room had been left on the kitchen fire for 'a vessel for the poor' he was seriously displeased, and sometimes he would leave his work in order to taste for himself the broth that was being prepared for them. In winter they were given ale and wine as well. Among the articles of clothing which he provided for the indigent, says Walton, were shirts made of strong coarse linen; 'and, that he might not give away what he himself could not thankfully receive, he always wore them himself first . . . after which they were washed and distributed'.

* *Notes and Materials for a Complete Biography of William Law.* London, 1848.

At noon in winter, at one in summer, the family dined.
Law ate very moderately and allowed himself only one glass
of wine. After dinner came the second instalment of family
devotions, followed by another period of retirement to the
study. At five o'clock Law would join the ladies, and while
they took tea would stand and engage them in cheerful conversation, eating nothing himself except a raisin or two from
his pocket. After tea 'exercises of piety were resumed, and
varied by the servants in turn reading a chapter from the
Bible'. Law would then go for a brisk walk; and after a
frugal supper, and more family devotions, he would retire
to his room once more, smoke one pipe, drink a glass of
water, and at nine o'clock go to bed. This was the routine
for four days out of seven: on Sundays, Wednesdays, and
Fridays there were church services, which Law and his ladies
never failed to attend. In the time they could spare from their
charities and private devotions Mrs Hutcheson and Miss
Gibbon copied out passages from edifying books and wrote
religious essays set them by their director of studies. They
seem to have been very ordinary and simpleminded women,
and Law was their oracle. One cannot help wondering if he
never hungered for more stimulating company.

It cannot be denied that for most of us today there is a
touch of absurdity in the picture, an excess of piety. But
we must take our saints as we find them: humour is seldom
their strong point. Law would allow no portrait to be made
of him, and the accounts of his person are oddly at variance.
Walton says that in stature he was rather over than under
the middle size, not corpulent but stoutly built, with a round
ruddy face, vivacious eyes, and a blunt felicitous expression;
that his normal manner was lively and unaffected; and that
though his walk and conversation among his friends was that
of a sage he talked freely with visitors. On the other hand
this same Walton quotes 'a sister of the Wesleys' as saying
that 'he was the very picture of the Law itself for severity

and gravity'. Possibly this last impression was heightened by 'the soberness of his dress, which was usually a clerical hat with the loops let down, black coat, and grey wig'. It is to be presumed, however, that he did not wear his hat in the house; and, as for the wig, what becomes of the rumour reported by Byrom 'that Mr Law [at Putney] was going to wear his own hair'? Perhaps the presence of ladies in the house had led him to resume the wig, as more seemly. But this is mere conjecture.

What we can be quite sure of is that under his grave exterior was a warm and gentle heart. He loved listening to music, was specially fond of singing, and held the curious opinion that everyone could sing if he wanted to. He had a humane sympathy with animals and hated to see a bird in captivity. He would have agreed with Blake that a robin redbreast in a cage puts all heaven in a rage. And the charity schools that he founded and financed were the fruit as much of a love of children as of his stern sense of duty. He loved to have children about him, was always delighted to see his great-nephews and nieces, one of whom remembered in old age being given 'rides on his foot'. So perhaps, after all, Miss Wesley's impression of his extreme severity of demeanour tells us only that he could not unbend except in congenial company. And this is consistent with what we certainly know of his unpretending sincerity, his total incapacity to behave otherwise than as he felt.

Retired and uneventful as his mode of existence was, he can never have lacked for occupation; for having acquired a wide reputation by his books he received many letters asking for advice in religious matters, some of them from complete strangers to him. A quotation or two from his answers will show how far he now was from exhibiting the 'morose and sour behaviour' which John Wesley, whether justly or not, had ascribed to him some twenty-five years earlier. 'My unknown friend in Christ Jesus, I am glad that you are so heartily affected, and so deeply instructed in the things of God. It is a happiness that no one knows, or can know, but he that is possessed of it. One of the surest signs of Divine light and true regeneration, is an inexpressible tenderness, an unfeigned love, an unchangeable compassion towards all that are under any hardness of heart, blindness, or delusion of our fallen nature. This is the necessary effect of regeneration; it brings forth nothing but the nature of Christ in the soul. All that Christ was towards sinners, is in its degree found in the truly regenerate man.' That Law himself was just such a man is evident in the tone of his answer to another unknown correspondent who in deep distress of mind had confessed himself addicted to lechery, a vice which we must suppose to have been peculiarly repugnant to Law. 'Poor honest man, whom I much love and esteem, your letter has been lost amongst a multiplicity of papers, and is but just found by me. I am not without hopes that God and time may have done that for you in a better way than it would have been done by me. To be left in distress is oftentimes the only way to be delivered from it; and, when help seems farthest off, then are we nearest to the place where it can only be had. Happy is that desolation, wheresoever it comes, that forces us to see no glimpse of relief but in giving up ourselves blindly, implicitly, and wholly, to the redeeming power and goodness of God, without the least thought or conceit of having any other or more goodness than what his Holy Nature and Spirit bring forth in us. . . .'

But Law was more discriminating in his tenderness to correspondents than he had been in his almsgiving. He will not be tricked into gratifying the self-important. To one such person he writes: 'There is hardly anything more hurtful to true spirituality (the life of God in the soul) than a talkative, inquisitive, active, busy, reasoning spirit, that is always at work with its own ideas, and never so content as when talking, hearing, or writing upon points, distinctions, and definitions of religious doctrines. . . . Bear with patience, my dear friend, this great and useful truth, viz. that all your letters to me are, from the beginning to the end . . . mere hasty, needless, fruitless words, brought forth by a talkative spirit, which is the spirit you want to have cast out of you.' And to Francis Okely, a Cambridge graduate who admired his books and proposed visiting him to converse on spiritual matters, he replied: 'An appointment for religious conversation has a taking sound, and passeth for a sign of great progress in goodness. But with regard to myself, such a meeting would rather make me silent, than a speaker in it. . . . I have wrote very largely of the spiritual life; and he that has read and likes it, has of all men the least reason to ask me any questions or make any visit on that subject. He understands not my writings, nor the end of them, who does not see that their whole drift is to call all Christians to a God and Christ within them, as the only possible life, light, and power of all goodness they can ever have; and, therefore, they turn my readers as much from myself as from any other.'

That last sentence is highly characteristic of him. Equally so is the fact that when Okely, not to be deterred, did visit him, he was kindly received, even though, according to his own account, Law did say to him: 'Sir, I am not fond of religious gossiping. My best thoughts are in my works, and to them I recommend you.' He added (with a smile, one imagines): 'If I should seem to you a positive old fellow, I cannot help it, well knowing the ground from which I write.'

§ 4

We have travelled a long way before coming to the heart of Law's matter; and even now there is one bridge left to cross. It is surprising, it surprised Law himself in retrospect, that a man so widely read in religious literature, and a master of many languages, should not have encountered the works of Boehme till late in life. George Cheyne, an eminent physician and himself something of a mystical philosopher, was the means of bringing them together.

Jakob Boehme (1575–1624), known to Law and his English contemporaries as Jacob Behmen, was born in a village of the hill country some ten miles from Goerlitz in Upper Lusatia. He had some elementary schooling at the near-by town of Seidenberg, was accustomed as a child to herding the cattle on his native hills, and at the age of thirteen became a shoemaker's apprentice. He seems to have shown no sign in youth of the strange genius that was to make him, after his death, so powerful an influence in religious thought. By the time he was twenty-four he was settled in Goerlitz as a master-shoemaker and a married man, and ten years later he was able to buy a house of his own. A few years after that, he gave up his shoemaking business and supported himself and his family by making and selling woollen gloves. Not till he was thirty-six did he begin writing. His first book was secretly copied and zealously circulated by a friend. It attracted to him a number of men far above him in culture and social status, and won for him the undying hostility of Gregorius Richter, pastor primarius of Goerlitz. He seems to have been utterly without personal ambition or spiritual pride. He was neither puffed up by admiration nor embittered by persecution. For five years he submitted to the edict of silence imposed on him by the authorities. Then he began writing again, but not publishing: the only things offered to the public during his lifetime and with his consent were some purely devotional pieces. He wrote much, however, during the last nine years of his short life (he died in his fiftieth year), in a style rendered obscure to the point of unreadability by the adoption of a crude pseudo-scientific symbolism. But of his profound mystical insight there can be no question.

An essentially humble man, he claimed nothing for himself in the way of supernatural apparitions or ecstatic experience. True, there is a story of a brilliant light which he saw reflected from a pewter dish; but that was clearly no more and no less than the external mode by which, on that occasion, he attained to the stillness of mind which commonly precedes inner illumination. He did claim, however, to have 'beheld' the root of all mysteries, the spiritual reality of which the natural world, with all its contrasts and discordancies, is an outbirth or manifestation. 'The whole outward visible world with all its being is a signature or figure of the inward spiritual world. Whatever is internally, and however its operation is, so likewise it has its character externally. As the spirit of each creature sets forth and manifests the internal form of its birth by its body, so does the Eternal Being also. . . . The Being of all beings is a wrestling power.' Distinguishing features of Behmen's thought are its emphasis on the stresses and strains in nature and its lavish use of physical concepts. These latter a reader does not always know whether to take literally or metaphorically; and it is improbable that Behmen himself, if challenged on the point, could have given a clear answer. The result is a fantastic mixture of 'natural' and 'divine' philosophy.

Law and other Behmenists believed that Newton owed something to their master; and since, in science as in philosophy, the greatest discoveries have a high imaginative quality, there is nothing intrinsically absurd in the suggestion. 'Sir Isaac ploughed with Behmen's heifer,' says Law. And again, in a letter to his friend Dr Cheyne: 'When Sir Isaac Newton died, there were found amongst his papers abstracts out of Jacob Behmen's works written with his [Newton's] own hand. This I have from undoubted authority. No wonder that attraction, with its two inseparable properties, which make in Jacob Behmen the first three principles of eternal nature, should come to be the grand foundation of the Newtonian philosophy.' Attraction in the physical universe is not merely an analogue of the Divine Love but an actual manifestation of it. 'Love,' says Behmen, 'supports the heavens and upholds the earth. . . . When thou art gone forth wholly from the creature, and from that which is visible, and art become nothing to all that is nature and creature, then thou art in that Eternal One which is God himself; and then thou shalt perceive and feel in thy interior being the highest virtue of love. . . . Thou shalt then see how love hath poured itself into all things,' and penetrateth all things, and is the most inward and most outward ground in all things: inwardly in the virtue and power of everything, and outwardly in the figure and form thereof. . . . Love enlarges the soul as wide as the whole creation of God. All things are from it, and in it, and by it. If thou findest it, thou comest into that ground whence all things are proceeded, and wherein they subsist; and thou art in it a king over all the works of God.'

To Law, with his almost fanatical disdain of that academic learning of which he himself had so conspicuous a share, Behmen's rustic uncouthness of mind was an additional attraction. And Law himself is sometimes perverse in his choice of terms. It is evident, for example, that the Reason against which he so industriously rants, even in his last and finest works, is very different from the Reason which the Cambridge Platonists consistently exalted as a God-given faculty for the apprehension of truth. At times Law seems to use 'reason' as a synonym for chop-logic and sceptical disputation, though probably all he means is that knowledge of God is grounded in experience, not in speculation; for he would have had to admit, had the point been put to him, that even his least controversial writings are chock-full of reasoning; and he himself, with comical inconsistency, invites us to observe with what good reason the illuminated Behmen tells us this or that. The best part of Law's mystical teaching is contained in *An Appeal to All that Doubt* (1740), mentioned earlier in this chapter, and in three later works: *The Spirit of Prayer* (in two parts, 1749 and 1750), its continuation in *The Way to Divine Knowledge* (1752), and, in the same year, *The Spirit of Love*. It is dominated by three main doctrines: (i) The world of created things is a manifestation of the Divine Life, and Man in his threefold nature a microcosm of that world. (ii) Man, being an effluence of God, was created perfect, and fell from perfection not by mere disobedience to an arbitrary command but by separating himself from God. His redemption consists in nothing else than 'a new birth of God in the soul'. (iii) God being all love, nothing but love can proceed from God.

'All creatures, whether intellectual, animate, or inanimate, are products or emanations of the Divine Desire,' says Law. The popular evangelical doctrine of the Atonement, which represents Jesus as dying for the sins of the world in order to appease the wrath of a Deity utterly separate from Man, was repugnant to him. 'Every creature of unfallen nature, call it by what name you will, has its form and power and state and place in nature, for no other end but to open and enjoy, to manifest and rejoice in, some share of the love and happiness and goodness of the Deity, as springing forth in the boundless height and depth of nature. From eternity to eternity he can will and intend nothing towards them, in them or by them, but the communication of various degrees of his own love, goodness, and happiness to them, according to their state and place and capacity in nature. This is God's unchangeable disposition towards the creature: he can be nothing else but all goodness towards it, because he can be nothing towards the creature but that which he is, and was, and ever shall be, in himself. God can no more begin to have any wrath, rage, or anger in himself, after nature and creature are in a fallen state, than he could have been infinite wrath and boundless rage everywhere and from all eternity. For nothing can *begin* to be in God, or to be in a *new state* in

him: everything that is in him is essential to him, as inseparable from him, as unalterable in him, as the triune nature
of his Deity.'

We see how this insight corroborates that of Julian, the
anchoress of Norwich, who declared it to be impossible that
God should be wrathful: 'I saw no manner of wrath in God,
neither for short time nor for long.' It is as good sense,
says Law ironically, 'to say that God, moved by a wrath in
and from himself, began the creation, as that a wrath in God
ever punished any part of it. Nature and creature is the only
source from whence, and the seat in which, wrath, pain, and
vexation can dwell. Nor can they ever break forth, either in
nature or creature, but so far as either this or that has lost
its state in God. God, considered in himself, is as infinitely
separate from all possibility of doing hurt or willing pain to
any creature, as he is from a possibility of suffering pain or
hurt from the hand of a man. The goodness of God breaking
forth into a desire to communicate good, was the cause and
the beginning of the creation. This is the amiable nature
of God: he is the Good, the unchangeable overflowing
Fountain of Good, that sends forth nothing but good to all
eternity. He is the Love itself, the unmixed unmeasurable
Love, doing nothing but from love, giving nothing but gifts
of love, to everything that he has made; requiring nothing
of all his creatures but the spirit and fruits of that Love
which brought them into being.' What, then, of heaven and
hell? 'There is no Hell but where the will of the creature is
turned from God, nor any Heaven but where the will of the
creature worketh with God.' We meet the same thought
again and again in the writings of the Cambridge Platonists,
more especially in Whichcote and John Smith: a parallel
passage from Smith's *The Nobleness of True Religion* has been
already quoted (see page 92).

Our will, says Law, is the seed of everything that can grow
in us. 'Whatever you are, or whatever you feel, is all owing

to the working and creating power of your own will. This is your God or your Devil, your Heaven or your Hell; and you have only so much of one or the other as your will, which is the First Mover, is either given up to the one or to the other. . . . The will of man hath the nature of divine freedom, hath the nature of eternity, and the nature of omnipotence, in it; because it is what it is, and hath what it hath, as a spark, a ray, a genuine birth of the eternal, free, omnipotent will of God. . . . And herein consisteth the infinite goodness of God, in the birth of all intelligent creatures, and also in the exceeding height, perfection, and happiness of their created state: they are descended from God full of divine power; they can will and work with God and partake of the divine happiness. They can receive no injustice, hurt, or violence either from nature or creature; but must be only that which they generate, and have no evil or hurt but that which they do in and to themselves. All things stand in the will, and everything, animate or inanimate, is the effect and produce of that will which worketh in it and formeth it to be that which it is. And every will, wherever found, is the birth and effect of some antecedent will; for will can only proceed from will, till you come to the first working will, which is God himself.' Behmen makes much use of the words *magic* and *magical*; but these, Law points out, are not to be understood in a bad or trivial sense. Behmen's *magic power* means nothing but the working of the will, whether it be the divine or the creaturely will. Prayer, the innermost desire of the heart, is itself a willing. 'As we pray, so we are; and as our will-spirit secretly worketh, so are we either swallowed up in the vanity of time or called forth into the riches of eternity. And therefore the spirit of prayer is most justly conceived, and most simply expressed, when it is said to be the rising of the soul out of the vanity of time into the riches of eternity.' The eternity Law speaks of is not a remote dream: it is here and now. 'Heaven is as near to our souls as this world is to our bodies; and we are created, we are redeemed, to have our conversation in it. God, the only Good of all intelligent natures, is not an absent or distant God, but is more present *in* and *to* our souls than our own bodies are; and we are strangers to Heaven and without God in the world for this only reason, because we are void of that spirit of prayer which alone can . . . unite us with the one only Good, and to open Heaven and the Kingdom of God within us.'

Mysticism is the inwardness of religion, and inwardness is the keynote of Law's later writings. 'All true knowledge, either of God or Nature, must be born in you. You cannot possibly know anything of God but so far as God is manifested in you; so far as his Light and Holy Spirit is born in you as it is born in him, and liveth and worketh in you as it liveth and worketh in him. A distant, absent, separate God is an unknown God.' And, equally: 'No Hell in any remote place, no Devil that is separate from you, no darkness or pain that is not within you, no Antichrist either at Rome or England, no furious beast, no fiery dragon, without or apart from you, can do you any hurt. It is your own Hell, your own Devil, your own beast, your own Antichrist, your own dragon, that lives in your own heart's blood, that alone can hurt you.' So, too, nothing can be truly known from without. 'Knowledge can only be yours, as sickness and health is yours: not conveyed into you by a hearsay notion, but the fruit of your own perception and sensibility of that which you are, and that which you have, in yourself.'

The eighteenth century, with its emphasis on seemliness and moderation and good sense, had a contempt for what it called 'enthusiasm' in religion. To the men most representative of that age the word stood for the frenzy, the mass-hysteria, the spiritual self-conceit, which have always been incidental features of popular religious revivals. In this sense the austere William Law was certainly no enthusiast. He was no friend to disorderly behaviour or to the antics of a self-

advertising 'spirituality'. On the other hand he waged cease-
less war on that spirit of expediency and compromise which
he believed to be the enemy of true religion; and, though
he disagreed with them on other points of doctrine, he was
at one with the Quakers in believing in the Inner Light, that
light 'which lighteth every man that cometh into the world'
—and by 'every man', when he quoted this text, he meant
every man from the beginning of time, without distinction
of race or creed, for the Christ of his worship was the
universal Spirit of God present in the First Man, a Christ
none the less universal because (for Law, who abated nothing
of his High Church orthodoxy) fully revealed in the second
Adam, Jesus of Nazareth. He not merely assented to the
doctrine of the Indwelling Love: he insisted on it and was
possessed by its dynamic power. In the best and deepest (and
etymological) sense of the word, therefore, he *was* an
enthusiast: that is, God-possessed. In *The Spirit of Prayer*
and *The Spirit of Love*, more especially in the expository
parts as distinct from the argumentative dialogues that follow
them, this enthusiasm expresses itself in a flowing lyrical
prose in which the same vital conviction, often in the very
same words, is stated again and again. It is all an amplification
of St John's great saying: 'God is love; and he that dwelleth
in love dwelleth in God, and God in him.'

If God is all love, and if God is—as Law so often declares—
the one Good, it follows that love and goodness are identical,
and goodness without love a contradiction in terms. 'There
is no peace, nor ever can be, for the soul of man but in the
purity and perfection of its first-created nature; nor can it have
its purity and perfection in any other way than in and by the
spirit of love. For as Love is the God that created all things,
so love is the purity, the perfection and blessing of all created
things; and nothing can live in God but as it lives in love.
Look at every vice, pain and disorder in human nature, it is
itself nothing else but the spirit of the creature turned from

the universality of love to some *self-seeking* or *own Will* in created things. So that love alone is, and can only be, the cure of every evil; and he that lives in the purity of love is risen out of the power of evil into the freedom of the One Spirit of Heaven.'

But how to attain to this condition? Law does not suggest that it is easy of attainment. 'You may indeed do many works of love, and delight in them, especially at such times as they are not inconvenient to you, or contradictory to your state or temper or occurrences in life.' That is not enough, for 'the spirit of love is not in you, till it is the spirit of your life, till you live freely, willingly, and universally according to it'. And its reward is in itself. 'As the sparks know no motion but that of flying upwards, whether it be in the darkness of the night or in the light of the day, so the spirit of love is always in the same course; it knows no difference of time, place, or persons; but whether it gives or forgives, bears or forbears, it is equally doing its own delightful work, equally blessed from itself. For the spirit of love, wherever it is, is its own blessing and happiness, because it is the truth and reality of God in the soul, and therefore is in the same joy of life, and is the same good to itself, everywhere and on every occasion.'

Chapter Seven

BLAKE

§ 1

FROM the militant moralism and anaemic holiness that mingle their darkness with the enlightenment of men like Fox and Law, we escape at last into an atmosphere more benign than the one and more bracing than the other. Words have a life of their own and in the course of centuries acquire new and sometimes contradictory layers of meaning. Thus *holy*, which is derived from the Middle English *hool* and therefore (like *hale*, to which it is closely related) should mean *whole*, in ordinary everyday usage carries quite a different meaning. So far from being a synonym for wholeness, health, spiritual integration, holiness to most people suggests almost the opposite of these things: a joyless solemnity involving the repudiation of all the delights of sense. Moral puritanism, which existed long before the Puritans, has at times carried that repudiation to its extreme point, so that all beauty, all pleasure, have been regarded as evil. The disease is now widely recognized as being rooted in fear of sex: which fear, in its turn, is rooted in a subconscious shame or guilt. Whether the origin of that guilt is social or personal, whether it is the price we pay for the necessary restraints of civilization or arises from the nature of man as man, we need not here try to determine: its existence and its malign effects are too obvious to need stressing. It has resulted in the radically false philosophy which by separating 'spirit' from 'sense', and representing them as opposed principles, can offer its adherents nothing better than a choice between disembodied negativism and gross sensuality.

Blake is conspicuous among mystics in being the declared

enemy of that philosophy. He denounced it again and again in unmeasured terms. He accepted the life of the body as frankly as Whitman was to do in a later century, and had nothing but hatred and contempt for the pallid negative pietism of religious moralists. Not only did he insist, as all true mystics have done, on the inwardness and universality of religious experience, on the immanence of the divine spirit and the essential unity of all life: he saw also, as some others did not, that a man's externalized God, that is his *idea* of God as distinct from the lived reality, is merely a projection of his own ideal notion of himself.* Theological formulations are fictions, for 'God only acts or is, in existing beings or men'. Blake is the most thoroughgoing of all English mystics. For him the whole universe of experience is a complex imaginative act. He does not, as some do, seek to arrive at a comfortable system of belief by leaving out inconvenient facts or by trying to explain them away. He is a realist of the realists, urging the necessity of the 'double vision', which sees a heavenly symbolism in every earthly thing, and accepting good and evil, darkness and light, innocence and experience, as 'contrary states of the soul' without which 'there can be no progression'. He distrusted and despised 'passive goodness'—by which he seems to have meant self-complacent righteousness or moral respectability—and exalted impulse above reason. Virtue is not virtue unless it is impulsive, and evil impulses are to be restrained not by regard for external rules but by the operation of contrary impulses. Like Boehme, whose writings he admired, he was profoundly aware that life and energy and all good things are generated by a tension between opposed principles. 'The being of all beings is a wrestling power,' said Boehme. It might equally well have been said by Blake.

Not that Blake was in any significant degree derivative

---

* This important truth is expressed in Blake's graphic art, as well as in his verse and prose. See J. H. Wicksteed's *Blake's Vision of the Book of Job*.

from Boehme or from any other man. He was highly indi-
vidualist, original, and eccentric. He was also, in the traditional sense, 'inspired', his intuitions appearing to him in
the form of visions and voices. That these were external, or
that he always believed them to be so, is a quite unnecessary
hypothesis. It was natural that a man who held that 'Imagination is not a state, it is all Human Existence' should speak
of his imaginings with the ingenuous literalism of a child.
According to his own account he consorted freely with angels,
prophets, Old Testament patriarchs, and demons of various
sorts and sizes; and some of his more portentous and
didactic (and least comprehensible) works were written at
the dictation, he tells us, of such personages. At the age of
four he saw God looking in at his bedroom window. In boyhood he incurred his father's wrath by saying that he had seen
a tree full of angels. One summer morning he saw angels in
a hayfield mingling with the haymakers. Many years later,
at Felpham, he watched a fairy's funeral, and gave an account
of it in casual conversation. 'I was walking alone in my
garden, there was a great stillness among the branches and
flowers and more than common sweetness in the air; I heard
a low and pleasant sound, and I knew not whence it came.
At last I saw the broad leaf of a flower move, and underneath
I saw a procession of creatures of the size and colour of green
and grey grasshoppers, bearing a body laid out on a roseleaf,
which they buried with songs, and then disappeared. It was
a fairy funeral.'

The child that dies or lives only intermittently in all of
us was very much alive in Blake. He never lost his child
vision. He was an innocent, but he was not *only* an innocent,
and he was not (as has been too often suggested) an innocent
in the pitiful or disparaging sense. His astonishing honesty,
the utter sincerity with which he spoke his mind, together
with his sometimes violent mode of expression, led to his
being regarded by men of his own time as mad. 'But,' said

Wordsworth, 'there is something in the madness of this man that interests me more than the sanity of Lord Byron and Walter Scott.' That Blake never for a moment lost his mental balance or became entangled in his own mythologies is more than we can confidently assert; but, despite all exuberancies, extravagances, and obscurities of expression, despite also a modicum of sheer silliness, it must be evident to any careful reader of and about Blake that he was essentially one of the sanest men that have ever lived. He laboured under many disadvantages, perhaps the chief of them being a lack of intellectual training. Even these, it is true, he was enabled by his native genius to turn to good account; but they did sometimes betray him into what can now be seen as errors of judgment; for example, the influence of Swedenborg on his thinking, and that of the preposterous *Ossian* on his later style, can only be regarded as lamentable, so far as they go. Such things, however, made no serious inroads on his originality; everything that he was willing to receive from others was instantly translated into Blake and given a new character; his life was a piece of sustained imaginative creation; and he attained, not without dust and heat, to a high degree of spiritual sanity—that is, of wholeness, or holiness. Not infrequently during his long life he was 'drunk with intellectual vision', and in the hour of his death he sang of the heaven that was opened to his sight. 'In truth he died like a saint,' said a contemporary, George Richmond.

The prophetic or visionary type of mind would seem to arrive at its formulations by a process in which rational or consecutive thinking plays at most a very minor part. It proceeds by leaps and bounds: in the vivid common phrase, it *jumps* to its conclusions, and whether they are well or ill founded is very much a matter of hit or miss. Against that it must be recognized that ideas which present themselves to the mind suddenly, with all the seeming inconsequence of guesswork, may in fact be the fruit of a long process of subliminal meditation, or in other words of inward experience. Blake, as we have seen, was a *seer* in a very real sense. Of the genuineness of his inspiration—that is, of his being able to tap the living water of truth at a deeper level than most men—there can be no sort of doubt. It is true that he was capable of saying foolish as well as wise things, and that his oracular pronouncements reflect his temperamental bias, his opinions and prejudices and psychological stresses, as well as his God-given vision; it is true too that he often goes out of his way to perplex us by using words in a sense directly opposed to their accepted meanings; it is true, in short, that he could be wilful, erratic, and perverse. Nevertheless, his most apparent follies are seldom more than verbal violences, overstatements of a truth, designed (it would seem) to irritate and startle us out of lethargy. They have, as the saying goes, nuisance value: like the catfish among the herrings, they keep us lively. And their truth, when they contain truth, carries its own authority. Blake himself says that truth 'can never be told so as to be understood, and not be believed'. To which we must add the paradox that we cannot receive truth unless we already possess it: that is, we cannot recognize a verbal formulation of truth unless the truth already exists unformulated within us.

Much of Blake has come to light in recent years that was never intended for publication. What is perhaps the most compact and luminous statement of the conviction in which and by which he lived was written casually, as a comment, in the margin of another man's book: 'God is in the lowest effects as well as in the highest causes; for he is become a worm that he may nourish the weak. For let it be remembered that creation is God descending according to the weakness of man, for our Lord is the word of God and everything on earth is the word of God and in its essence is God.' In another place he says: 'All deities reside in the human breast'. Is there a contradiction here? By no means. That brief sentence is capable of sustaining two diverse but not contradictory interpretations. It can mean, as has been already said in other words of Blake's, that God only acts, or is, in existing beings or men. It can also mean, and in its context does mean, that all notions or conceptions of deity are man-made, the products of the human mind, or, at a deeper level, the projections of human needs. Both meanings are profoundly true and equally important.

§ 2

He was born in London on the 28th of November 1757, the second son of a Nonconformist hosier. He had three brothers and a sister; but his first biographer, Gilchrist, ventures the plausible guess that William was a solitary child, much given to going off on his own into the fields and country lanes which in those days were comparatively near at hand. From the very first he seems to have possessed that highly developed power of visualization which is the mark of the born graphic artist and which as vividly informs his poems as his pictures. As soon as he could hold a pencil he began to draw, and almost as soon as he had acquired a manageable vocabulary, it would seem, he began to write. His bent towards art was so unmistakable that at the age of ten his general elementary education was discontinued and he was sent by his surprised but percipient parents to 'Mr Pars's drawing-school in the Strand'. He enjoyed four years of this tuition, supplemented by much work done at home with his father's active encouragement; and then Blake senior decided to apprentice him to an engraver. After an abortive interview with a man of whom the boy said to his father: 'I do not like that man's face: it looks as if he will live to be hanged'—and hanged he eventually was, for forgery— William Blake, at fourteen, became the working pupil of James Basire, of Lincoln's Inn Fields.

Before and during the years of apprenticeship he wrote
the *Poetical Sketches by W. B.*, privately printed in 1783
through the kindness of a friendly clergyman, who explained
in a preface that their author, an untutored youth, had begun
writing them in his twelfth year and continued at intervals
till his twentieth, and that his friends, though conscious of
irregularities and defects to be found on almost every page,
still believed them to possess 'a poetic originality which
merited some respite from oblivion'. It is easy to poke fun
at this tepid commendation of poems that include *How sweet
I roamed from field to field* (said to have been written when
the poet was twelve years old), to name only one among
half a dozen exquisite and immortal things; but how many
of us, I wonder, at that time, would have proved to be more
perceptive than the Reverend Henry Mathew? For poetry,
in the seventeen eighties, was in the doldrums. The Augustan
Age had dwindled to a dull decline. Genteel correctitude and
slavish imitation were the order of the day. Feathered song-
sters carolled tediously in verdant groves, or disported
themselves with remorseless mechanical precision upon floral
carpets. Small wonder then if Mr Mathew, coming upon such
lines as these to Spring:

> *The hills tell each other, and the listening*
> *Vallies hear*

or these to the Evening Star:

> *Smile on our loves, and, while thou drawest the*
> *Blue curtains of the sky, scatter thy silver dew*
> *On every flower that shuts its sweet eyes*
> *In timely sleep. Let thy west wind sleep on*
> *The lake; speak silence with thy glimmering eyes,*
> *And wash the dusk with silver*

—small wonder if he was more conscious of 'irregularities
and defects' than of a new freedom, a new musical accent,
breaking at last into English poetry. Nothing more unex-

pected can have happened in the history of literature than that
the first poems of an uneducated or self-educated boy should
so artlessly and triumphantly ignore the prevailing fashions.
Scarcely a trace of contemporary influence is discernible: in
so far as Blake had models, they were of an earlier and better
time.

John Flaxman—'Dear Sculptor of Eternity'—shared with
Mathew the cost of printing the little book. Since the end
of his apprenticeship Blake had earned a precarious living
by engraving for 'booksellers' (i.e. publishers), and among
his friends in the same line of business were Stothard and
Flaxman. It was Flaxman who introduced him to Mrs
Mathew, at whose house in Rathbone Place young artists
were received and patronized. In this at first congenial
atmosphere he found an audience for his verses, which he
would sing to airs of his own devising. These airs, said to
have been 'most singularly beautiful', have not survived. In
drawing Blake had always preferred stark strength to the
rational elegance of the age he lived in; Raphael and
Michelangelo were his spiritual masters; his visits to Westminster Abbey in prentice days had inflamed him with a
passion for Gothic art, whose 'living form' had for him more
life, and therefore more stimulus to his genius, than any
statically posed living model could have. He disliked drawing
from life: it distracted him, he said, from his visions. Throughout his long life he followed his own bent, held to his own
opinions, with inflexible tenacity. The notions of art current
in Rathbone Place soon became intolerable to him, and he
broke away; but the Mathews have put all posterity in their
debt by printing, and so perhaps preserving from oblivion,
the *Poetical Sketches*.

In the previous year, 1782, Blake had married a comely
illiterate girl, Catherine Boucher, he being then twenty-five
and she twenty. The story of their coming together has been
often told but is worth telling again because it so vividly

A PAGE FROM 'SONGS OF INNOCENCE,' 1789

illustrates the impulsiveness which he practised as well as
preached. He met Catherine at a friend's house when he was
suffering from his first attack of jealousy. He had been
'walking out' with a young woman, and when he discovered
that she extended her favours to others besides himself he
reproached her. 'Are you a fool?' she retorted scornfully.
Catherine, hearing this sad story, declared that she pitied him
from her heart. 'I love you for that,' he answered; and, as
Gilchrist remarks, a second and more prosperous courtship
began. At the time of her marriage Catherine could neither
read nor write: in the parish register she could only make
her mark. Blake taught her both accomplishments, and even,
in later years, the elements of his own craft of engraving. She
was a deeply devoted wife, and needed to be; for years of
laborious poverty lay ahead, and no worldly consideration
could deflect Blake from his visionary course. That she was
also jealously possessive of him is probable but not proved.
If the story is true that he once proposed to introduce a
second wife into the household and was persuaded by
Catherine's distress to abandon the idea, the queer poem
significantly entitled *William Bond* is a piece of allegorical
autobiography. The thing may well never have happened,
but those who regard the mere suggestion of its possibility
as an infamous libel on Blake have quite evidently never
come within miles of accepting him for what he was. Only
by reading some of his plainest passages with one eye carefully shut can you avoid seeing that the morality which makes
a virtue either of sex-repression on the one hand, or of a
social expedient (monogamy) on the other, was utterly
obnoxious to him. An apostle of energy—'Energy is Eternal
Delight'—he would neither worship a vacuum nor allow that
love could suffer the bondage of external rules without losing
its essential quality.

> *Abstinence sows sand all over*
> *The ruddy limbs and flaming hair,*

and, what is worse, debilitates the mind with unfruitful fantasies of lust,

> *But Desire Gratified*
> *Plants fruits of life and beauty there.*

Jealous possessiveness, no less than enforced abstinence, he held to be the very negation of love. Love is of its nature 'lawless, wing'd, and unconfined'. But note that this rhetorical statement is made of love, not of mere sex; of love which includes sex, of sexual love in short, but not of sex without love. A trivial promiscuous carnality activated by a mere itch for sensation would certainly have been as repulsive to Blake as to the most severe of the moralists who looked askance at his libertarian philosophy. What he repudiated was the doctrine, stated or implied, that 'woman's love is sin', something to be reluctantly permitted under safeguards (since it cannot be entirely stamped out) but always to be spoken of obliquely, in hushed tones, as belonging to our 'lower nature'. This notion of sex as a shameful necessity permeated all official religious thought. To Blake it was a kind of blasphemy. He knew, without instruction from psychologists, that the repression or frustration of desire, so far from being virtuous, was evil in principle and pernicious in its effects. He believed, too, that women had been hoodwinked into collaborating with the priests into making an intolerable bondage of a relationship which could be fruitful of joy only if it were free. But though he believed in freedom, and preached it, he was realistic enough to recognize that it could be bought at too high a price. As the story of William Bond shows, he could not practise cruelty in order to obtain the sun of his desire:

> *I thought Love liv'd in the hot sun shine,*
> *But O, he lives in the Moony light!*
> *I thought to find Love in the heat of day,*
> *But sweet Love is the Comforter of Night.*

Seek Love in the Pity of others' Woe,
In the gentle relief of another's care,
In the darkness of night and the winter's snow,
In the naked and outcast, Seek Love there!

Was William Bond making a virtue of necessity? It may be so. The poem was probably never intended for publication.

Six years after the *Poetical Sketches* had been privately printed and circulated—it is more than likely that copies may have reached and influenced Coleridge and Wordsworth, whose *Lyrical Ballads* in 1798 marks the official beginning of a new epoch in English poetry—Blake brought out his *Songs of Innocence* (1789) in a volume of which both text and decorations were etched on copper by the poet himself, the pages printed from these plates being then illuminated by hand. The *Songs of Experience* followed in 1794. The method was a new one which Blake believed had been communicated to him by his dead brother, Robert, to whom he had been deeply attached. When William set up shop as print-seller and engraver in partnership with James Parker, young Robert came to live with the Blakes as an apprentice. One day, a dispute arising between Robert and Catherine, Catherine used words which stirred William to anger. 'Kneel down,' he said, 'and beg Robert's pardon, or you will never see my face again!' Instead of boxing her husband's ears or flouncing out of the room, as a more spirited or less devoted wife would have done, Catherine actually did kneel down, and said meekly: 'Robert, I beg your pardon. I am in the wrong.' 'Young woman,' retorted Robert, 'you lie! *I* am in the wrong.' It is to be hoped that the episode ended in laughter. Two and a half years after joining his brother's household Robert died, in his twenty-fifth year. William had nursed him devotedly, sitting with him day and night without sleep, to be rewarded at last by seeing Robert's soul fly away to heaven through the ceiling, 'clapping its hands for joy'. Whatever may have been the strains and stresses of Blake's

married life, whatever he may have found wanting in
Catherine of inspiration and intellectual stimulus, there can
be no doubt that he and his wife were in the end deeply
involved with each other, by habit and affection and a long
shared life of trouble and triumph. The whole truth about
any marriage is known to no one, not even, perhaps, to its
participants. Swinburne's verdict, that Catherine was 'about
the most perfect wife on record', is little more than guesswork. But we do know that on his deathbed, at the age of
seventy, Blake called for his drawing materials and made a
last sketch of her, saying 'You have always been an angel
to me'. And it is fitting that we should allow him the last
word on the subject.

§ 3

Not that 'angel' was always, with Blake, a term implying
love or admiration. Often it suits his perverse fancy to put
the wisest of his sayings into the mouths of 'devils'. He
adopts this device in *The Marriage of Heaven and Hell*, which
contains in small compass the most luminous prose exposition
of his wisdom (though mixed with some fantastical silliness)
and is second in value only to the lyrics. It is 'The Voice of
the Devil' that declares, uttering Blake's profoundest convictions, that 'Man has no Body distinct from his Soul, for
that call'd Body is a portion of Soul discern'd by the five
Senses, the chief inlets of Soul in this age', and that Energy
'is the only life' and Reason 'the bound or outward circum-
ference of Energy'. The key to this method, this attribution
of vital wisdom to devils, is contained in his view of Milton's
Paradise Lost. 'Those who restrain desire, do so because
theirs is weak enough to be restrained; and the restrainer
or reason usurps its place and governs the unwilling. And
being restrain'd, it by degrees becomes passive, till it is only
the shadow of desire. The history of this is written in
Paradise Lost, and the Governor or Reason is call'd Messiah.'

God, in Milton's poem, is for Blake the repressive Reason
which is at war with Impulse, Energy, or Desire, personified
in Satan. And 'the reason Milton wrote in fetters when he
wrote of Angels and God, and at liberty when of Devils and
Hell, is because he was a true Poet and of the Devil's party
without knowing it'.

By calling the things he admires 'evil', and the things he
resents 'good', Blake plunges an impatient or unwary reader
into a state of hopeless confusion. For it is clear that Blake
would claim that he himself was 'of the Devil's party' and
a zealous advocate of that 'Evil' which is 'the active springing
from Energy'. Does this mean that he enjoyed and admired
all that the rest of us call evil—cruelty, oppression, lust of
power, inordinate pride, lasciviousness, and the rest?
Obviously it does not. His whole life and work contradicts
such an absurdity. The truth is that in his use of words he
was more provocative than consistent. Elsewhere he wrote,
not for publication: 'As I understand Vice it is a Negative.
It does not signify what the laws of Kings and Priests have
call'd Vice; we who are philosophers ought not to call the
Staminal Virtues of Humanity by the same name that we call
the omissions of intellect springing from poverty. Every
man's leading propensity ought to be call'd his leading
Virtue and his good Angel . . . the omission of act in self
and the hindering of act in another, this is Vice, but all Act
is Virtue. To hinder another is not an act; it is the contrary;
it is a restraint on action both in ourselves and in the person
hinder'd, for he who hinders another omits his own duty at
the same time. Murder is Hindering Another. Theft is
Hindering Another. Backbiting, Undermining, Circumvent-
ing, and whatever is Negative is Vice.' It is easy to criticize
Blake's use of words in such passages. The statement 'All
act is Virtue' logically implies that there can be no such thing
as a vicious act, and that murder, to take the first of his
examples, is not an act at all. That is plainly not true. It is,

on the face of it, nonsense to say that hindering another is not an act. But Blake's intention, though clumsily expressed, becomes clear after a moment's reflection. He means that all *creative* or *life-enhancing* action is virtuous; and by the statement that 'Vice is a Negative' he means, not quite what he says, but that vice is that which is the opposite of creative, that which impoverishes or destroys life. This philosophy finds its focal point in his conception of art as the divine function of man. Art *is* creation, the outward manifestation of inward vision; and in this sense the whole life of every man should be a continuous work of art. Man, as a creature, is a microcosm of the universe of which he is part; and in his creativity he participates in the eternal divine imagining which all creation is. But the creative impulse of man is in chains: the enemies of impulse have persuaded him to neglect or deny his visions, so that his sense of the eternal, of eternity not hereafter but here and now, the reality in and behind all appearances, is dimmed and lost.

That vision will be recovered, Blake says, by an improvement of sensual enjoyment. 'If the doors of perception were cleansed, everything would appear to man as it is, infinite. For man has closed himself up, till he sees all things through narrow chinks of his cavern.' Rationalism (not to be confused with reasonableness) is the chief obstacle to true vision. 'He who sees the Infinite in all things, sees God. He who sees the Ratio only, sees himself only.' Moreover: 'As the true method of knowledge is experiment, the true faculty of knowing must be the faculty which experiences. This faculty I treat of.' He treats of it in a series of seven propositions entitled *All Religions Are One*, and he calls it the Poetic Genius, arguing that there exists a universal Poetic Genius [that is, generating power] from which all religions and philosophies are derived, their various forms representing adaptations to 'the weaknesses of every individual'. As all men, though infinitely various, are alike, so all religions have this one source. 'The true Man is the source, he being the Poetic Genius.' This True Man of Blake's is presumably, whether he knew it or not, the Platonic Idea of Man existing in the mind of God.

Blake's didacticism too often defeats itself by muddled thinking and obscure mythology. But poetry is always liable to break in, to illuminate the darkness. There is more illumination in his purely lyrical utterances and in the haphazard aphorisms scattered throughout *The Marriage of Heaven and Hell* and elsewhere than in those later elaborate performances which meant so much more to him than they can ever mean to anyone else, no matter how diligently they are studied and disputed over. His shining sense of an ever-present eternity, with the ecstatic joy and the aching desire which that vision involves, sings again and again in poems and fragments of poems that become instantly part of one's own experience and seem not so much to have been written as to have happened spontaneously, like the sudden hedgerow flowers that startle one with pleasure on a country walk in springtime. They are windows through which one may see eternity itself. 'Ah sunflower, weary of time'—it seems hardly necessary to go on. All we need is there. And if we take one line more:

> *Ah sunflower, weary of time,*
> *That countest the steps of the sun—*

every sunflower is henceforward transfigured for us into a flaming symbol of our own unappeasable desire, 'the lost traveller's dream under the hill'. Eternity, in Blake's conception, is no static or passionless affair: energy and delight are of its essence. Nor is its blessedness to be won by trying to grasp and possess it for oneself:

> *He who binds to himself a joy*
> *Does the winged life destroy:*
> *But he who kisses the joy as it flies*
> *Lives in eternity's sun rise.*

In one of the *Songs of Innocence* we are shown a child's bed-time paradise. Over the silent fields, at nightfall, move 'the feet of angels bright'.

> *They look in every thoughtless nest,*
> *Where birds are covered warm;*
> *They visit caves of every beast,*
> *To keep them all from harm.*
> *If they see any weeping*
> *That should have been sleeping,*
> *They pour sleep on their head,*
> *And sit down by their bed.*
>
> *When wolves and tygers howl for prey,*
> *They pitying stand and weep;*
> *Seeking to drive their thirst away,*
> *And keep them from the sheep;*
> *But if they rush dreadful,*
> *The angels, most heedful,*
> *Receive each mild spirit,*
> *New worlds to inherit.*
>
> *And there the lion's ruddy eyes*
> *Shall flow with tears of gold,*
> *And pitying the tender cries,*
> *And walking round the fold,*
> *Saying 'Wrath by his meekness*
> *And by his health sickness*
> *Is driven away*
> *From our immortal day.*
>
> *'And now beside thee, bleating lamb,*
> *I can lie down and sleep;*
> *Or think on him who bore thy name,*
> *Graze after thee and weep.*

For, wash'd in life's river,
My bright mane for ever
Shall shine like the gold
As I guard o'er the fold.'

In these verses there is a reminiscence of Isaiah's vision of
an ultimate peace, 'when the wolf shall dwell with the lamb,
and the leopard shall lie down with the kid, and the calf and
the young lion and the fatling together; and a little child
shall lead them'. Another poem of reconciliation, very different in tone, is spoken by a 'little vagabond' in *Songs of
Experience*. He begins by contrasting the coldness of the
church with the pleasant warmth of the alehouse:

But if at the Church they would give us some Ale,
And a pleasant fire our souls to regale,
We'd sing and we'd pray all the live-long day,
Nor ever once wish from the Church to stray.

Then the Parson might preach, and drink, and sing,
And we'd be as happy as birds in the spring;
And modest Dame Lurch, who is always at Church,
Would not have bandy children, nor fasting, nor birch.

And God, like a father rejoicing to see
His children as pleasant and happy as he,
Would have no more quarrel with the Devil or the Barrel,
But kiss him, and give him both drink and apparel.

The allegory is a simple one. God (Reason) and Satan
(Desire) are not irreconcilable. Only fear and diseased
notions of piety make them seem so. For 'every thing that
lives is holy'.

It is perhaps a pity that the Reverend William Law had
no chance of reading Blake. It would have administered a
wholesome shock to his puritanism. 'Shame is Pride's cloak.

M

Prisons are built with stones of Law, brothels with bricks of Religion. The pride of the peacock is the glory of God. The lust of the goat is the bounty of God. The wrath of the lion is the wisdom of God. The nakedness of woman is the work of Gòd.' But there are many among these *Proverbs of Hell* that Law would have approved of. 'A fool sees not the same tree that a wise man sees. Eternity is in love with the productions of time. The most sublime act is to set another before you. Joys impregnate: sorrows bring forth. The cistern contains: the fountain overflows. One thought fills immensity. The tigers of wrath are wiser than the horses of instruction. To create a little flower is the labour of ages. The soul of sweet delight can never be defiled.' Blake did not spend his strength in bemoaning the unalterable nature of things: he believed that man himself is the author of his worst woes.

> *In every cry of every Man,*
> *In every Infant's cry of fear,*
> *In every voice, in every ban,*
> *The mind-forged manacles I hear.*

The mind-forged manacles. The timidities, misconceptions, greeds, hates, cruelties, prides, and prohibitions. All these are products of a dearth or distrust of imagination, the master faculty of man. Equally mind-forged are the manacles that bind the street-walker to her dreary trade:

> *. . . most thro' midnight streets I hear*
> *How the youthful Harlot's curse*
> *Blasts the newborn Infant's tear,*
> *And blights with plagues the marriage hearse—*

these desolations being the price we pay for the moral complacency that acquiesces in the existence of poverty and for the moral puritanism that by not allowing love its natural fulfilment except under special licence (and then grudgingly) makes of sex a furtive vice and a marketable commodity.

Whether we agree with him or not, this is unquestionably
Blake's view. The precise meaning of that unexpected phrase
'marriage hearse' is not clear; but it suggests that he did not
regard the institution of marriage, as it was in his day, with
unmixed favour. The poem about the Garden of Love, where

> *Priests in black gowns were walking their rounds,*
> *And binding with briars my joys and desires*

points to the same conclusion.

Blake hated secrecy, believing that an impulse denied
expression and hidden from view must turn to poison. He
was no advocate of violence; he knew the value of meekness
and forbearance when these graces flowered spontaneously
from the heart; but he loathed a pretended meekness, a politic
or merely dutiful forbearance, behind which resentment fes-
tered. He insists on the danger of 'nursing unacted desires'.
Anger, no less than love itself, must be vented, not hidden
away.

> *I was angry with my friend:*
> *I told my wrath, my wrath did end.*
> *I was angry with my foe:*
> *I told it not, my wrath did grow.*
>
> *And I water'd it in fears*
> *Night and morning with my tears;*
> *And I sunned it with smiles,*
> *And with soft deceitful wiles.*
>
> *And it grew both day and night,*
> *Till it bore an apple bright;*
> *And my foe beheld it shine,*
> *And he knew that it was mine,*
>
> *And into my garden stole*
> *When the night had veiled the pole:*
> *In the morning glad I see*
> *My foe outstretch'd beneath the tree.*

Blake might with justice have made the further point: that the 'poison tree' is as poisonous to him who watches and waters it as to him who eats of its fruit. But, since murder ensues, that is clearly implied.

§ 4

It is inevitable, and right, that we should accept from Blake what we recognize as true and valuable for ourselves, while rejecting, or at any rate ignoring, what looks like grotesque nonsense. No one can swallow him whole. But in introducing him to others, as I attempt to do here, one must make it clear that what is offered *is* only a selection: a few salient features of his mind, not a detailed portrait. Blake was a multitude and his ideas are a riot. To see his whole mind one must read everything he wrote and ponder everything he drew and painted. He was often a profound but never a tidy or rational thinker; and, though the cardinal principles of his philosophy are definite enough, in the exposition of those principles it never seems to have occurred to him to bother about verbal consistency. Having an instinct to dramatize everything, he resorted too freely for our comfort to myth, allegory, and a symbolism which, when it falls short of the high poetry of the early *Songs*, is too often cumbrous and arbitrary. Even in his use of personification, which is the most elementary of allegorical devices, he is not consistent. Satan, who stands for Energy or Desire in *The Marriage of Heaven and Hell*, becomes later the Accuser of Mankind. Christ 'comes to deliver Man the Accused, and not Satan the Accuser. We do not find anywhere that Satan is accused of Sin; he is only accused of Unbelief and thereby drawing Man into Sin that he may accuse him. Such is the Last Judgment—a deliverance from Satan's Accusation. Satan thinks that Sin is displeasing to God; he ought to know that nothing is displeasing

to God but Unbelief and Eating of the Tree of Good and
Evil.'

Hell suffers the same diversity of interpretation. We have
seen that some of Blake's wisest utterances are labelled
Proverbs from Hell. Yet in 1809, in the *Descriptive Catalogue*
just quoted, we are told: 'In Hell all is Self Righteousness;
there is no such thing there as Forgiveness of Sin; he who
does forgive Sin is crucified as an Abettor of Criminals, and
he who performs Works of Mercy in any shape whatever
is punish'd and if possible destroy'd, not through envy of
Hatred or Malice, but through Self Righteousness that thinks
it does God service, which God is Satan. . . . Forgiveness of
Sin is only at the Judgment Seat of Jesus the Saviour, where
the Accuser is cast out, not because he sins, but because he
torments the Just and makes them do what he condemns as
Sin and what he knows is opposite to their own Identity. . . .
Thinking as I do that the Creator of this World is a very
Cruel Being, and being a worshipper of Christ, I cannot help
saying: "The Son, O how unlike the Father!" First God
Almighty comes with a Thump on the Head. Then Jesus
Christ comes with a balm to heal it.' Yet, in the very next
paragraph, Blake says that when the sun rises he sees, not
a round disk somewhat like a guinea, but 'an innumerable
company of the heavenly host crying: Holy, holy is the Lord
God Almighty!'. Why they should ascribe holiness to 'a very
Cruel Being' is not clear, unless we are to infer that they are
all in a conspiracy together. By 'the Creator of this World'
Blake seems to mean the creator of error. 'Error is Created.
Truth is Eternal. Error, or Creation, will be burned up, and
then, and not till then, Truth or Eternity will appear.' But
if God Almighty is the creator of error, either he is identical
with Satan, whose function is described above, or Satan is
out of a job.

Confused by this kind of haphazard mythology, an impatient reader will be inclined to plead with Blake that he

shall give didacticism a rest and return to his singing. The famous opening couplets of *Auguries of Innocence*—

> *To see a world in a grain of sand,*
> *And a heaven in a wild flower,*
> *Hold Infinity in the palm of your hand*
> *And Eternity in an hour*—

say more in their simplicity than any amount of such elaborate exegesis. Incidentally, they throw doubt on Blake's later assertion that the outward creation was a hindrance to him. 'I question not my corporeal or vegetative Eye any more than I would question a Window concerning a Sight. I look through it and not with it.' True, but a window is no hindrance: it is even useful, in that it supplies a frame, definition. And one cannot see heaven in (or through) a wild flower, unless one sees the wild flower. Another question arises: does Creation, the work of that 'very Cruel Being', include the grain of sand and the wild flower, or does it not? 'Eternity exists, and all things in Eternity, independent of Creation which was an act of mercy.' We are left now with three statements about Creation from which to take our choice. It was the act of a cruel being. It was an act of mercy. It is error.

I do not contend that these inconsistencies go very deep. They arise from Blake's trick of changing the sense of his key-words without troubling to warn us of the fact. It is all of a piece with his oracular self-confidence, his persuasion of being a man instructed by visions and voices. It can irritate the reader, but it does not seriously obscure the essentials of Blake's mystical philosophy. From what has been said it will be evident that a neat summary of those essentials would effect nothing but a misleading simplification. They have already been stated, where possible in Blake's own words. But there is one conspicuous feature about which something more must be said—Blake's emphasis on the idea of forgiveness.

Blake had a profound distrust of what he called Moral
Virtue, his notion of which may be defined as living by rule
of thumb and in a spirit of self-righteousness. He would not,
I suppose, have denied that certain rules of conduct have some
trifling practical utility; but he resented their being invested
with a pseudo-religious sanctity. As for the pretence that
morality had anything to do with Christ, he would have none
of it:

> *If Moral Virtue was Christianity,*
> *Christ's pretensions were all vanity,*
> *And Caiaphas and Pilate men*
> *Praiseworthy . . .*

In a prefatory note to this strange poem, *The Everlasting
Gospel*, he makes his point very clearly. 'There is not one
Moral Virtue that Jesus inculcated but Plato and Cicero did
inculcate before him. What then did Christ inculcate? Forgiveness of Sins. This alone is the Gospel, and this is the
Life and Immortality brought to light by Jesus, even the
Covenant of Jehovah, which is this: If you forgive one another
your Trespasses, so shall Jehovah forgive you, that he himself
may dwell among you; but if you avenge, you murder the
Divine Image, and he cannot dwell among you . . .' So, too,
in the preamble to *Jerusalem*: 'The Spirit of Jesus is continual
forgiveness of Sin. He who waits to be righteous before he
enters into the Saviour's kingdom, the Divine Body, will never
enter there. I am perhaps the most sinful of men. I pretend not
to holiness: yet I pretend to love, to see, to converse with
daily, as man to man . . . the Friend of Sinners.'

At the beginning of the fourth section of the same work
he addresses some searching remarks *To the Christians*, of
which the following is an abridgement: 'I know of no other
Christianity and of no other Gospel than the liberty both of
body and mind to exercise the Divine Arts of Imagination:
Imagination, the real and eternal World of which this

Vegetable Universe is but a faint shadow, and in which we shall live in our Eternal or Imaginative Bodies when these Vegetable Mortal Bodies are no more. The Apostles knew of no other Gospel. What were all their spiritual gifts? What is the Divine Spirit? Is the Holy Ghost any other than an Intellectual Fountain? What are the Treasures of Heaven which we are to lay up for ourselves, are they any other than Mental Studies and Performances? What are the Gifts of the Gospel, are they not all Mental Gifts? O ye Religious, discountenance every one among you who shall pretend to despise Art and Science! What is the Life of Man but Art and Science? What is Mortality but the things relating to the Body which Dies? What is Immortality but the things relating to the Spirit which Lives Eternally? What is the Joy of Heaven but Improvement in the things of the Spirit? What are the pains of Hell but Ignorance, Bodily Lust, Idleness, and devastation of the things of the Spirit? Answer this to yourselves, and expel from among you those who pretend to despise the labours of Art and Science, which alone are the labours of the Gospel.'

A summing-up, after all, must be risked. All life is one life, outward and various manifestation of that One which is within us and in whose eternal being we are. The contraction and hardening of consciousness round its several centres results in the illusion and assertion of selfhood as an absolute, a self-subsistent independent reality sufficient unto itself. Self-assertion in this sense of self-isolation cuts us off, while it lasts, from communion with that Eternal which is here and now, shining through the things of time, and so frustrates the deepest desire of the human-divine spirit. The only escape from this self-imprisonment is by way of what Blake calls Imagination; for Imagination (not to be confused with mere fancy) is nothing less than the vision of Eternity. In practice man's salvation (spiritual health) lies neither in conventional religious observances nor in adherence to an arbitrary moral code, but in imaginative (or creative) work, of which art in its various forms is the type. The artificial repression of natural desire belongs to expedient negative morality, not to virtue, true virtue being from within, and positive. The diverse impulses which are at war in man (sometimes, for fun, Blake calls them God and the Devil) can be brought into ultimate accord by the spirit of Jesus, whose whole gospel, where it differs from that of earlier teachers, is of love and the forgiveness of sins.

Chapter Eight

WORDSWORTH

§ 1

No two men could have been more different, on a superficial view, than Blake and Wordsworth. And even at a deeper level a great difference persists. That in spite of it they were both mystics, in the sense defined in our first chapter, is as reassuring as the concord underlying all divergencies of expression between Taoist and Hindu, or between Quaker revolutionary and Catholic saint. In the letter of their works the dissimilarity is extreme, the one seemingly so wild, the other in general so tame; for if Blake's besetting sin is fantasticality, Wordsworth's is a tendency to lapse into prosiness and complacent moralizing while remaining sublimely unaware of the lapse. Yet they were at one in essentials; they both strongly repudiated the mechanistic conception of man and nature which prevailed in their day, seeking to replace it in the minds of men by a philosophy that differed from primitive animism (to which it was in some sense a return) in its subtlety of apprehension, its intellectual discipline, and above all its recognition of a unity in all things. For Wordsworth, as for Blake, the universe was alive in all its parts and alive with one life. Nature was *naturans*, not *naturata*: a living organism suffused with that which in its higher manifestations we call mind or consciousness. As a mere idea this was no novelty: Wordsworth's value for us lies not in any new contribution to thought but in his quality as a poet. It is true that didacticism too often breaks in, and the tone of the lecture-room makes an end of poetry; but in his greatest moments, moments that come and go with unpredictable and disconcerting suddenness, the majesty that inspires him finds majestic utterance. It should be remembered, however, that in these inspired moments Wordsworth is still (and pre-eminently) a poet, not a dialectician. Much of the criticism levelled against his poetic philosophy turns on the meaning to be attached to the term Nature. He has been accused of romantic vagueness, of paganism, of pantheism, of sentimental nature-worship; and no doubt there is a grain of truth in each of these charges. But they do not go to the root of his matter. For what, in fact, does 'Nature' mean in Wordsworth's verse? Not always the same thing. The meaning not only varies with the context but is defined by it, so that the context is our only clue to it. Sometimes it means, quite simply, the natural scene. More often it means that same natural scene regarded as a living manifestation of a divine life or spirit. In 'Nature and the language of the sense' Wordsworth recognizes

> *The anchor of my purest thoughts, the nurse,*
> *The guide, the guardian of my heart, and soul*
> *Of all my moral being.*

If Nature here meant merely the external physical universe, the sum of natural phenomena, there would be some excuse for dismissing these lines as empty romantic rhetoric. But it clearly does not mean that. It is a statement that can be understood only in relation to the lines that precede it:

> *a sense sublime*
> *Of something far more deeply interfused,*
> *Whose dwelling is . . .*

not only in external Nature, the light of the sun, the round ocean, the living air, but also, and significantly, 'in the mind of man'. In short, Nature, of which Man is a part, is for Wordsworth, as for Erigena and others, a theophany, or manifestation of God.

As mysticism is the inwardness of religion, so poetry is the language—and the only verbal language—of mysticism. (I say the only 'verbal' language, because music and the graphic arts are also ways of communicating spiritual sensation incommunicable by plain prose statement.) Poetry, though it normally embodies plain statement, begins at the point where statement ends; and though its form be 'musical' its spirit speaks in the silences that punctuate and in the stillness that follows the music. What poetry 'says' can therefore never be stated in other words, or in another manipulation of the same words; and what mysticism *is* can never be expressed in a doctrinal formula. The attempt to do these things cannot always be avoided, but the results are never satisfactory and often they are disastrous. Phrases like 'eternity in time' and 'the unity of all life', when offered and received as mere intellectual propositions, are not only barren of vital meaning but too easily degenerate into empty catchwords: their truth has a living and dynamic quality only for those who, however dimly, have seen it or felt it for themselves. Poetry cannot be exhaustively defined in terms of literary technique: it is something that happens when words are so used as to communicate an aspect or nuance of reality otherwise incommunicable. The operative word is 'happens'. I say poetry happens, because in the last analysis it is an event beyond the poet's conscious contriving. The chances are that but for his disciplined skill, his command of language, and above all his self-dedication to the arduous business of meditation, it would *not* happen; but when it does it is something given, something that comes by grace. This is most conspicuously true of Wordsworth. The direct pursuit of poetry is as self-defeating as the direct pursuit of happiness: the poet must content himself, therefore, with putting into words what he sees, what he feels, what he thinks, knowing that the eventual illumination must come, if it come at all, from beyond him and as if by accident.

It follows that the poetic impulse and mystical religion have much in common. Both poet and mystic are concerned to find the universal in the particular, the eternal aspect of temporal things. Both are intent upon the Real. Blake's maxim that if the doors of perception were cleansed (but surely he meant 'windows'?) everything would be seen as it is, infinite, exactly describes the poet's vision, given to him, and to us through him, in rare flashes of insight, and so communicating to us that sensation of eternity which is at once the soul of poetry and the essence of mystical illumination. Wordsworth, in several famous passages, has recorded such an experience:

> *that blessed mood*
> *In which the burthen of the mystery,*
> *In which the heavy and the weary weight*
> *Of all this unintelligible world,*
> *Is lighten'd, that serene and blessed mood*
> *In which the affections gently lead us on*
> *Until, the breath of this corporeal frame*
> *And even the motion of our human blood*
> *Almost suspended, we are laid asleep*
> *In body, and become a living soul:*
> *While with an eye made quiet by the power*
> *Of harmony, and the deep power of joy,*
> *We see into the life of things.*

§ 2

Enthralled by the sublimity of his few great poems, or deceived by the ambling monotony of the blank verse in which some of his most miraculous passages are embedded, most of us too easily think of Wordsworth either as a tranquil 'poet of Nature', gathering everywhere the 'harvest of a quiet eye', or as a sober, moralizing, self-satisfied old gentleman who had known nothing of spiritual storm and stress and who ruthlessly subordinated all other interests, including the consideration due to his too devoted wife and sister, to his self-appointed mission to instruct and edify the world. There is some truth in both these versions of him, but they fall so far short of the whole truth that either of them, or both together, can be no more than a caricature.

Everyone knows that he outlived his inspiration; that during the ten years from 1798, when the *Lyrical Ballads* were written and published, to 1807, when he read to Coleridge the unpolished but already much worked-on first draft of *The Prelude*, all his greatest work was done; and that though he remained a craftsman to the end, capable of a magnificent line here and there, something like a hardening of the poetic arteries set in, those ten fruitful years being followed by forty-three comparatively barren ones. They were barren, these later years, not of verse but (in general) of poetry; and the poet himself, though resisting the knowledge, was at times despondently aware of it. Ingenious explanations of this aridness have been advanced; but the more picturesque of them belong, in my opinion, rather to imaginative fiction than to biography. The theory that Wordsworth's creativeness was frustrated, his manhood undermined, by a (conscious or subconscious) regret or remorse for his eventual abandonment, with her consent, of Annette Vallon, the young Frenchwoman with whom he fell in love in his twenty-first year and who bore him a child in 1792, is almost certainly an over-simplification of the truth, if not a complete distortion. That fiery episode happened at a time of youthful intoxication and generous revolutionary idealism, in a France 'standing on the top of golden hours'; it was, moreover, Wordsworth's first experience of passionate love, and as such must have made a deep and permanent mark on his psyche. We may be inclined to regret, romantically, the vein of caution in him that prevented his marrying Annette out of hand, without waiting for his guardian's consent and with no prospect of being in a position to support a wife and child; but, once divided from her by uncontrollable circumstances (he left France because his money was running out, and a few months later the two countries were at war), it was almost inevitable that his first ardour, given time, should cool somewhat, or be worn away by his hope's too long deferment. This kind of thing has happened to other young men without disastrously affecting the whole course of their lives.

Nevertheless, it may well be true that the fading of his poetic vision was the result of a more general violence done (by himself) to his nature, a violence in which his acquiescence in the loss of Annette was but one incident, though possibly the first. For Wordsworth, who in a long perspective looks so quietly contemplative, so tamely respectable, was in his original make-up a wild and passionate creature, full of animal energy and eager for active delights. He confesses himself to have been also, in early boyhood, 'of a stiff, moody, and violent temper'. His mother has left it on record that he was the only one of her five children about whose future she felt anxious. It is no doubt to be admired in him that he took such stern control of himself; but is it not possible that in insisting on being a totally different kind of man from that which Nature seems to have designed him for, he wrought his ultimate undoing? He was resolved to be a great poet, and great poet he became; but in the end the very excess of his resolution defeated him. Seeing himself as a dedicated spirit he was at pains to contrive, with the zealous help of his womenfolk, that nothing in the world should for a moment interrupt his pursuit of poetry: all must be sacrificed to that. The sequence of events is well known. In 1795 a legacy from a friend, Raisley Calvert, and the generosity of 'a Mr Pinney' and later of Thomas Poole, who saw to it that he had somewhere to live at little or no rent, eased him of economic anxiety; and his sister Dorothy, of whom he wrote, saying no more than the truth,

> *She gave me eyes, she gave me ears,*
> *And humble cares, and delicate fears,*
> *A heart, the fountain of sweet tears,*
> *And love, and thought, and joy—*

was now domesticated with him, after a separation of sixteen years. In 1799 he and Dorothy moved to Dove Cottage, Grasmere; in August 1802 they spent a month with Annette and her ten-year-old daughter Caroline at Calais; and in the following October Wordsworth was married to Mary Hutchinson, whom he had known as a little girl, his school-fellow at a dame's school in Penrith. That the marriage was an eminently comfortable one seems well attested; and it was none the worse for being a marriage of convenience as well as affection. It served two important purposes: it made a decisive end in Wordsworth's mind of the Annette chapter, and it provided him with possibly the only wife whom Dorothy could have persuaded herself to share him with. Dorothy's love for her brother was tender, passionate, boundless. She had, moreover, no less than he, a sense of his exalted destiny. Mary was her most intimate woman friend, and the two now devoted the rest of their lives (until his death in 1850) to keeping the candles alight on the altar of his high ambition.

Such a degree of womanly devotion was more 'natural' in a wife than a sister, and Dorothy in the end had to pay a bitter price for her part in it. And may it not be that she and Mary, and certainly Wordsworth himself, cosseted his Muse too much? Freedom is the breath of life to a poet, and faith in his powers the staff he leans upon; but freedom extended without limit reaches a point at which it becomes a spiritual vacuum, and a sense of greatness that is hourly fostered by veneration from the other members of a tiny

WILLIAM WORDSWORTH IN 1798

enclosed community is in perpetual danger of becoming both selfconscious and selfcomplacent. Wordsworth's sense of possessing great powers was abundantly justified, as was later his uneasy fitful sense of having not fully realized them. Such an endowment as his was a heavy responsibility, and his recognition of the fact can only be applauded. Yet one cannot quite resist the suspicion that there was something a thought too deliberate, too methodical, too thorough, about the way he set up shop as a great poet. It was in truth a solemn business, but he overdid the solemnity. Someone has aptly said that if Blake had had a little of Wordsworth's sobriety, and Wordsworth a little of Blake's madness, both would have been better poets. But the perfect complement to Wordsworth's mind was that of Coleridge, whom he found in 1797 and lost (through a misunderstanding) in 1810. The two men were made for each other. Coleridge, with his enthusiasm, his wealth of exciting ideas, his soaring imagination, his flow of vivid and challenging talk, consciously needed the stabilizing influence of Wordsworth's massive wisdom, of which he was instantly aware; and the deeply ruminating Wordsworth needed the sparkle and stimulus of Coleridge's company to keep his mind fresh and alert. Their loss of each other was a disaster for both. It left Wordsworth with no one who was a match for him, no one to sharpen his wits against; and he gradually subsided into taking himself for granted as bard and oracle.

Thoroughness, an excess of resolution, was perhaps his undoing. Technique, which is the poet's instrument, can be worked upon without limit; but poetry cannot be commanded, nor can it be achieved by taking thought. Wordsworth gives the impression, not exactly of taking his work too seriously, but of worrying and theorizing about it too much. The poet in him had to contend with a too active conscience, which was for ever reminding him of his duty and getting in the way of his doing it. Some of his 1798 poems suffer from having

N

been written in conscious conformity with a theory, though it is not to be supposed that they were written for theory's sake. He could handle prose with mastery as well as verse; his preface to the second edition of *Lyrical Ballads* enriched our literature with certain great critical generalizations; but, fine imaginative critic though he was, he was apparently incapable, craftsmanship apart, of discriminating between good and bad in his own work. There is no reason to suppose that he was even dimly aware that the poem written near Tintern Abbey was worth all the rest of his *Lyrical Ballads* put together.

J. K. Stephen's

> *Two voices are there: one is of the deep,*
> *And one is of an old, half-witted sheep,*

is a cruelly apt comment on Wordsworth's total output of verse. But not merely were there two voices: it is almost as if there were two distinct beings in Wordsworth, and that during the years that followed Coleridge's departure the busier of the pair, by unremitting industry, succeeded at last in talking the other, the seer, into silence. But no sooner is that said than one sees it to be at most only half the truth. For, though good things came so seldom in his later years, the poet in Wordsworth, the power of great utterance, never died. The sonnet on *Mutability*, which after an indifferent opening rises to a superb height, belongs to his fifth decade:

> *Truth fails not; but her outward forms that bear*
> *The longest date do melt like frosty rime*
> *That in the morning whitened hill and plain*
> *And is no more; drop like the tower sublime*
> *Of yesterday, which royally did wear*
> *His crown of weeds, but could not even sustain*
> *Some casual shout that broke the silent air,*
> *Or the unimaginable touch of time.*

And, as de Selincourt discovered for us, and pointed out in his edition (1926) of the 1805 and 1850 versions of *The Prelude*, the poet was over sixty when he wrote, of Newton's statue:

> *The marble index of a mind for ever*
> *Voyaging through strange seas of Thought, alone.*

Such things silence criticism, and other examples could be found. Yet it remains true, despite individual exceptions, that by far the best of Wordsworth belongs to that one decade, beginning with the year of *Tintern Abbey*, his twenty-ninth, and ending with the completion of the autobiographical *Prelude* which he revised yet again, during his last year of life, for posthumous publication, improving its literary craftsmanship at many points, at some other points altering it stylistically for the worse, and, most lamentable of changes, watering down his ecstatic immanentism, his vision of God in Nature, in a timid endeavour to bring it into line with conventional Anglicanism.

§ 3

It is with the Wordsworth that 'died' at about the age of forty that we have to do: what followed scarcely concerns us. The early years of any man's life are decisive, and Wordsworth, being destined for poetry, was singularly lucky in his antecedents and environment. Born within sight and sound of the lakes and fells and singing waters of Cumberland, he was uniquely sensitive to the impact of these wonders on his eager, ardent spirit:

> *Fair seedtime had my soul, and I grew up*
> *Foster'd alike by beauty and by fear:*
> *Much favour'd in my birthplace, and no less*
> *In that beloved Vale to which ere long*
> *We were transplanted.*

He had three brothers and a sister, all near him in age; his father was a substantial lawyer, his mother a woman of deep nature and great natural sagacity; and their social station was the best that could have been chosen, the middle station, at once sturdily independent and immune from false pride. They were of true country stock, deep-rooted through several generations in their native soil, and mixing with their neighbours, whether gentle or simple, in a democratic equality untainted by doctrine or selfconsciousness. The child Wordsworth grew up, as he tells us, fostered not only by beauty but by fear; but the fear, the awe, was perhaps an effect of the beauty, or rather of the grandeur, that environed him. One evening, a schoolboy on holiday, wandering by Patterdale, to which he was a stranger, he found a shepherd's boat tied to a willow tree in a cave, and, unloosing the tether, stepped in and pushed from the shore:

> It was an act of stealth
> And troubled pleasure. Not without the voice
> Of mountain-echoes did my boat move on,
> Leaving behind her still, on either side,
> Small circles glittering idly in the moon
> Until they melted all into one track
> Of sparkling light. A rocky steep uprose
> Above the cavern of the willow tree,
> And now, as suited one who proudly row'd
> With his best skill, I fix'd a steady view
> Upon the top of that same craggy ridge,
> The bound of the horizon, for behind
> Was nothing but the stars and the grey sky.
> She was an elfin pinnace; lustily
> I dipp'd my oars into the silent lake,
> And, as I rose upon the stroke, my boat
> Went heaving through the water like a swan;
> When from behind that craggy steep, till then

The bound of the horizon, a huge cliff,
As if with voluntary power instinct,
Uprear'd its head. I struck, and struck again,
And, growing still in stature, the grim shape
Rose up between me and the stars, and still,
With measured motion, like a living thing,
Strode after me.

Trembling, he turned back; moored the boat in the place
from which he had taken it; and walked home in 'serious
mood' through the meadows. And for many days, he says:

for many days my brain
Worked with a dim and undetermined sense
Of unknown modes of being. O'er my thoughts
There hung a darkness, call it solitude
Or blank desertion. No familiar shapes
Remained, no pleasant images of trees,
Of sea or sky, no colours of green fields;
But huge and mighty forms, that do not live
Like living men, moved slowly through the mind
By day, and were a trouble to my dreams.

Nature was already wonderful and awful in his eyes; but
he was not yet conscious of her as an intimate presence or
as the nurse of his moral being. Nor did he even dimly
surmise at that time that he was to give himself to poetry.
Outwardly, with his passionate energy and his delight in
strenuous games, he was little different from other boys. On
the death of his mother, when he was eight, the family had
broken up, brothers and sister being, as fifteen-year-old
Dorothy ruefully put it, 'squandered abroad'. Dorothy was
entrusted to the care of her grandmother at Penrith, and
William and his elder brother were sent to school at Hawkshead, near Esthwaite Water. The boys lodged with people

in the village and attended school daily: an arrangement perfectly suited to one of Wordsworth's temperament, for it combined in equal proportions the joys of companionship with those of solitude, and he had a powerful appetite for both. These years at Hawkshead were perhaps the richest of all his life in spiritual growth. The transition from child-hood to adolescence must anywhere have been the most critical stage of his development; but at Hawkshead he had everything, it would seem, that could conduce to the full flowering that was to come: the salutary discipline of school routine, abundant freedom, and the presence of incomparable natural beauty for senses and imagination to feed on. These things did their work unseen, and only later, in retrospect, did he become fully aware of what it had meant to him.

The great poem (unequal though it is, with many flat passages) in which he records the growth of his mind was written for the eye of the intimate friend, Coleridge, to whom it was addressed; and partly for that reason, as well as because it was designed as prelude to a still larger work (never completed), he hesitated to make it public, thinking that to less partial readers it might seem like the ebullition of a too-complacent egoism. This we do well to bear in mind as we read the poem: that it is, in effect, a long confidential letter from friend to friend. If he had the self-confidence that is born of conscious power, Wordsworth was yet by no means lacking in humility. Like a priest, for as such in some sense he regarded himself, he reverenced his office but, so far from being conceited, strove unremittingly to make himself worthy of it. The trouble in later years was that he fell into the delusion of supposing that everything he wrote had high value. Southey complained, with justice, that he consistently overrated his work, though even Southey knew that his best was beyond praise. For all that, he was never satisfied with *The Prelude*, to which, at intervals for over forty years, he returned again and again, though well knowing towards the

end that it would never appear during his lifetime. The
legend of his elderly self-importance and pompousness must
not obscure—indeed it sharpens—the tragedy of his last
years. In de Selincourt's view, he could not but have known
that *The Excursion*, which was to have been his masterpiece,
represented a sad falling-off, a loss of power.

His father dying in 1783, Wordsworth in his fourteenth
year became subject to the guardianship of two uncles. By
then he had spent five school years at Hawkshead, and was
to spend three or four more before going to Cambridge. His
sense of a vital affinity with Nature gradually developed
during those nine years. In the early morning, before school
began, he used to walk round Esthwaite Water, a distance
of five miles, sometimes alone, sometimes with a particular
friend. And sometimes at night, he says, he would walk alone
under the quiet stars, or, when a storm threatened, stand

> *Beneath some rock, listening to notes that are*
> *The ghostly language of the ancient earth,*
> *Or make their dim abode in distant winds.*
> *Thence did I drink the visionary power;*
> *And deem not profitless those fleeting moods*
> *Of shadowy exultation: not for this,*
> *That they are kindred to our purer mind*
> *And intellectual life, but that the soul,*
> *Remembering how she felt, but what she felt*
> *Remembering not, retains an obscure sense*
> *Of possible sublimity.*

The changing seasons, day and night, sleeping and waking,
and 'thought from sources inexhaustible', all contributed

> *To feed the spirit of religious love*
> *In which I walked with Nature.*

It was, in Wordsworth's view, a real communion that he

enjoyed: he was not passively receptive. Coleridge's cry of disenchantment,

> *we receive but what we give,*
> *And in our life alone does Nature live:*

is a flat contradiction of Wordsworth's doctrine. But Wordsworth—the fact is reassuring rather than otherwise—was aware of giving as well as receiving. He was aware of a light within him responsive to the light without and in essence one with it:

> *An auxiliar light*
> *Came from my mind, which on the setting sun*
> *Bestowed new splendour. The melodious birds,*
> *The fluttering breezes, fountains that ran on*
> *Murmuring so sweetly in themselves, obeyed*
> *A like dominion, and the midnight storm*
> *Grew darker in the presence of my eye.*
> *Hence my obeisance . . .*
> *Thus did my days pass on, and now at length*
> *From Nature and her overflowing soul*
> *I had received so much, that all my thoughts*
> *Were steep'd in feeling; I was only then*
> *Contented, when with bliss ineffable*
> *I felt the sentiment of Being spread*
> *O'er all that moves, and all that seemeth still,*
> *O'er all that, lost beyond the reach of thought*
> *And human knowledge, to the human eye*
> *Invisible, yet liveth to the heart;*
> *O'er all that leaps and runs, and shouts and sings,*
> *Or beats the gladsome air; o'er all that glides*
> *Beneath the wave, yea in the wave itself*
> *And mighty depth of waters. Wonder not*
> *If such my transports were; for in all things now*
> *I saw one life, and felt that it was joy.*

'In all things . . . I saw one life, and felt that it was joy.'
This is the first, the distinguishing feature of Wordsworth's
quality: that he found in Nature 'a never-failing principle of
joy, and purest passion'. But it is by no means the whole
story. Not less important, perhaps more so, is his profound
sense of the (potential) greatness of the human soul and his
recognition of that greatness in ordinary humble men and
women. That was a later vision, the mellow fruit of his young
maturity. It is the 'moral' implicit in nearly all his *Lyrical
Ballads* and supplied the motive for his perhaps too conscious,
too deliberate resolve, which was to make himself the poet
of the ordinary, to show that the ordinary is alive with
meaning and high value. But if his incidental banalities are
to be blamed upon this resolve, his sublimest moments are
informed by the impulse that prompted it. I quote the oft-
quoted invocation to the Spirit of the Universe for the sake
of its last line, noting that in the phrase 'mean and vulgar
works of man' a discriminating stress falls on the adjectives,
not on 'works of man'. Wordsworth is not saying that the
works of man, as such, are mean and vulgar, but only that
some of them are.

> *Wisdom and Spirit of the universe,*
> *Thou Soul that art the eternity of thought,*
> *That givest to forms and images a breath*
> *And everlasting motion, not in vain*
> *By day or starlight thus from my first dawn*
> *Of childhood didst thou intertwine for me*
> *The passions that build up our human soul:*
> *Not with the mean and vulgar works of man,*
> *But with high objects, with enduring things,*
> *With life and nature, purifying thus*
> *The elements of feeling and of thought,*
> *And sanctifying, by such discipline,*
> *Both pain and fear, until we recognize*
> *A grandeur in the beatings of the heart.*

In *Tintern Abbey* and in the *Ode on Intimations of Immortality*, which with the *Prelude* (or parts of it) put Wordsworth among the greatest poets of all time, the two objects of his insight, which we may label (very roughly) the Spirit in Nature and the Spirit of Man, are seen to be one, fused in his vision. There they are treated in universal terms and in a spirit of high exultation. But elsewhere, in quietly reflective pieces which are apt to be undervalued because they so narrowly escape (and they do not always escape) triteness, the same imaginative philosophy is implicit. It is no use being impatient with Wordsworth when, for no adequate reason as it seems, he puts his singing robes away and settles down to being a metrical moralist. Dullness cannot be defended, and much dullness is to be found, heaven knows, in the great mass of his verse. But except when he reverts, in defiance of his own critical doctrine, to the weary periphrasis and abstract language of the poetic convention he so decisively broke away from in his best work, his simplest 'thoughts' have a profundity and a quality peculiarly his own: they seem shallow only when, dressed up in borrowed clothes, they pretend to be grander than they are. We miss a good half of Wordsworth's value if we fail to appreciate the quiet composure of his normal speaking voice, the fidelity of his observation, and the directness of his approach. One minor example will suffice: fourteen simple lines entitled *Animal Tranquillity and Decay*:

> *The little hedgerow birds,*
> *That peck along the road, regard him not.*
> *He travels on, and in his face, his step,*
> *His gait, is one expression: every limb,*
> *His look and bending figure, all bespeak*
> *A man who does not move with pain, but moves*
> *With thought. He is insensibly subdued*
> *To settled quiet: he is one by whom*

All effort seems forgotten; one to whom
Long patience hath such mild composure given
That patience now doth seem a thing of which
He hath no need. He is by nature led
To peace so perfect that the young behold,
With envy, what the Old Man hardly feels.

That belongs to 1798, when Wordsworth was himself a young man, not yet thirty. It is not an exciting poem. It is a poem such as perhaps no one but Wordsworth would have thought worth writing down, and its versification is unremarkable except for simplicity and unpretentiousness; but these still waters run deep. Wordsworth calls it a 'sketch', and so it is. But it is more than a mere faithful description of something seen: it is an imaginative experience, the divination of a state of being of which the poet at that time can have had only intuitive knowledge. It is, in a word, Wordsworthian.

§ 4

Before going further into his life and thought, let us pause to admire that beautiful bareness and directness of diction which gives to his best things not only splendour and dignity, as of great sculpture or great music untainted by the vulgarity of adventitious ornament, but also an almost dateless, anonymous quality, such as poetry attains to only in its highest moments: moments when the voice of the poet, losing its local or individual accent, becomes as it were the vehicle for a universal utterance. It is as though not a man but Man himself, the embodiment of all men, were speaking. Wordsworth in his great Ode gave expression not only to 'intimations of immortality from recollections of early childhood' but to intimations of an impending loss of the vision that sustained him. Impending may seem to be the wrong word, since the poem's whole burden is to the effect that the loss has already happened; but if indeed it had, at that time, the bereavement was so recent, the memory of the early divine apprehension so fresh and glorious, that the regret is everywhere suffused with the radiance of recollection. Coleridge's comparable Ode, with its catalogue of wonders of which he says 'I see, not feel, how wonderful they are', a statement not very different at first blush from Wordsworth's 'The things which I have seen I now can see no more', is significantly entitled *Dejection*. Dejection alone cannot inspire poetry, but there *is* dejection (as well as eloquence) in Coleridge's poem, whereas in the *Intimations* there is none. Dated 1803–1806, it is the immortal swan-song of that mystical apprehension which had irradiated Wordsworth's late adolescence and early manhood and was so soon to grow dim.

> *There was a time when meadow, grove, and stream,*
> *The earth, and every common sight,*
> > *To me did seem*
> > *Apparelled in celestial light,*
> *The glory and the freshness of a dream.*
> *It is not now as it hath been of yore:*
> > *Turn wheresoe'er I may,*
> > *By night or day,*
> *The things which I have seen I now can see no more.*

> > *The Rainbow comes and goes,*
> > *And lovely is the Rose,*
> > *The Moon doth with delight*
> *Look round her when the heavens are bare,*
> > *Waters on a starry night*
> > *Are beautiful and fair;*
> > *The sunshine is a glorious birth;*
> > *But yet I know, where'er I go,*
> *That there hath passed away a glory from the earth.*

How simple in diction; how true in feeling; how masterly, effortless, inevitable, the weave of the alternating rhythms. Except for one phrase, 'of yore', which however does not trouble us in this particular context, there is not a word that belongs more to the nineteenth century than to our own, and not a vestige of that applied decoration which is the mark of straining after effect, of weariness or selfconsciousness— in a word of artistic insincerity. Nor is there anything deliberate in the abstention, any conscious adherence to Wordsworth's own doctrine, the doctrine promulgated in the preface to the second edition of *Lyrical Ballads* of 'fitting to metrical arrangement a selection of the real language of men in a state of vivid sensation'. It is as if (as we noticed with Blake's finest lyrics) the poem wrote itself: an effect which, with 'inspiration' aiding, is the crown of skilful patient workmanship.

In its technical accomplishment and poetic integrity, its blend of fresh feeling with classical formalism and of generalization with vivid imagery, this is perhaps the most consistently satisfying of all Wordsworth's poems. It has been the fashion to see in its theme a reminiscence of Vaughan's *Retreat*, which Wordsworth certainly knew; but there is so much more in Wordsworth's poem than that, that the fact, if fact it is, is of very trifling significance. He has even been mildly scolded, by the orthodox, for seeming to give countenance to a doctrine—that of pre-existence—which official Christianity will have none of. To that there are two answers. First, that Wordsworth was under no obligation to conform to Christian dogma, and until his late middle age seems to have made no pretence of doing so; second, that he uses pre-existence rather as a convenient poetic myth, providing the rationale of his conception of infantile blessedness, than as something in which he wishes to engage the reader's literal belief. A third point, perhaps more important than these, is that if he did in any sense believe in pre-existence it was not *individual* pre-existence that he had in mind. The famous passage, which has figured so often in the discourses of nonconformist divines:

> *Our birth is but a sleep and a forgetting:*
> *The Soul that rises with us, our life's Star,*
> *Hath had elsewhere its setting,*
> *And cometh from afar:*
> *Not in entire forgetfulness,*
> *And not in utter nakedness,*
> *But trailing clouds of glory do we come*
> *From God, who is our home . . .*

is susceptible of quite another interpretation. It is a poet's statement of the ancient doctrine of the universal incarnation of the Divine Spirit in persons and things, the eternal self-division of the One into the Many.

Unqualified pantheism presents difficulties both intellectual and moral. It tends to substitute a featureless undifferentiated oneness for the glorious diversity which is a pre-condition of the only life we know or can conceive, and the source equally of pain and delight. It tends, in the moral sphere, to blur the distinction (vitally necessary in practice, whether logically valid or not) between good and evil. It encourages, especially in the eastern hemisphere which was its first home, a certain spiritual languor, a disdain and consequent neglect of the practical business of living. Wordsworth's pantheism, never formulated in strictly intellectual terms, was not of this uncompromising kind. The universal 'presence' or 'spirit' of which he is aware in Nature is not conceived by him as being confined within Nature: he would have agreed, I think, had he been forced into theological argument, that God is self-manifested in the universe but not contained (enclosed) in it; or even that the universe is identical with God (and this is pure pantheism) but does not, and cannot, constitute the whole Being of God. In the later revisions of *The Prelude* he did his best to soften the vitalizing (and blameless) pantheism of his young manhood, thereby in some degree falsifying the story. One among many changes, 'Nature's self, which is the breath of God' (1805) suffers in 1850 the feeble addition of: 'Or His pure Word by miracle revealed.' The younger Wordsworth would never have tolerated that anti-climax.

I have suggested that the Ode is the swan-song of Wordsworth's mystical rapture. But it is something more than that, something more profound and more complex. Its mood is a blend of chastened exultation and noble acceptance. It is at once a lament for what is gone, the beatific vision, and a paean of thanksgiving for what nevertheless remains, be it only a memory. It is very far from being, however, the expression (and enjoyment) of a merely romantic regret. With the humility of mature wisdom, a wisdom born of the very experience it treats of, it recognizes loss and suffering, the fading vision and the 'earthly freight' of custom, as belonging ineluctably to our human lot. By these, as well as by shared joys, we are bound to each other in a natural sympathy. Respond as we may to the divine mystery manifested in Nature—and how could we so respond were we not ourselves part of it?— it is by 'the human heart' that we live. This mystical humanism, which is central in Wordsworth and the chief source of his power, finds explicit utterance in the majestic closing lines of the Ode:

> *The clouds that gather round the setting sun*
> *Do take a sober colouring from an eye*
> *That hath kept watch o'er man's mortality;*
> *Another race hath been, and other palms are won.*
> *Thanks to the human heart by which we live,*
> *Thanks to its tenderness, its joys, and fears,*
> *To me the meanest flower that blows can give*
> *Thoughts that do often lie too deep for tears.*

The bereavement of which the poet tells in this poem, though grievous, is not ultimately desolating. The immortal light once seen, its loss can never be absolute. There is in our nature something that remembers, and so retains, the fugitive gleam.

> *The thought of our past years in me doth breed*
> *Perpetual benediction:*

not for the unthinking innocence of childhood, but for 'these obstinate questionings of sense and outward things', and for

> *Those shadowy recollections,*
> *Which, be they what they may,*
> *Are yet the fountain light of all our day,*
> *Are yet a master light of all our seeing;*
> *Uphold us, cherish, and have power to make*
> *Our noisy years seem moments in the being*
> *Of the eternal Silence . . .*

> *Though nothing can bring back the hour*
> *Of splendour in the grass, of glory in the flower,*
> *We will grieve not, rather find*
> *Strength in what remains behind;*
> *In the primal sympathy*
> *Which having been must ever be;*
> *In the soothing thoughts that spring*
> *Out of human suffering;*
> *In the faith that looks through death,*
> *In years that bring the philosophic mind.*

§ 5

In his nineteenth year Wordsworth consciously dedicated himself to poetry; during his twentieth, just down from the

SAMUEL TAYLOR COLERIDGE IN 1799

University, he enjoyed a strenuous walking holiday in Europe with a Cambridge friend; and by November of the following year, 1791, he was in Orleans, and already intoxicated with the revolutionary ardour, the sense of a renascent freedom for mankind, which animated all the generous spirits of that time. Annette Vallon, the object of his first passionate love and the mother of his first child, was royalist in her sympathies; but this difference of opinion did not divide the lovers. The story of that sojourn in France, so full of searching and dramatic experiences, and so different in general character from anything he had known before, has been told too often and too recently to need re-telling here. So too has the story of his inevitable disenchantment when, as is the way with violent revolutions, libertarian enthusiasm gave place to a brutal and bloody tyranny. Wordsworth has been accused of 'apostacy'; but, however much we may deplore the senile Toryism into which he finally lapsed, only the most infatuate political doctrinaire can blame him for hating the cruelty and corruption which attend unbridled power, or wish that he had joined in the sentimental adulation, in later years, of Napoleon.

One of the most momentous events in the lives of both was the restoration to each other of Wordsworth and his sister Dorothy. He had been her favourite brother in infancy; they had been parted by family circumstances and grown to manhood and womanhood away from sight of each other; and the blend of familiarity and strangeness made their mutual rediscovery a deep romantic delight, as well as an occasion for lasting satisfaction. Wordsworth's lifelong debt to Dorothy, apart from his specific acknowledgment of it, can be clearly read in a comparison between her *Journals* and his shorter poems. Dorothy, with her exquisite sensibility and her gift of minute observation, did, as he confessed, give him eyes and ears. On many occasions, indeed, she did his seeing and his hearing for him. Not only did she provide him with subjects for some of the lyrics: sometimes her very phrases are embodied in the resulting poem. It was she who saw the 'dancing daffodils', she who remembered after twenty years their shared delight in the sparrow's nest, she herself who told him that though as a child she had chased the butterflies she had always been careful not to catch them lest she should brush the dust from their wings. Greatest benefaction of all, it was she who comforted his spirit in its hour of perplexity and sick reaction and fortified his resolve:

> *She in the midst of all preserved me still*
> *A Poet, made me seek beneath that name,*
> *And that alone, my office upon earth.*

And it was to her, fittingly, that he addressed the greatest of his contributions to the 1798 volume: a volume first tentatively planned by Wordsworth, Coleridge, and Dorothy herself—'three persons and one soul' as Coleridge said—during an excursion, full (we may be sure) of glowing excited talk, which they made together from Nether Stowey to Linton. The impact of Dorothy's rare spirit on two major poets is something for which we must always be grateful.

And so we come back to the *Lines composed a Few Miles above Tintern Abbey*. They are a hundred and fifty-nine in number, and never again, not even in *The Prelude*, was Wordsworth to sustain in blank verse, a form that lends itself too easily to slack writing, so long a flight of continuously inspired poetry. The tribute to Dorothy is explicit and beautiful:

> *in thy voice I catch*
> *The language of my former heart, and read*
> *My former pleasures in the shooting lights*
> *Of thy wild eyes. Oh, yet a little while*
> *May I behold in thee what I was once,*
> *My dear, dear Sister! And this prayer I make . . .*

let the moon
Shine on thee in thy solitary walk;
And let the misty mountain-winds be free
To blow against thee; and, in after years,
When these wild ecstasies shall be matured
Into a sober pleasure, when thy mind
Shall be a mansion for all lovely forms,
Thy memory be as a dwelling-place
For all sweet sounds and harmonies—oh then,
If solitude, or fear, or pain, or grief,
Should be thy portion, with what healing thoughts
Of tender joy wilt thou remember me,
And these my exhortations! Nor perchance—
If I should be where I no more can hear
Thy voice, nor catch from thy wild eyes these gleams
Of past existence—wilt thou then forget
That on the banks of this delightful stream
We stood together; and that I, so long
A worshipper of Nature, hither came
Unwearied in that service: rather say
With warmer love—oh, with far deeper zeal
Of holier love. Nor wilt thou then forget,
That after many wanderings, many years
Of absence, these steep woods and lofty cliffs,
And this green pastoral landscape, were to me
More dear, both for themselves and for thy sake.

Dorothy was passionate as well as tender. The riches of her nature found perforce their chief outlet in sisterly devotion. And if anyone unacquainted with her tragic history should ask why she and Coleridge did not marry, the painfully simple answer, that Coleridge was already married, and disastrously, must be supplemented by a further question. Would she, had Coleridge been a free man, have herself felt free to leave William, whose need of her she knew to be so great? Here, all is conjecture. We do not know.

§ 6

Among the many discoveries made by that great Wordsworthian Ernest de Selincourt is a fragment of blank verse
from which, in his introductory essay, he quotes the following
lines:

> *the one interior life*
> *In which all beings live with God, themselves*
> *Are God, existing in the mighty whole,*
> *As indistinguishable as the cloudless east*
> *Is from the cloudless west, when all*
> *The hemisphere is one cerulean blue,*

which constitute (and no doubt for that very reason were
suppressed by the poet) the most explicitly pantheistic
passage that we know in Wordsworth. But the quotation,
as given, is edited, in that between 'the one interior life' and
'In which all beings live with God' there are lines which,
though of inferior quality, are valuable as supplying a gloss
upon a not sufficiently noticed phrase in the one passage in
Tintern Abbey which anthologists have made known to
everybody. Restoring de Selincourt's 'cut', we read:

> *the one interior life*
> *That lives in all things, sacred from the touch*
> *Of that false secondary power by which*
> *In weakness we create distinctions, then*
> *Believe that all our puny boundaries are things*
> *Which we perceive and not which we have made . . .*

lines which, in an amended version, found a place in *The
Prelude*. Add to this:

> *the mighty world*
> *Of eye and ear—both what they half create*
> *And what perceive,*

and we see, in a simple contrast, the sharp conflict between the mystic and the materialist, the poet and the purely analytical philosopher, the one seeking and finding unity in all things, the other always busy with his dissecting knife. We need not trouble to trace the ancestry of the idea that the visible universe is in part a mental creation: it is familiar enough to students of academic philosophy. Wordsworth's conviction is that such 'creation' is the work of a 'false secondary power', and that the learned analysis of living things, though it may have utility in its own narrow sphere, becomes palpably false, and deadly, when it presents itself in philosophic guise. He is conscious always of one informing Life or Spirit:

> For I have learned
> To look on Nature, not as in the hour
> Of thoughtless youth but hearing oftentimes
> The still, sad music of humanity,
> Nor harsh nor grating, though of ample power
> To chasten and subdue. And I have felt
> A presence that disturbs me with the sense
> Of elevated thoughts, a sense sublime
> Of something far more deeply interfused,
> Whose dwelling is the light of setting suns,
> And the round ocean and the living air,
> And the blue sky, and in the mind of man:
> A motion and a spirit that impels
> All thinking things, all objects of all thought,
> And rolls through all things. Therefore am I still
> A lover of the meadows and the woods
> And mountains, and of all that we behold
> From this green earth . . .

Chapter Nine

COMMENTS AND CONCLUSIONS

§ 1

In Wordsworth's later years the view of life which regards consciousness as a by-product of matter had already gained much ground. During the second half of the century it became firmly entrenched. It is nowadays the fashion either to blame avowed atheists and agnostics for this state of affairs, or to represent it as a glorious victory of science over religion. Dogmatic theoretical atheism, which incontinently denies the possibility of God's existence, admits of no rational defence. But atheism in practice seldom goes so far as that. It is not the denial of a divine redeeming element in life, but merely the repudiation, on logical grounds, of the particular concepts of God that happen to be current at any given time. As an intellectual attitude it differs only in name from agnosticism, which affirms, as Christian mystics too have affirmed, that the ultimate mysteries are beyond human knowledge, though not, the mystic would add, beyond apprehension. The man who coined the word agnostic, Thomas Henry Huxley, was a man with an abiding sense of the human sanctities. His approach was intellectual, not mystical, but he was at one with the mystics in recognizing the limitations of intellect. Mystical or spiritual insight is far from being inconsistent with intellectual agnosticism: its discoveries relate to realities which the language of poetry and symbolism may dimly suggest, but which cannot without distortion be intellectually formulated. And the paradox of the situation is, that when, in the realm of theology, it resorts (as it must) to negations, saying that God is not this, not that, not the other, the total effect of these negations is quite other than negative.

As for the nineteenth-century 'conflict between science and religion', that was little more than a display of shadow-boxing. The combatants were at one in regarding the natural world as a piece of clockwork: the only (very minor) point in dispute was whether or not the clock had been designed and wound up by a remote almighty hand. Institutional religion, with its cast-iron categories of natural and super-natural, body and spirit, Creator and creature, had therefore nothing to oppose to the materialism based on physical science but a counter-materialism, a system of symbolic dogma of which the symbolic character had been lost sight of, so that imaginative ideas metaphysically or poetically expressed had hardened into literal-minded fictions. Having already conceded the 'deadness' of the physical universe, it had taken refuge in an 'unseen world' conceived not as being 'within us' (as Jesus said it was) but as an actual somewhere or other to which, after death, we might hope to go, the mystical insight of the eternal manifesting in time, here and now, having been lost. Nor, by the religious world in general, has that insight yet been recovered. Yet it is surely evident that we can escape from the mess into which our moral (not philosophical) materialism has landed us, not by stubborn adherence to the principle of *credo quia absurdum*,* but only by realizing the inward law of our being and by learning to put first things first: a process that involves not merely self-knowledge—the only road to knowledge of others—but individual self-discipline. These remarks imply no disparage-ment of organized religion as such. I am only pleading that the emphasis should be upon inward experience, the life of the spirit, the contemplation of eternal things, rather than upon the letter of a creed. This does not mean either pre-occupation with one's own soul or fixing one's gaze upon

* Or, in Tertullian's actual words, *credibile quia ineptum est.*

a remote hereafter: quite the reverse. 'Eternal things,' says Dr Santayana,* in an essay on Platonism, 'are not other material things by miracle existing in another world; eternal things are the essences of all things here, when we consider what they are in themselves and not what, in the world of fortune, they may bring or take away from us personally. That is why piety and prayer are spiritual, when they cease to be magic operations or efforts of a celestial diplomacy.'

A religion that would substitute an imaginary world for the reality of living experience can only evade, not answer, the challenge of those who tell us that human behaviour, including the 'illusion' called thought, is nothing but a series of mechanical reactions to external stimuli. We need not dwell on the Behaviourist philosophy beyond noting that it is the *reductio ad absurdum* of materialistic monism. The behaviourist says in effect: 'I think that I think, but I don't really think. What really happens is a series of thoughtless physiological movements.' But to think that one thinks is to think: to have the illusion of consciousness is to be conscious. In the very act of appealing to reason the behaviourist assumes the validity of reasoning; but if all so-called thought is merely mechanical, the thought-process embodied in the statement of the fact is as mechanical as everything else, and such words as 'reason' and 'truth' and 'meaning' become empty noises. But, whether logically tenable or not, the doctrine that denies the reality of spirit has certainly coloured the mind and behaviour of mankind in recent years. Being a doctrine of pure despair, it cannot be tolerated indefinitely, and the revolt against it has taken various forms, some romantic, some pathetic, some infantile. Astrology, spiritualism, the humourless particularities of theosophy: all are attempts to enliven a dismal scene.

The mystical apprehension of a unity in multiplicity, of eternity in time, runs like a thread of light through the works

---

* *Soliloquies in England*. Constable, 1922.

of many nineteenth and twentieth century poets not regarded
primarily as mystics, as well as in the more explicit utterances
of Emily Brontë, Francis Thompson, and the rest. Only by
virtue of a high artistic integrity in its expression does it
escape—when it does escape—being a poetical cliché. The
more explicit the doctrine, the less persuasive the poetry.
Shelley's *Adonais*, with its invocation of

> *that sustaining love*
> *Which, through the web of being blindly wove*
> *By man and beast and earth and air and sea,*
> *Burns bright or dim, as each are mirrors of*
> *The fire for which all thirst*

is perhaps, after Wordsworth, the most famous example. But
Adonais himself, even more than Shelley, had an intense
imaginative and passionate sympathy with all forms of life.
Keats's 'O for a life of sensations rather than of thought!'
is the cry not of an Epicurean, and not (emphatically not) of
a man deficient in intellectual power, but of one animated
by the mystic's hunger for living reality and by a distrust
of all doctrine not rooted in real experience. 'The setting
sun will always set me to rights,' he wrote to a friend, 'or if
a sparrow come before my window I take part in its existence
and pick about the gravel.'

Appearance and reality, time and eternity, matter and
mind, body and spirit: these pairs represent distinctions in
human thought, not oppositions in the nature of things. The
'single vision' stigmatized by Blake is a one-eyed vision,
resolved to see only one aspect of an unimaginably complex
and many-sided reality. In philosophy it makes for quarrel
and confusion; in life it makes for a kind of death. Mysticism,
at its best, rejects these false antinomies and follows 'the
unitive way', the way of integration. But there are abortive
or aberrant forms of mysticism, as of everything else. In the
whole man, reason does not exclude intuition, nor intuition

exclude reason: feeling and thinking, mind and soul, body and spirit, are resolved in harmony. Any undue emphasis on one element at the expense of the others disturbs the balance and sets up a counter-emphasis. Fear of emotion gives rise to arid intellectualism, fear of the body to an anaemic spirituality; and these, by force of reaction, produce their opposites. In the nineteen-twenties the revolt against these two extremes found fiery expression in the writings of D. H. Lawrence: a man of genuine vision and, despite impatience and a certain peevishness, essentially a man of love, as those who knew him have testified. 'We must have the courage,' he wrote in a private letter, 'to cast off the old symbols, the old traditions. What we want is the fulfilment of our desires, down to the deepest and most spiritual desire. The body is immediate, the spirit is beyond: first the leaves and then the flower: but the plant is an integral whole: therefore *every* desire, to the very deepest.' To say that the body is immediate, and the spirit beyond, seems almost to concede the very dualism that Lawrence is repudiating; but the context makes his meaning clear. 'I shall find my deepest desire to be a wish for pure unadulterated relationship with the universe, for truth in being. It is this establishing of pure relationships which makes heaven, wherein we are immortal, like the angels, and mortal, like men, both. And the way to immortality is in the fulfilment of desire. God works in me (if I use the term God) as my desire. He gives me the understanding to discriminate between greater and lesser desire.' Many a Christian mystic of earlier centuries might have written something very like that. But Lawrence did not stop there. He believed 'in the blood, the flesh, as being wiser than the intellect', and regarded sex as the central and sacramental mystery, as others have done in times both ancient and modern. 'The source of all life and knowledge is in man and woman, and the source of all living is in the interchange and the meeting and mingling of these two: man-life and woman-life, man-knowledge and woman-knowledge, man-being and woman-being.'*

Lawrence was serious in grain, with the seriousness of a child, the startling insight of a child, and a child's incapacity for sustained rational thought. He detested prudery and pruriency with an equal detestation, seeing them for what they are, two symptoms of the same disease. Dominated by his one idea, he either failed to see, or too often forgot, that to exalt the body at the expense of the mind is as foolish as the converse error, that to attack intellect as such is to attack reason and so open the door to madness, and that if we abandon ourselves to the 'dark gods' of the blood they will swell to unimaginable proportions and end by demanding a blood-tribute. Since his death this has actually happened: had he lived to see it no one would have been more horrified than he. Though there is truth and value in his mystique of sex, it is far from being the whole truth; but it supplied a psychological need of the time and so won him the reputation of a prophet.

§ 2

The sense of a basic unity in all things, and of love as the principle of attraction perpetually working towards the actualization of that unity, does not imply that the dualities apparent in everyday experience are meaningless illusions, and that the whole universe of being is an unimaginable featureless One. Unimaginable in its essence and totality it doubtless is, but no proposition can be true of it that denies or belittles the fascinating diversity of things. Things may be conceived scientifically as incidents in a process or flux, or mythologically as thoughts in a universal thinking; but whatever metaphor or image be chosen we cannot without

* All the Lawrence quotations are from *The Letters of D. H. Lawrence*, edited by Aldous Huxley. Heinemann, 1932.

self-deception embrace a theory which seeks to resolve the inescapable paradox of our condition by merely denying one of its terms, as for example the Indian philosopher Sankara seems to do in his commentaries (9th century, A.D.) on the ancient Upanishads. To accept the necessity of paradox is a first condition of any vital philosophy: the alternatives are solipsism, nihilism, or pure materialism. A metaphysical formula is worse than useless if it denies or diminishes, instead of deepening, the significance of human life. We may say, if we choose, that reality is the eternal operating in time; but to declare that the eternal is real and time only an appearance does not advance the argument, unless we add that the world of appearance necessarily partakes of the reality which informs it. It is true that whatever we can truly know is one with ourselves, true knowledge being identical with love, and love being 'the motion of things towards their final rest, which is also their first source' (Erigena); but it is also true that we cannot know or love anything except under the form of not-self.

The mystic, as such, is not concerned with systems of thought. The special value of his witness is that he speaks to us of something intimately felt, seeking not to expound a theory but to record an intuition. True, the practical and philosophical implications of what he has to say cannot be entirely neglected, except at peril of losing oneself in a region of private fantasy; we cannot and should not rest satisfied until intuition and reason are seen, so far as sight can carry, to be in harmony; but we are under no obligation to embrace the Neoplatonic or any other particular metaphysical system. Nor are we obliged to choose between the Materialist denial of mind and the Illusionist denial of matter. 'In Europe and in India, respectively,' a distinguished philosopher of our own day* has said, these extreme points of view 'have sought to assert themselves as the sole truth. In India, if the result

* Sri Aurobindo, *The Life Divine.* Calcutta, 1939.

has been a great heaping up of the treasures of the Spirit
—or of some of them—it has also been a great bankruptcy
of Life. In Europe, the fullness of riches and the triumphant
mastery of this world's powers and possessions have pro-
gressed towards an equal bankruptcy in the things of the
Spirit.' These errors of emphasis have had some limited value
for mankind; for materialism itself has been largely inspired
by a passion for exact knowledge of particulars; but truth
can be found only in the modification and synthesis of the
two. 'The affirmation of a divine life upon earth and an
immortal sense in mortal existence' can have no basis unless
we recognize, not only eternal spirit, but matter as its
mutable form. 'Nor is this, even, enough to guard us against
a recoil from life in the body unless, with the Upanishads,
perceiving behind their appearances the identity in essence
of these two extreme terms of existence, we are able to say
in the very language of those ancient writings, *Matter also
is Brahman*, and to give its full value to the vigorous figure
by which the physical universe is described as the external
body of the Divine Being.'

In short, Illusionist theories, either of matter or of
spirit, cannot hold water. The one is an idle fancy, susceptible of neither proof nor disproof: the other denies the
one reality of which we are immediately aware, namely
our own awareness. 'The world of Matter is affirmed by
the experience of the physical senses which, because they
are themselves unable to perceive anything immaterial or
not organized as gross Matter, would persuade us that the
suprasensible is the unreal. This vulgar or rustic error of
our corporeal organs does not gain in validity by being
promoted into the domain of philosophical reasoning.' Moreover, 'it will be evident that *essential* Matter is a thing
non-existent to the senses, and only a conceptual form of
substance; and in fact the point is increasingly reached [in
modern physics] where only an arbitrary distinction in

thought divides form of substance from form of energy'. The conclusion is that 'Matter expresses itself eventually as a formulation of some unknown Force. Life, too, that yet unfathomed mystery, begins to reveal itself as an obscure energy of sensibility imprisoned in its material formulation: and when the dividing ignorance is cured which gives us the sense of a gulf between Life and Matter, it is difficult to suppose that Mind, Life and Matter will be found to be anything else than one Energy triply formulated. Nor will the conception then be able to endure of a brute material Force as the mother of Mind. The Energy that creates the world can be nothing else than a Will, and Will is only consciousness applying itself to a work and a result.'*

To deny that matter is the sole reality is not to deny that it is a form or appearance of reality. 'Phenomenon is not phantasm: phenomenon is the substantial form of a Truth.' The point is vital, for 'if we assert only pure Spirit and a mechanical unintelligent substance or energy, calling one God or Soul and the other Nature, the inevitable end will be that we shall either deny God or else turn from Nature. For both Thought and Life, a choice then becomes imperative. Thought comes to deny the one as an illusion of the imagination or the other as an illusion of the senses; Life comes to fix on the immaterial and flee from itself in a disgust or a self-forgetting ecstasy, or else to deny its own immortality and take its orientation away from God and towards the animal.'† There is in practice a third alternative, repugnant to philosophy, and that is to accept an absolute ultimate dualism. This is what Christian theology as popularly expounded has too often been content to do. Mind and matter, spirit and body: each of these pairs is represented not as two aspects of one reality but as absolute self-subsistent entities between which there is an inexplicable (and in the last analysis unmeaningful) correspondence. Spirit is asserted

* Aurobindo, *op. cit.*   † *Ibid.*

to be good, the 'higher self', and body to be evil, the 'lower self'. This notion may seem at first sight to be supported by the fact implied in such expressions as 'self-control'; but on reflection we see it is not so, for the self that is controlled is as indubitably spirit as the will that controls it. Evil proceeds not from the body as such, but from the ego. It is not that the ego is evil in itself, but that the existence of egos, separated units of spirit, makes evil possible. It is not made *necessary* by the nature of things, but its contingency being implicit in the existence of a world of finite beings it would be surprising if in fact it never occurred.

In its understandable anxiety not to belittle the actuality and evilness of evil, popular pulpit-Christianity presents us with an absolute dualism which is expressly repudiated, however, by such Christian saints and philosophers as Augustine, Dionysius, Erigena, and Julian of Norwich, as well as by Plotinus before them. They have seen and affirmed that the One, or Absolute, is beyond good and evil, because beyond all categories. At the same time they agree with Plotinus that the One is also the Good. The inconsistency here is only apparent. For while what is beyond good cannot conceivably be evil, what is beyond evil cannot be conceived otherwise than as in some sense good. The goodness of that which is beyond the categories is a goodness which, lacking the counterpart of evil, has real but not logical being. Goodness, harmony, wholeness, is implicit in the 'eternal joy' which is, the mystics tell us, the very being of God. They tell us, further, that by humility and charity, which is to say by realizing our true nature, we can be partakers in that joy, not in a remote hereafter but here and now, and become members in the communion of Love, whose service is perfect freedom, and in whose will is our peace.

§ 3

Humility and charity: if these be lacking there is less than
no profit in following the fitful gleam of mystical vision.
United with them it can transform both the inner and the
outer life of man: divorced from them it becomes either a
private pastime or (worse) a means of evading the duties
of everyday life. So soon as one begins to fancy oneself a
'favourite of God', or to preen oneself on the possession of
a special insight, the deadliest of the seven devils enters in
and takes command. Compared with pride of spirituality, the
state of the most unimaginative materialist is a state of grace.
Mysticism, like any other good thing, can be distorted,
vulgarized, turned to base or trivial uses. It can be made
a pretext for intellectual laziness, spiritual self-sufficiency,
and arrogant disdain of simple human pleasures. It can open
the door to magic and superstition. But all this is utterly
alien to the spirit of genuine mysticism. Nothing, for example,
could be further removed from pride, from indifference, from
sentimental daydreaming, from facile optimism, than the
practice of disciplined meditation of which the author of *The
Cloud of Unknowing* gives a precise and vivid account. That
'acute psychologist and humorous critic of manners'* tells
his brothers of the cloister: 'A man may not be fully active
but if he be in part contemplative, nor yet fully contemplative
but if he be in part active.' And he warns them plainly, time
and again, against indulging in devout-seeming capers or
hearkening to the deceits of fantasy. For the work of divine
contemplation 'is far from any fantasy, or any false imagination or quaint opinion: the which be brought in, not by a
devout and a meek blind stirring of love, but by a proud,
curious, and imaginative wit. Such a proud, curious wit
behoveth always be borne down and stiffly trodden under

* As Evelyn Underhill calls him, in the introduction to her edition of *The
Cloud of Unknowing* (Watkins, 1922), to which I am indebted for my quotations.

foot, if this work shall truly be conceived in purity of spirit'. Vain bodily exercises and imaginings are to be avoided, and metaphors interpreted with intelligence. 'A young man or a woman new set to the school of devotion heareth how that a man shall lift up his heart to God and unceasingly desire for to feel the love of his God. And as fast in a curiosity of wit they conceive these words not ghostly, as they be meant, but fleshly and bodily; and travail their fleshly hearts outrageously in their breasts', and so either fall into frenzies, and so into weariness of body and soul, or by this misruling of their bodies become feverish, 'or else they conceive a false heat wrought by the Fiend, their ghostly enemy', and suppose it to be the fire of love, kindled by the Holy Ghost. Of which deceit, and of its many branches, spring many mischiefs, for 'as fast after such a false feeling cometh a false knowing in the Fiend's school, right as after a true feeling cometh a true knowing in God's school. For I tell thee truly, that the Devil hath his contemplatives as God hath his.' Modern psychologists do not talk of 'the Fiend': they follow a newer fashion in mythologies. But though their language would be different their verdict would be essentially the same.

This unknown fourteenth-century writer had a sharp eye for the antics of selfconscious pietism. He remarks how some misguided devotees 'stare as they were mad, and leeringly look as if they saw the Devil', adding crisply: 'Surely it is good they be wary, for truly the Fiend is not far off.' There follows this racy description: 'Some set their eyes in their heads as if they were sturdy sheep beaten in the head, and as if they should die anon. Some hang their heads on one side as if a worm were in their ears. Some pipe when they would speak, as if there were no spirit in their bodies: and this is the proper condition of an hypocrite. Some cry and whine in their throats, so greedy and hasty they be to say what they think: and this is the condition of heretics, and of them that with presumption and curiosity of wit will

P

always maintain error.' From this we may infer that sancti-
moniousness was not the invention of seventeenth-century
Puritans and Dissenters: it has flourished in all periods and
places. So, too, has selfrighteous censoriousness, the itch to
rebuke sin in others. 'Some men,' says the author of *The
Cloud*, 'the Fiend will deceive on this manner. Full wonderfully he will inflame their brains to maintain God's law, and
to destroy sin in all other men. He will never tempt them
with a thing that is openly evil; he maketh them like busy
prelates watching over all the degrees of Christian men's
living, as an abbot over his monks. All men will they reprove
of their defaults, right as they had cure of their souls. And
they say that they be stirred thereto by the fire of charity,
and of God's love in their hearts: and truly they lie, for it
is with the fire of hell, welling in their brains and in their
imagination.' The Devil, he repeats, so inflames the imagination of his contemplatives with the fire of hell, 'that suddenly
without discretion they shoot out their curious conceits, and
without any advisement they will take upon them to blame
other men's defaults over soon'. This, he says, is because
they have only one spiritual nostril—a good example of his
genius for homely illustration. For the division in a man's
nose, parting the one nostril from the other, 'betokeneth that
a man should have ghostly [spiritual] discretion', so that
he can 'dissever the good from the evil, and the evil from
the worse, and the good from the better', before arriving
at a judgment upon anything said or done by those about him.

Six hundred years of human history have done nothing to
diminish the value and importance of that piece of advice.

§ 4

And now, at the end of this all-too-brief survey of a vast
subject, we have to ask ourselves what it all amounts to. The
answer is: everything and nothing. Everything, because it

gives meaning to human life: nothing, because that meaning
must always elude precise definition. But this much, I hope,
will have emerged clearly from what has been said: that the
true, the sane mysticism is essentially realistic, is a discipline
no less than an inspiration, is not eager credulity or wishful
thinking, and does not absolve us from the duty which we
owe to ourselves and each other of exposing all conclusions
to the cold light of reason. Any verbal formulation is rightly
subject to logical analysis and criticism, and the worst that
the sceptic can do must be welcomed by every honest mind.
He cannot, however, do very much; for even if he succeed
in demolishing your mystical philosophy, as he well may,
he cannot dispose of the fact, the experience, of which that
philosophy is a more or less accidental by-product. Mysticism
in its essence is not a dialectic and therefore cannot be destroyed dialectically: it is something sensually and spiritually
felt, and only afterwards reasoned about. The mystic is a
man in love, a man in love with what, if he must give it
a name, he will call beauty, reality, the eternal, God,
according to his individual predilection. Whatever it be, he
finds it both in his deepest self, the light of his being, and
beyond him, manifested in the things of time. But these are
mere words, and it is the ultimate paradox of mystical
experience that though we must speak of it nothing we
can say can encompass its reality. 'The highest thought,'
runs an entry in Butler's *Notebooks*, is 'ineffable; it must be felt
from one person to another but cannot be articulated. All
the most essential and thinking part of thought is done
without words. It is not till doubt and consciousness enter
that words become possible. Our profoundest and most
important convictions are unspeakable.'

Mysticism establishes no precisely articulated system of
thought: it is not a belief but a life. The recurring features
of the event of which it is born are a loss of separateness,
a sense of union with all spirit, and an intuition or sensation

of immortality: not necessarily of one's own immortality as a local and individual person, but rather of an immortal reality to which one already belongs. Reality, however much logicians may cavil at the word, is of the essence of the matter, so far as one may gather it from report. This is more real, the mystic feels, than anything else that has ever happened to him before: it is the very heart and touchstone of reality. And about that there is no arguing with him, any more than there is with a man who discovers all the beauty of earth and heaven in the face of his beloved. Such a man may in time lose his beatific conviction; but who can say which of the two brought him nearer to eternal things, the vision or its loss? If the word eternal be objected to as a beggar of the question, let us say *real*; and if real is disallowed for the same reason, let us concede that neither term, nor any other that may be substituted for it, is adequate or exact. Verbal exactness in this matter is not merely difficult but impossible. If a word is to effect communication it must carry an agreed meaning, and a meaning agreed among two or more people derives from their common experience of what the word stands for. Without that community of experience meaning is lacking. The word *sky* to a man blind from birth cannot mean the actual sensual perception which sky is to the rest of us. The words *love* and *joy* could not be understood in their inwardness by one who had never felt love and joy in his own person. And no attempt to describe the sensation or intuition that we have agreed to call mystical can convey any true notion of its nature, still less conviction of its reality, to those—they are perhaps fewer than is generally supposed —in whom the mystical sense is always and utterly lacking.

No stranger to pain and grief, no dealer in pipe-dreams or shallow optimism, the mystic yet brings us, throughout the ages, news of an 'eternal joy', a 'heaven within', a light shining in the very heart of our darkness and beyond it. If we ourselves have ever known the least pulse of that joy, caught the least fragmentary glimpse of that glory, we shall listen to him; but if what he says strikes no bell in us his words will seem idle and empty. In this realm of the spirit we can learn nothing from the report of another that we have not seen, however dimly, or felt, however dumbly, for ourselves.

BIBLIOGRAPHY

Of the many writers who touch on mysticism, only a few need be mentioned here. The following short list includes all the principal works cited in the text and some others which readers coming new to the subject may find worth while.

ANONYMOUS

The Cloud of Unknowing (14th century). Edited by Evelyn Underhill. Watkins, 1912.

AUROBINDO, SRI

The Life Divine. Arya Publishing House, Calcutta, 1939.

BARCLAY, ROBERT

An Apology for the True Christian Divinity, 1678.

BLAKE, WILLIAM

Poetry and Prose of William Blake, edited by Geoffrey Keynes. Nonesuch Press, 1927. Gilchrist's *Life of Blake,* edited by Ruthven Todd for Everyman's Library. *Blake's Vision of the Book of Job* and *Blake's Innocence and Experience,* both by Joseph H. Wicksteed. Dent.

BOEHME, JAKOB

The Signature of All Things, in Everyman, provides a handy way of making acquaintance with this inspired but difficult writer.

CAMBRIDGE PLATONISTS

Tulloch's *Rational Theology in England in the 17th Century.* Blackwood, 1874. *The Cambridge Platonists.* Edited with an introduction by E. T. Campagnac. Clarendon Press, 1901. *Select Discourses,* by John Smith. Edited by H. G. Williams. Cambridge University Press, 1859.

CARPENTER, EDWARD

Preface to *Towards Democracy.* Allen & Unwin, 1883.

DONNE, JOHN
Sir Herbert Grierson's Oxford Press edition of the *Poems*. Logan Pearsall Smith's Clarendon Press volume of selections from the *Sermons*. See also the Nonesuch volume, *Complete Poetry and Selected Prose*, edited by John Hayward, 1929.

ERIGENA, JOHANNES SCOTUS
Henry Bett's *Johannes Scotus Erigena: a study in mediaeval philosophy* (Cambridge, 1925) contains a life of Erigena, a detailed summary of his system, and a valuable commentary.

FOX, GEORGE
The Journal of George Fox. A revised text prepared and edited by Norman Penney, with an introduction by Rufus M. Jones. Dent, 1924. *The Fells of Swarthmoor Hall*, by Maria Webb. *Life of George Fox*, by Thomas Hodgkin.

HERBERT, GEORGE
The Temple (poems) and *A Priest to the Temple* (prose). One volume, Everyman's Library.

HILTON, WALTER
The Scale of Perfection. Edited from MS sources with an introduction by Evelyn Underhill. Watkins, 1923.

HOOKER, RICHARD
The Laws of Ecclesiastical Polity.

INGE, WILLIAM RALPH
Christian Mysticism. Methuen, 1899. *Personal Idealism and Mysticism*. Longmans, 1924. *The Platonic Tradition in English Religious Thought*. Longmans, 1926. *Light, Life and Love* (selections from the German mystics of the Middle Ages, with a long introduction). Methuen, 1904.

JAMES, WILLIAM
Varieties of Religious Experience. Longmans, 1905.

JEFFERIES, RICHARD
The Story of My Heart. Longmans, 1883.

JULIAN OF NORWICH

Revelations of Divine Love. A version from the British Museum MS, edited by Grace Warrack. Methuen, 1901.

LAO-TZU

The *Tao Tê Ching.* Since the Chinese text admits of a wide variety of interpretation, more than one of the many English versions should be consulted.

LAW, WILLIAM

Works. In 9 vols. Edited by G. B. Morgan. London, 1892–3. Apart from selections, only his inferior works, such as the *Serious Call,* are easily accessible. John Byrom's *Private Journal* and Christopher Walton's *Notes and Materials for a Complete Biography of William Law* are the earliest sources for the life. They were used to excellent purpose by Canon Overton in his *William Law: Nonjuror and Mystic,* 1881.

LAWRENCE, D. H.

In addition to the novels and poems, his *Letters* (Heinemann, 1932), edited with an introduction by Aldous Huxley, are vital to anything like a full understanding of Lawrence.

PLOTINUS

The only tolerable English translation of the *Enneads* (which are at best difficult reading) is Stephen Mackenna's. It is not easily come by. Bouillet's French version (Paris, 1857–61) includes Porphyry's life of Plotinus. *The Essence of Plotinus,* a volume of selected passages based on the Mackenna text, with an introduction by its editor, is published by the Oxford University Press.

ROLLE, RICHARD

The Fire of Love and *The Mending of Life,* in one volume. Richard Misyn's 15th-century translation (from the Latin) paraphrased by Frances Comper. Methuen,

1914. Also by Frances Comper is: *The Life and English Lyrics of Richard Rolle*. Dent, 1928.

RUSSELL, BERTRAND

Mysticism and Logic. Allen & Unwin, 1918. Excellent medicine for the over-credulous. The same author's *Problems of Philosophy*, in the Home University Library, 1911, provides the perfect introduction to its subject.

SACKVILLE-WEST, V.

The Eagle and the Dove. Michael Joseph, 1943. A study of two sharply contrasted personalities: Teresa of Avila and Thérèse of Lisieux.

SANTAYANA, GEORGE

Soliloquies in England (for the essay, 'Reversion to Plotinus'). Constable, 1922. *Platonism and the Spiritual Life*. Constable, 1927.

SHAW, GEORGE BERNARD

Saint Joan. Constable, 1924. More particularly the Preface.

TRAHERNE, THOMAS

Centuries of Meditations. Dobell, 1908. Printed from a 17th-century manuscript discovered (and its value instantly discerned) by Bertram Dobell. Also, but less valuable, *Poems of Felicity*.

TREVELYAN, G. M.

England under the Stuarts. Longmans, 1904. For the ecclesiastical history of 17th-century England, see also Masson's *Life of Milton*.

UNDERHILL, EVELYN

Mysticism. London, 1911. *The Mystic Way* (described by the author as 'a psychological study in Christian origins'). Dent, 1913. *The Essentials of Mysticism and Other Essays*. Dent, 1920.

VAUGHAN, HENRY

The poems are published in 2 vols. by the Oxford Press, 1914, edited by L. C. Martin. The fullest and most

recent biography is F. E. Hutchinson's *Henry Vaughan*.
Oxford, 1947.

WALTON, IZAAK

Walton's *Lives* include lives of Donne, George Herbert,
and Richard Hooker.

WORDSWORTH, WILLIAM

The poems are available in various popular editions.
There is a good selection by Matthew Arnold (Golden
Treasury Series), prefaced by his deservedly famous
critical essay. Professor de Selincourt's edition (1926)
of the 1805 and 1850 versions of *The Prelude* is indispensable to the serious student. New light was shed
on the poet's early life in *Wordsworth and Annette
Vallon*, by Emile Legouis. Dent, 1922. See also
Dorothy Wordsworth's *Journals* and Catherine Maclean's
biography of her.

INDEX

Absolute Reprobation, doctrine of, 68, 69, 70, 71
Adams, Dr, Provost of King's College, 130
Adonais, 217
Agnosticism, 214
Alfred the Great, 45
All Religions are One, 174
Anamnesis, 40
Animal Tranquillity and Decay, 202, 203
Anne, Queen, 130, 131
Apology for the True Christian Divinity, An, 92
Appeal to All that Doubt, An, 144, 154
Arminius, Arminianism, 67, 117
Ascension Hymn, 108
Asceticism, 31, 32
Astrology, 216
Atheism, 68, 69, 124, 125, 214
Auguries of Innocence, 182
Augustine, 25, 59, 60, 61, 62, 70, 223
Aurobindo, 220–222

Bacon, Francis, 69
Bangor, Bishop of, 135
Barclay, Robert, 70, 71, 92
Basire, James, 166
Behaviourism, 216
Behmen, see Boehme
Bemerton, 101
Bett, Henry, 46
Beza, Theodore, 71
Bhagavadgita, 25
Bibliolatry, 72, 91
Blake, Catherine, 168, 169, 171, 172
Blake, Robert, 171
Blake, William, 30, 36, 161–185, 186, 189, 193, 205, 217
Blasphemy Law, 78, 79
Boehme, Jakob, 29, 129, 135, 139, 140, 143, 152, 153, 154, 157, 126

Book of Common Prayer, 49 (footnote)
Bourignon, Antoinette, 139
Brahman, 221
Brontë, Emily, 217
Browning, Robert, 21
Butler, Samuel, 227
Byrom, John, 130, 134, 137, 138, 139, 140, 149
Byrom, Phebe, 139
Byron, Lord, 164

Calvert, Raisley, 191
Calvin, Calvinism, 67, 69, 70, 71, 127
Cambridge Platonists, 89, 92, 113–128, 154
Carlyle, 82
Carpenter, Edward, 26, 28
Centuries of Meditations, 110–112
Charles the Bald, 44, 45
Charles the First, 66, 73, 104
Charles the Second, 66, 73, 84, 86
Cheyne, Dr George, 152, 153
Christian Perfection, 135, 141, 142, 144
Civil War, 87, 88
Cloud of Unknowing, The, 25, 34, 47, 54, 64, 224–226
Coate, Wiltshire, 22
Coleridge, S. T., 171, 190, 193, 198, 200, 204, 210, 211
Collins, Dr, Provost of King's, 117
Conventicle Act, 86
Copernicus, 33
Cowper, 69
Crashaw, Richard, 103
Cromwell, Oliver, 73, 86
Cudworth, Ralph, 120, 123, 124, 128
Culverwel, Nathanael, 121

Dalton, Sir John, 51
Dante, 89
De Divisione Naturae, 45

Deism, 24, 46
Dejection, Coleridge's Ode, 200
   (quotation from), 204
Derby, 79, 85
Descriptive Catalogue, Blake's, 181
'Dionysius the Areopagite', 25, 44,
   45, 60, 223
Divine Dialogues, 128
Dominicus, 70
Donne, Ann, 98, 99
Donne, John, 94–100, 101
Doomsdale, 85
Dove Cottage, 192

Eagle and the Dove, The, 20
Ecclesiastical Polity, Of the Laws of,
   90, 91
Eckhart, 15, 25, 33, 140
Ecstasy, The, 94
Egerton, Sir Thomas, 98
Eliot, T. S., 60
Emanation, doctrine of, 42
Emmanuel College, 115, 118, 123,
   130, 136
Enchiridion, 61 (footnote)
England under the Stuarts, 85
Enneads of Plotinus, 41, 44
Erigena, Johannes Scotus, 25, 32, 33,
   44, 45, 46, 60, 187, 233
Essentials of Mysticism, 44
Esthwaite Water, 197, 199
Eustochius, 42
Everlasting Gospel, The, 183
Excursion, The, 199

Fairy funeral, 163
Fell, Judge, 81
Fell, Margaret (from 1669 wife of
   George Fox), 81
Felpham, 163
Fenny Drayton, 73
Flaxman, John, 168
Fox, Christopher, 73
Fox, George, 29, 65–93, 96, 115, 121
Francis of Assisi, 30, 50

Galileo, 33
Genesis, 45
Geneva, 68
George the First, 131
Gibbon, Edward (the elder), 136,
   139, 143
Gibbon, Hester, 143, 145, 148
Gilchrist, William, 166, 169
Gosse, Edmund, 99
Guyon, Jeanne Marie, 139

Hampole, 52
Hawkshead, 197, 198, 199
Herbert, George, 101, 102, 103, 105,
   106
Herbert, Lady Magdalen, 101
Hilton, Walter, 47, 49, 50, 53, 64
Holy Sonnets, 99
Honorius, Pope, 45
Hooker, Richard, 89, 90, 91
Hutcheson, Mrs, 145, 148
Hutchinson, F. E., 105 (footnote)
Hutchinson, Mary, 192
Huxley, Aldous, 219 (footnote)
Huxley, Thomas Henry, 214

Inge, William Ralph, 17, 32, 35, 44
Intimations of Immortality, 40, 202,
   203, 204, 206, 207, 208
Inward Light, 88, 159

Jacobitism, 130, 131, 137
James the First, 86, 101
James, William, 21, 27
Jefferies, Richard, 22, 24, 25, 28
Jerusalem, 183
Jesus, 20, 34, 49, 155, 159, 215
Johannes Scotus, see Erigena
John of the Cross, 21
Journal, George Fox's, 81, 83
Julian of Norwich, 47, 49, 50, 55–64,
   96, 129, 156, 223

Keats, 217
Kempis, Thomas à, 142
King's Cliffe, 130, 143, 144

Kollmann, Johann, 67
Krishna, 25

Lampitt, Parson, 81
Lao-Tzu, 25
Laud, William, 66
Launceston, 84
Law, George, 131
Law, William, 29, 92, 129–160
Lawrence, D. H., 218, 219
Life Divine, The, 220–222
Life Force, 54
Little Gidding, 60
Luther, 30, 68
Lyrical Ballads, 171, 190, 194, 201, 205

Malebranche, Nicolas, 139
Marcus Aurelius, 34
Marriage of Heaven and Hell, The, 172, 175, 180
Marvell, Andrew, 107
Mathew, Rev. Henry, 167
Methodism, 134
Michelangelo, 168
Milton, 89, 172, 173
More, Sir George, 98
More, Henry, 120, 126
Morton, Thomas, 98
Mutability, sonnet, 194

Napoleon, 209
Nayler, James, 80
Neoplatonism, 41, 42, 43, 44, 47, 220
Nether Stowey, 210
Newman, F. W., 21
Newton, Isaac, 30, 153, 195
Newton, near Skethrog, 103
Nicholas the First, Pope, 45
Night, The, 108–110
Nobleness of True Religion, The, 156
Nottingham, 77

Okely, Francis, 151
Orleans, 209
Ossian, Macpherson's, 164

Overton, J. H., 139, 141

Pantheism, 46, 187, 206
Paradise Lost, 172, 173
Parker, James, 171
Patrick, Simon, 121, 122
Pattison, Pringle, 17
Paul, the Apostle, 32, 44
Pembroke, Earls of, 101
Penn, William, 82, 83
Penrith, 192, 197
Philosophy of Plotinus, The, 44 (footnote)
Piemont, William, 146, 147
Pippa passes, 21
Plato, Platonism, 35, 40, 41, 42, 115, 121, 216
Platonism and the Spiritual Life, 35 (footnote)
Plotinus, 15, 25, 41, 42, 43, 44, 46, 60, 115, 127, 223
Poetical Sketches, 167, 168, 171
Poison Tree, The, 179 (quotation from)
Pond, The, 139
Poole, Thomas, 191
Porphyry, 41
Praemunire, 86
Praise (Herbert), 105
Praise (Vaughan), 105
Predestination, doctrine of, 68, 69, 70, 71
Pre-existence, 205
Prelatism, 67, 114
Prelude, The, 43, 190, 195, 196, 197, 198, 199, 200, 201, 202, 206, 210, 212
Proclus, 25
Proverbs of Hell, 178, 181
Pulley, The, 105
Puritans, 65, 66, 67, 71, 72, 76, 89, 114, 161
Pursuit, The, 105
Pythagoras, 30

Quakers, 66, 70, 86, 92, 159
Queen's College, 121

Ranters, 80
Raphael, 168
Rational Theology in the Seventeenth Century, 114
Reason, 30, 89, 91, 115, 116, 118, 121, 154, 172, 173, 177
Recusants, Catholic, 67
Retreat, The, 40, 104, 205
Revelations of Divine Love, 55–64
Richmond, George, 164
Richter, Gregorius, 152
Righteous Overmuch, Danger of Being, 134
Rolle, Richard, 47, 49, 50, 51, 52, 53, 96

Sackville-West, V., 20
Saint Joan, 29, 30
Sankara, 220
Santayana, George, 35 (footnote), 216
Satan, 180, 181
Sawrey, Judge, 81
Scale of Perfection, The, 64
Scott, Sir Walter, 164
Select Discourses, 122
Selincourt, Ernest de, 195, 212
Separatists, 67, 79
Serious Call, A, 135, 136, 139, 141
Sermon on the Mount, 105
Shaw, Bernard, 29
Shelley, 217
Silex Scintillans, 104
Sin, 31, 38, 59, 60, 61, 69, 72
Single Vision, 217
Smith, John, 92, 120–123, 124–126
Smith, Logan Pearsall, 21
Society of Friends, 87, 89
Socrates, 30, 42, 114
Soliloquies in England, 216 (footnote)
Songs of Experience, 171, 177
Songs of Innocence, 171, 176
Southey, Robert, 198
Spirit of Love, The, 155, 159
Spirit of Prayer, The, 155, 159
Spiritualism, 216

Stephen, J. K., 194
Story of My Heart, The, 22–24, 26
Superstition, 124, 125
Swarthmoor Hall, 81
Swedenborg, 30, 164
Swinburne, 172
Synod of Dort, 67

Tao, 25
Tauler, 140, 141
Temple, The, 102
Tennyson, 27
Teresa of Avila, 20 (footnote), 103
Tertullian, 215 (footnote)
Theism, 18
Theologia Germanica, 127
Theosophy, 216
Thompson, Francis, 217
Tillotson, Archbishop, 118
Tintern Abbey, 194, 195, 202, 210, 211, 212
Toleration Act, 86
To the Christians, 183
To the Evening Star, 167
Towards Democracy, 26
Traherne, Thomas, 32, 110–112
Trapp, Dr Joseph, 134, 135
Trevelyan, G. M., 85 (footnote)
Trinity, doctrine of, 49 (footnote)
True Way of Attaining Divine Knowledge, 122
Tuckney, Antony, 115, 116
Tulloch, John, 114 (footnote), 120

Underhill, Evelyn, 32, 44, 50, 224 (footnote)
Unlawfulness of Stage Entertainment, The, 133
Upanishads, 25, 220
Usk, river, 103, 107
Utrecht, Treaty of, 130

Vallon, Annette, 190, 191, 209
Vallon, Caroline Wordsworth, 192
Varieties of Religious Experience, 27

Vaughan, Henry, 40, 102, 103, 104–
    110, 115, 205
Vedantist, 17

Walton, Christopher, 147, 148
Walton, Isaak, 98, 101
Warrack, Grace, 61 (footnote)
Way to Divine Knowledge, The, 155
Wesley, John, 141, 142, 143, 149

Whichcote, Benjamin, 92, 113–120,
    121
Whitman, Walt, 21, 28, 32, 133, 162
Wicksteed, J. H., 162 (footnote)
William Bond, 169, 170, 171
Woman Suffrage, 54 (footnote)
Wordsworth, Dorothy, 192, 197, 209,
    210, 211
Wordsworth, William, 40, 42, 43,
    104, 164, 171, 186–213, 214